SCHOOL DEVELOPMENT SERIES
David Hopkins and David Reynolds

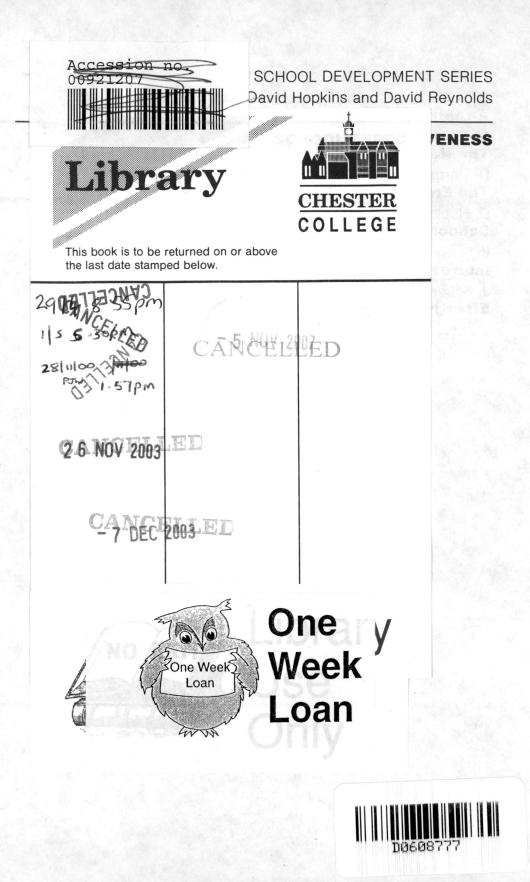

OTHER TITLES IN THE SCHOOL DEVELOPMENT SERIES

R. Bollington, D. Hopkins and M. West:
An Introduction to Teacher Appraisal

M. Fullan:
The New Meaning of Educational Change

D. Hargreaves and D. Hopkins:
The Empowered School

D. Hopkins:
School Improvement in an Era of Change

K.S. Louis and M.B. Miles:
Improving the Urban High School

J. Scheerens:
Effective Schooling

SCHOOL EFFECTIVENESS
Research, Policy and Practice

Edited by
David Reynolds
and Peter Cuttance

CASSELL

Cassell
Villiers House
41/47 Strand
London WC2N 5JE
England

387 Park Avenue South
New York
NY 10016-8810
USA

First published 1992

British Library Cataloguing in Publication Data
School effectiveness: research, policy and practice. –
(School development series).
1. Schools. Effectiveness
I. Reynolds, David *1949-* II. Cuttance, Peter III. Series
379.154

ISBN 0-304-32295-4
0-304-32276-8 pbk

Library of Congress Cataloging-in-Publication Data
School effectiveness: research, policy, and practice/edited by
David Reynolds and Peter Cuttance
p. cm. – (School development series)
Includes index.
ISBN 0-304-32295-4 – ISBN 0-304-32276-8 (pbk.)
1. Schools – Great Britain. 2. Schools – United States.
3. Schools – Netherlands. 4. School improvement programs – Great Britain. 5. School improvement programs – United States. 6. School improvement programs – Netherlands. I. Reynolds, David, 1949- .
II. Cuttance, Peter. III. Series.
LA632.S28 1991
371′.00941 – dc20 91-4405
CIP

Typeset by Colset Private Limited, Singapore
Printed and bound in Great Britain by
Dotesios, Trowbridge, Wilts.

Contents

List of Contributors

Bill Badger, Highland Region Education Authority, Inverness, Scotland
Louise S. Blakey, The Training Agency, Sheffield, England
Bert P.M. Creemers, RION, University of Groningen, the Netherlands
Peter Cuttance, Education Review Unit, State of South Australia
Carol T. Fitz-Gibbon, School of Education, University of Newcastle upon Tyne, England
Anthony F. Heath, Nuffield College, Oxford, England
Daniel U. Levine, Department of Education, University of Missouri, USA
Peter Mortimore, Institute of Education, London, England
Joseph Murphy, Peabody College, Vanderbilt University, USA
Anthony Packer, School of Education, University of Wales College of Cardiff, Wales
David Reynolds, School of Education, University of Wales College of Cardiff, Wales

Preface and Introduction

Seven years ago a number of us collaborated to produce a book which we entitled *Studying School Effectiveness*, which sought to review progress in the field of school effectiveness research and to look also at the areas towards which future research should have been directed. This book is a continuation of that effort to make the knowledge base of school effectiveness research more systematically ordered for the researcher or academic, and at the same time more easily accessible for the practitioner and/or policy-maker.

There is no doubt that the sub-discipline of school effectiveness as a 'specialty' within the world of education is now very different in its characteristics from the creature of the 1980s. Whereas in Britain in the mid-1980s there were still doubts as to the validity of some of the earlier research, such as our own and that of Michael Rutter and colleagues, in the early 1990s there has accumulated a considerable volume of further research studies showing substantial school effects and suggesting the nature of some of the within-school factors responsible for them from researchers such as Mortimore, Smith, Tomlinson, Nuttall and Goldstein.

As the body of knowledge in the field has increased, the changed set of British educational policy concerns has resulted in the public and political debate about education being re-located increasingly close to the concerns of school effectiveness researchers. Discussion of performance indicators, development planning, school self-evaluation and improved efficiency, and the concern with the effectiveness of the educational system so often voiced within political discourse are clear examples of this.

The other trend that has become increasingly obvious since the mid-1980s is the increased internationalization of the school effectiveness community. Five or six years ago there were generally isolated communities of researchers in five or six different cultures, namely the United Kingdom, the United States, Australia, the Netherlands, Canada and Scandinavia. Research results and findings rarely crossed national boundaries, which hampered the growth in understanding of school processes and school effects internationally.

The effect of these developments in educational climate and of the internationalization of the field has not, though, merely been the affirmation of the validity of the existing knowledge base of the discipline. As paradigms have been exposed to different educational policy climates, some of the basic tenets of the school effectiveness community of the 1980s have become increasingly redundant. Most importantly, as findings from different countries have crossed national boundaries they have thrown up many examples of conflicting findings, exemplified by the consistent inability of Dutch researchers to establish in their schools the importance of the firm instructional leadership characteristic of effective American schools.

This book aims to reflect all these changes in the field. It begins with three international overviews of the literature in the United Kingdom, the United States and the Netherlands. The United Kingdom review paints a picture of a heavily academically dominated, research-based school effectiveness enterprise, with a strong knowledge base and with little application of that knowledge into programmes of school improvement. In Britain, the school improvement paradigm has been one of celebration of practitioner lore, of naturalistic enquiry and of school self-evaluation or self-determination of goals, rather than being based on an empirical identification of success at outside-school determined educational goals. Many of the early certainties in the British research paradigm have also eroded as the field has developed, the chapter argues, and present uncertainties relate to the size of school effects, their consistency over time, the interrelationship of outcome variables and the precise factors responsible for differentially effective school processes.

Levine in his review of the literature paints a very different picture of American school effectiveness research. The volume of literature on school effectiveness is clearly much larger than in Britain, yet Levine is still able to note the consistent tendency for certain school effectiveness 'correlates' or factors to appear in virtually all the studies as being linked with effectiveness. The volume of improvement studies where application of effective schools knowledge has been attempted is also very large, leading to the creation of a knowledge base about how actually to create effective schools that has no British or Dutch parallel. Levine also identifies areas of deficiency in the American research tradition, including the neglect of conceptualizing and measuring higher order skills, and the lack of classification of the effective instructional or classroom processes within effective schools.

Creemers in his review of school effectiveness and school improvement concerns in the Netherlands paints a picture of rapid growth in the knowledge base about effective schools. Early innovatory and experimental projects had largely disappointing results and minimal effects upon student outcomes, which is probably to be explained by the inability of the reform programmes to alter the instructional interaction between teacher and pupil within classrooms. Later school effectiveness research in the Netherlands that followed the failure of these educational policies tested out the importance of numerous of the effective school factors derived from American research and found that very few of them appeared to explain why certain Dutch schools were effective. Creemers argues that school effectiveness research in his country and in others needs to pay attention to the instructional processes that go on in classrooms and to the ways in which these interact with, are determined by and in turn determine factors at the level of the school.

Peter Cuttance in the next chapter looks in detail at various different ways that have been utilized to assess whether individual schools are effective or not. The simple 'standards' model reflected in the provisions of the British 1980 and 1988 Education Acts, whereby school examination results are the criteria for judging a school's effectiveness, is seen as highly inadequate as a basis for informed evaluation, since apparently 'good' or 'effective' schools judged on examination results criteria may be so only because they take pupils from advantaged catchment areas, not as a result of their more effective management or functioning. A second method of evaluating effectiveness, based on looking at the mean or average scores of pupils as they enter their schools (to see if effective schools are taking more able pupils, for example), also suffers from defects in as much as the substantial range or variation between pupils is hidden and therefore statistical analysis is likely to be highly restricted. The third and preferred method of school evaluation uses data upon each *individual* pupil as he or she enters and leaves school, permitting both a more scientific assessment of the effects of the schools and an assessment of whether the schools are more or less effective with the different types of individual pupils within them.

Using this third model, Scottish data reported by Cuttance show that between 7½ and 10 per cent of the variation between pupils in their examination attainment is due to the effects of their schools, a not inconsiderable and potentially modifiable figure. Differences in examination results between various different sectors of education with different levels of selectivity, reported by Cuttance, clearly favour the more selective sectors of education, but it is not clear whether this superiority may be due to unmeasured characteristics of the children attending these schools which further advantage the selective sectors.

Chapter 5, by Carol Fitz-Gibbon, reports her findings from the COMBSE project (Confidential, Measurement Based, Self-Evaluation), which collected data on the intakes and academic outcomes at A level and O level of a large number of pupils and schools. Schools appeared to have substantial effects on their pupils in this large-scale database and interestingly this effect varied by subject, with the effects being much more pronounced for mathematics than for English. Attitudes to school were more affected by the nature of the school environment than was the academic development of pupils. The chapter concludes with an interesting discussion of those resources that schools need to use in order to appraise their own effectiveness, and will be useful for any educational practitioners wanting guidance on the information systems that are necessary to undertake this, since the questionnaires and tests used in the project are described in full detail.

The next chapter in the collection reports some findings of the Oxford School Effectiveness project. The authors note the large differences that they have found in the academic effectiveness of a sample of fifteen comprehensive schools, differences that are only slightly reduced when allowance is made for the most effective schools' socially superior intakes. The difference in mean academic achievement between the most effective school and the least effective school was of the order of two O level passes, even after allowing for differences in intake quality. Differences are also in evidence between the schools as to how effective they are with different types of pupil - some schools seem in Louise Blakey and Anthony Heath's study to be equally effective or ineffective across ability ranges, but two schools exist that are called by the authors 'egalitarian' schools, since they do better than average for less able pupils but worse than average for more able pupils. Differences between schools in their overall effectiveness seem interestingly to be heavily related to the entry rates that the schools show for public examinations, suggesting that academic outcomes from schools may be very much determined by school decision-making and its effects upon pupils.

The next chapter is concerned with the separate but related theme of how the knowledge gained from school effectiveness work can be translated into school improvement and change strategies that will ultimately make schools more effective in terms of producing higher levels of pupil academic and social development. Bill Badger firstly describes the changes in the ways in which disruptive behaviour had been explained by researchers during the 1980s and goes on to look at the evidence from one school in the north of England concerning the possible ways in which the school itself and its environment may be responsible for this problem. Badger helped the school staff to collect data on when disruption occurred, on the perceived causes of disruption that pupils and teachers gave and on the school-based organizational factors that may be linked to pupil behaviour. Out of this 'epidemiology' of disruptive incidents have come proposals for changing the school, originating from a special school committee and subsequently considered both by full staff meetings and by the school management team. Change followed that attempted to minimize movement around the school, to increase staff time for dealing with any problem pupils, to follow up systematically those pupils referred to the 'quiet room' and to change aspects of the school's punishment system. The potential of these linked methods of school effectiveness, evaluation and school improvement for school practitioners is clear from the account in the chapter.

The final three chapters of the book all attempt to review the past of the field of school effectiveness and to look forward at the ways in which the field needs to develop, to overcome some of the problems in research methodology and in the application of that methodology of the 1980s. Mortimore in the first of these chapters argues for more representative samples of schools to be used in research, for the use of more outcome measures, for the use of multi-level modelling, for better linkages to be made between outcomes and processes, and for the continued growth of international studies of school effectiveness that will continue the field's existing rapid intellectual development.

Joseph Murphy argues in his chapter that the effective schools movement in the United States and elsewhere needs to think beyond the continued recitation of the effective schools 'correlates' that have been associated with school success, since these are likely to be of limited use in the 1990s. School effectiveness has generated major advances in our thinking about schools, he argues: in its belief that all students can learn, in its focus on equity issues, in its belief that schools are responsible for student failure and success, and in its focus upon the need for collegiality within teacher groups. His future research agenda encompasses the need to address the instructional and curriculum processes that may be linked with effectiveness, and to think more radically about how the American 'school restructuring movement' may have implications for our discipline.

The final chapter argues that many issues from the 1980s still wait to be resolved by school effectiveness research, concerning the size of school effects, their consistency over time, the relationship between school performance on different outcome measures and the impact of school experience for different sub-groups of pupils. The 1990s, the chapter argues, are also likely to generate further problems for researchers with their need for new educational outcomes, and the rapid educational changes that are going on in virtually all industrialized societies make it very unlikely that the 'effective headteacher' or the 'effective school' of the year 2000 will look much like the rather simplistic creature at present described in school effectiveness research. The chapter concludes by arguing for the intellectual bankruptcy of the traditional approach to school improvement of the 1980s in the changed climate of the 1990s, perhaps a rethinking that is representative of much of the thinking and philosophy that permeates the book as a whole. School effectiveness research and school improvement practice need to look forward and change as rapidly as the educational systems being described. We hope that this volume succeeds in facilitating that change.

David Reynolds, *Cardiff*

Chapter 1

School Effectiveness and School Improvement: An Updated Review of the British Literature

David Reynolds

It is important to make clear at the outset of this chapter that only in the 1980s did a body of research findings in this area begin to emerge in Britain. This is in marked contrast with the United States, for example, where both school effectiveness and school improvement have been large and established disciplines from the mid-1970s onwards. There is not space to consider the detailed reasons for this here (see Reynolds, 1985) but a few explanations for this retarded development may be instructive:

1 There had been some difficulty in the past in gaining access to schools in Britain for comparative research purposes, as shown by the unhappy experience of Michael Power (Power *et al.*, 1967, 1972) in the London Borough of Tower Hamlets, in which research access to schools was refused after large differences were found in schools' delinquency rates.

2 Early research findings in the United States (Coleman *et al.*, 1966; Jencks *et al.*, 1971) and in Britain (Department of Education and Science, 1967) showed very limited school effects on academic outcomes and created a climate of professional educational opinion which held that variation in individual school organizations had minimal effects upon pupils' development.

3 The absence of reliable and valid measures of institutional climate, again in marked contrast to the situation for researchers in the United States (see details of the OCDQ and OHI questionnaires in Hoy *et al.*, 1991, for example) hindered the understanding of within-school processes and the measurement of the characteristics of effective organizational processes.

4 The popularity in Britain of determinist sociology of education, as reflected in the work of Bowles and Gintis (1976) and of Bourdieu and Passeron (1977), led to a sociological neglect of the school as an institution independent from the wider society that lasted throughout the 1970s and early 1980s, with the result that the pioneering work into the independent effects of school organizational processes of Hargreaves (1967) and Lacey (1970)

had no subsequent elaboration or development until the studies of Ball (1981) and Burgess (1983) published over a decade later.

5 The intellectual hegemony of traditional British educational research, with its psychologically determined paradigm as to the primacy of individual, family and community based explanations for children's 'educability', created a professional research climate somewhat hostile to school effectiveness work, a hostility which showed in some of the critiques of the Rutter *et al.* (1979) study *Fifteen Thousand Hours* (see, for example, those of Acton, 1980, and Goldstein, 1980), and in some of the reception given to early work from South Wales, which, for example, Musgrove (1981) called 'widely applauded but highly implausible'!

Indeed, when research findings were generated which showed the independence of children from the various socio-psychological influences of family background and environmental factors, the evidence was tailored to fit with the basic tenets of the paradigm. An example of this is the National Child Development Study of 1958 (Davie *et al.*, 1972), where although great emphasis was put in the study publications upon the *dependence* of the child upon his or her environment, the excellent reading performance of the Scottish children who came from the worst housing conditions in the sample showed clearly the *independence* of children from their outside school environment. Attention was not drawn to this finding.

While school effectiveness research has begun to gain momentum later in Britain than in some other countries, then, the 1980s have seen the growth of a substantial knowledge base in the field. Although that growth in knowledge has produced as many unanswered questions as questions answered, there is a sense of a genuine progression in the body of knowledge and in the methodological sophistication of the work over time, as will emerge below as we investigate some of the key areas and questions that work in the field has illuminated.

DO SCHOOLS HAVE EFFECTS UPON PUPILS?

At one level answering this question is not difficult, since we have good evidence that the *amount* of schooling or instruction consumed by pupils will have an effect upon their academic and social development. Fogelman (1983) noted that school attendance had an independent influence upon levels of children's attainments and patterns of behaviour, and (Fogelman, 1978) that children's attainment is related to the quantity of schooling they have received, particularly in such school-dependent subjects as mathematics.

While schools clearly matter in affecting development, the question above is normally held to refer to a slightly different issue: whether variation in the *quality* of their educational institutions has effects upon pupils. The regression analyses conducted for the Plowden Committee (Department of Education and

Science, 1967) suggested that there was little differential effect of schools on pupils, and that parental factors such as social class and particularly parental attitudes were the key determinants. In the United States, it was the *uniformity* of schools' organizational effects that was emphasized by Coleman *et al.* (1966) and Jencks *et al.* (1971).

The early British school effectiveness studies (Reynolds, 1976; Reynolds and Sullivan, 1979; Rutter *et al.*, 1979) sought to show that the outcomes of individual schools were not determined by the academic and social backgrounds of their intakes of pupils, yet there were in many people's minds doubts as to whether enough detailed information on the intakes of pupils had been collected to prove that the large differences in the outcomes of the schools studied did not only reflect the effects of unmeasured differences in the quality of the intakes of pupils. More recently, however, studies which have collected a very wide range of data concerning the intakes into different schools have still found large differences in the outcomes of the schools, even when allowance has been made for differences in intakes. The Inner London Education Authority Junior School Project of Mortimore *et al.* (1988) has data on the attainment, social class, sex and race of pupils on entry to their junior schools and still finds that this detailed individual information is a poor predictor of what progress the children will make over their next four years, without the addition of further data on the organizational character of their schools. Both Smith and Tomlinson (1989) and Nuttall *et al.* (1989) have recently reported substantial variations between schools in their effectiveness, even after multiple factors were measured relating to the pupil intakes.

WHAT IS THE SIZE OF SCHOOLS' EFFECTS ON THEIR PUPILS?

Early studies showed - in the views of their authors - very large school effects. Power *et al.* (1967) reported a twenty-fold difference in the delinquency rates of London schools, a difference which they argued was virtually independent of catchment area characteristics, and Gath *et al.* (1977) reported substantial variation in the child guidance referral rates of schools. Reynolds (1976) reported large differences between schools in their effectiveness, which were again argued to be virtually completely due to the effects of the schools themselves, since there was evidence that the schools were taking from similar catchment areas. The variation in delinquency rates across the schools was three-fold and in attendance rates was from 90 per cent attendance at the 'top' school to only 77 per cent at the 'bottom' school. The Rutter team (Rutter *et al.*, 1979) also emphasized the scale of their school effects, and the early work of Gray (1981), using already available local education authority databases, produced an estimate that the 'competitive edge' possessed by the most effective fifth of state secondary schools (as against the least effective fifth) amounted to approximately the equivalent of $1\frac{1}{2}$ of the old O level public examination passes per child. Substantial school effects on pupils' examination results were also reported by Gray *et al.* (1983) in their analysis of data from secondary schools in Scotland and by Brimer *et al.* (1978) using examination passes as their measurement of effectiveness.

Indeed, the latter study of variation in the public examination performance of pupils at the old O and the still used A level examinations showed some of the highest estimates of 'school effects' ever reported in the international literature, with a range of between-school variation of from 5 per cent to 42 per cent in eleven O level subjects, after allowing statistically for the effect of pupils' family backgrounds. In eight of the eleven subjects, 80 per cent of the between-school difference was further explicable by a range of data that had been collected on school and instructional variables such as teaching methods, school curricular provision and teacher beliefs.

After these early studies, however, came a large number of British studies in the 1980s that showed much smaller school effects, although these studies were in turn followed by a further wave of research in the last few years which suggests the existence of quite substantial school effects. The earlier research suggesting only small effects appeared as follows:

1 Comparisons of the academic 'outcomes' of local education authorities showed that social, economic and environmental factors accounted for up to 80 per cent of the variation in pupil academic attainment (Department of Education and Science, 1983, 1984; Gray *et al.*, 1984).
2 Comparisons of school systems which were selective with those which were comprehensive showed minimal differences, as shown by the National Children's Bureau Studies (Steedman, 1980, 1983) and the work from the Scottish Education Data Archive (Gray *et al.*, 1983).
3 Comparisons of the outcomes of individual schools suggested small differences in effects, as shown by the Scottish data of Willms (1986), in which schools only explained 2 per cent of the variation in the academic achievement of pupils. The work of Gray *et al.* (1986) suggested much more limited school effects than their earlier study, with the difference between the most effective and least effective schools being only one very low-grade CSE examination pass in size. The seminal study of Aitken and Longford (1986) also reported that only 2 per cent of the variance in pupil attainment was due to the effects of school.
4 What appeared to be important in many studies was the 'balance' of the pupil intake into schools or the catchment area's effect in raising or lowering pupils' expected performance levels, as in the findings from Willms (1986) noted above, where there were large school contextual effects upon performance in English and in mathematics. Willms (1985) also noted that students of average ability in high-ability schools scored more than a full examination grade higher than comparable students in schools where the majority were pupils of lower ability. It was not so much the organization of the school that was seen as

important in the mid-1980s as the characteristics of the pupil *group*, in terms of affecting outcomes.

More recent work, however, has begun to support the earlier suggestions of large school effects. Cuttance's recent Scottish data (reported in Chapter 4 of this book) suggest that up to 8 per cent of the variance in pupils' examination attainments is school related and that the difference between the 'most effective quarter' and 'least effective quarter' of schools is of the order of two of the old O level grades. Reynolds *et al.* (1987) reported large school system effects upon pupils, in particular a major deficiency in the non-academic outcomes of comprehensive schools when their pupils' outcomes were compared with those of pupils from the selective system. Mortimore and his colleagues (1988) also report substantial school effects, not upon attainment *at a point in time* but upon *progress over time* where, in the case of mathematics for example, the influence of the school was ten times more important than the influence of the home. Even in reading, which is likely to be more dependent upon the general cultural background of the child's family, the school's influence on pupil progress was four times greater than that of the child's home.

Smith and Tomlinson's (1989) study also shows large differences in the effects of schools, with for example a child of above average ability who managed to obtain an old CSE grade 3 in English at one school obtaining an old O level grade B in the same examination at another school. For certain groups of pupils, in fact, the variation in examination results between individuals in different schools was as much as one quarter of the total variation in examination results. Both Tizard *et al.* (1988) and Nuttall *et al.* (1989) have also recently reported large school effects, with the former based upon a sample of pupils in infant schools and the latter based upon the examination performances of over 30,000 students drawn from 140 schools, although Gray *et al.* (1990) have recently generated estimates of variation between schools that are at the lower end of the range.

ARE SCHOOLS EQUALLY EFFECTIVE UPON DIFFERENT ASPECTS OF PUPIL DEVELOPMENT?

The early work of Rutter *et al.* (1979) and of Reynolds (1976) reported high intercorrelations between schools' academic effectiveness and their social effectiveness as measured by attendance and delinquency rates. However, more recent work has suggested that schools may be differentially effective in different areas. Gray *et al.* (1983) showed that the social outcomes of schooling such as pupils' liking for school or school attendance rates were partially independent of schools' academic outcomes, as did the National Children's Bureau research in the area of comprehensive/selective system comparisons (Steedman, 1980, 1983), in which the comprehensive schools were performing academically as well as those of the selective system, but were under-performing socially in comparison. Our own work (Reynolds *et al.*, 1987) shows small academic, but large behavioural and attitudinal, differences in the effectiveness of the same two systems. The ILEA study (Mortimore *et al.*, 1988) shows that schools can be differentially effective upon their pupils' academic and social outcomes. Although much of the discussion of the findings of the study has concentrated upon the group of fourteen schools which were effective in terms of both academic and social outcomes, in fact there is almost a complete independence of effectiveness in the various academic and social areas of development. Galloway's (1983) study of four schools with very low levels of behavioural problems is also illuminating in this respect, since one of the schools also possessed very low levels of academic achievement, a result no doubt of the imposition of a policy of minimal demands on the pupils!

Even if we look only at one discrete area of schools' effectiveness - the academic outcomes from schooling - there is substantial variation in the Mortimore *et al.* (1988) study between schools' effectiveness on one academic outcome, such as oracy (heavily school influenced) and another, such as reading skills (less heavily school influenced). Smith and Tomlinson (1989) also report substantial variation in the departmental success rates at different schools in public examinations, with these differences not just being a function of the overall effectiveness of the individual schools. In fact, schools are reported in this study as differing more in their achievement at particular subjects than in the aggregate, since out of the eighteen schools the school that was 'first' overall on mathematics attainment (after allowances had been made for intake quality) was 'fifteenth' in English and since the school that was 'second' in mathematics achievement came 'tenth' in English achievement.

The work of Fitz-Gibbon and colleagues reported in this volume and elsewhere (Fitz-Gibbon, 1985; Fitz-Gibbon *et al.*, 1990) also shows a substantial variation between the effectiveness of different schools' subject departments of English and mathematics.

ARE SCHOOLS CONSISTENTLY 'EFFECTIVE' OR 'INEFFECTIVE' OVER TIME?

Early work suggested that schools were consistent over a number of years in their outcomes (Reynolds, 1976; Rutter *et al.*, 1979), although of course this is not the same as being consistent in their effectiveness.

More recently it has seemed that schools can vary quite markedly in their performance over time, as originally noted by Goldstein (1987). Nuttall *et al.* (1989) note that their sample of 140 London schools exhibit unreliability in their performance over the period 1985-7, and conclude sensibly that their analysis

> gives rise to a note of caution about any study of school effectiveness that relies on measures of outcome in just a single year, or of just a single cohort of students. Long time series are essential for a proper study of stability over time.
>
> (Nuttall *et al.*, 1989, p. 775)

The Scottish data analysed by Willms and Raudenbush (1989) also suggest a picture of schools as changing, dynamic and relatively unstable enterprises, which are changed by children as they change the children themselves. Statistical estimates of the correlation between school effects over time vary from 0.59 to 0.96 to 0.87, depending on the method used, but it is clear that there is more 'movement' in school performance than might have been supposed from the early work in this field.

DO SCHOOLS HAVE THE SAME EFFECTS UPON ALL PUPILS?

Early work (Reynolds, 1982; Rutter *et al.*, 1979) suggested that a school was equally effective or ineffective for all types of pupil in the school, irrespective of their social background or their ability.

More recently, however, Aitken and Longford (1986) found that schools can differ in their regression line slopes (the line reflecting the statistical relationship between their intakes and outcomes), suggesting that some may be more effective for pupils of a certain ability level than for others. Also, Cuttance (this volume, Chapter 4) notes that advantaged pupils from homes of high socio-economic status are more affected by their schools than pupils from a disadvantaged background, and Gray *et al.* (1986) note that high-ability pupils were more affected by their schools than those of lower ability. McPherson and Willms (1987) show that the effects of comprehensivization in Scotland varied considerably according to the social class of pupils, with working class pupils gaining more over time than others. All these more recent studies suggest that schools may not have consistent organizational effects upon different kinds of pupil, a finding supported by the hints in Willms and Cuttance's (1985) data concerning the existence of a few schools that might have been effective for high-ability children and a few for lower-ability children, and vice versa.

Using the techniques made possible by the adoption of a multi-level modelling methodology, Nuttall *et al.* (1989) show large differences for different types of pupils in the relative effectiveness of schools in London. If we take the experience of abler pupils (or VR Band One) and the experience of the less able pupils (or VR Band Three), in some schools the difference in the groups' performances as they leave school is as small as 11 VRQ points and in others as large as 28 points, even after adjusting for differences in the pupils' abilities at the time of joining their schools. In this study, the performances of schools were also found to vary in the ways that they impact upon boys and girls and in their effects upon pupils of different ethnic groups, with some schools narrowing the gaps between these different groups over time and some widening the gaps in both instances. In Smith and Tomlinson's (1989) study there is also evidence of differential effects of schools upon different pupils, particularly on those of both above average and below average prior attainment, but although the effects were statistically significant they were substantively smaller than those found by Nuttall *et al.*, mentioned above.

Gray *et al.* (1990) report different findings, however, in that in a wide range of local education authorities they could find little evidence of differential effectiveness of schools. As they note themselves,

> What is more surprising is the similarity of our findings across data sets of very different characteristics. We found this to be the case for those [LEAs] with large numbers of pupils in a relatively large number of schools and with prior attainment as an

> explanatory measure. We also found similar results with small numbers of pupils in a smaller set of schools, again using prior attainment.
>
> (Gray *et al.*, 1990, p. 150)

On the issue of school differential effects - as on some other issues that began to attract researchers' attention during the 1980s - the jury is still clearly out!

WHAT ARE THE CHARACTERISTICS OF EFFECTIVE SCHOOL ORGANIZATIONS?

It is important to note that we know at present far more about the factors associated with academic effectiveness than about those factors that are associated with social outcomes. Rutter *et al.* (1979) identified over twenty factors associated with academic effectiveness but only seven associated with social effectiveness as measured by a school's possession of a low delinquency rate. The Inner London Education Authority study of Mortimore *et al.* (1988) found only six school factors associated with behavioural effectiveness (such as low rates of misbehaviour) and thirteen school factors associated with academic effectiveness judged in terms of good reading scores, even though the schools' overall effect *sizes* were the same on the two different outcomes. Our relative ignorance of the factors making for social effectiveness is also unlikely to be remedied by work from abroad, since virtually all the North American studies (with the notable exception of Brookover *et al.*,1979) look only at academic effectiveness (see reviews in Anderson, 1982; Purkey and Smith, 1983; and Levine, Chapter 2 in this volume).

It is also important to note that we have only three studies in Britain which have been able to collect data systematically on a wide range of school processes in effective and ineffective school organizations, two on processes in secondary schools (Rutter *et al.*, 1979; Reynolds, 1976, 1982) and one on effective primary school processes (Mortimore *et al.*, 1988), although as we will see later there are a number of small-scale studies which focus upon particular aspects of school organization.

The Rutter study found that certain factors are not associated with overall effectiveness, among them class size, formål academic or pastoral care organization, school size, school administrative arrangements (i.e. whether a school is split site or not), and the age and size of school buildings.

The important within-school factors determining high levels of effectiveness were argued by Rutter (1980) to be:

1 The balance of intellectually able and less able children in the school, since, when a preponderance of pupils in a school were likely to be unable to meet the expectations of scholastic success, peer group cultures and an anti-academic or anti-authority emphasis may have formed.
2 The system of rewards and punishments - ample use of

rewards, praise and appreciation being associated with favourable outcomes.

3 The school environment - good working conditions, responsiveness to pupil needs and good care and decoration of buildings were associated with better outcomes.

4 Ample opportunities for children to take responsibility and to participate in the running of their school lives appeared conducive to favourable outcomes.

5 Successful schools tended to make good use of homework, to set clear academic goals and to have an atmosphere of confidence in their pupils' capacities.

6 Outcomes were better where teachers provided good models of behaviour by means of good time-keeping and willingness to deal with pupil problems.

7 Findings upon group management in the classroom suggested the importance of preparing lessons in advance, of keeping the attention of the whole class, of unobtrusive discipline, of a focus on rewarding good behaviour and of swift action to deal with disruption.

8 Outcomes were more favourable when there was a combination of firm leadership with a decision-making process in which all teachers felt that their views were represented.

Our own work in South Wales, although undertaken in a group of secondary modern schools and in a relatively homogeneous former mining valley that is very different in its community patterns from the communities of inner London, has produced findings that in certain ways are parallel to those of Rutter. We studied the school processes of eight secondary modern schools, each of which was taking the bottom two-thirds of the ability range from clearly delineated catchment areas. We found substantial differences in the quality of the school outputs from the eight schools, with a variation in the delinquency rate of from 3.8 per cent of pupils delinquent per annum to 10.5 per cent, in the attendance rate of from 77.2 per cent average attendance to 89.1 per cent and in the academic attainment rate of from 8.4 per cent to 52.7 per cent proceeding to further education.

The early analysis (Reynolds, 1976) of the intake data showed no tendency for the schools with the higher levels of performance to be receiving more able intakes on entry. In fact, high overall school performance was associated with *lower* ability intakes as measured by the Ravens Standard Progressive Matrices test of non-verbal ability. Although subsequent full analysis of our full range of intake data revealed a tendency for the higher-performance schools to have intakes of slightly higher verbal and numerical ability, the personality variables for these schools' intakes (higher extroversion and higher neuroticism scores) suggested, on the contrary, a poor educational prognosis. Although our sample sizes were too small to permit the use of more than basic statistical methods, and although the study was cross-sectional in that data were collected from different pupils at intake and outcome, the intake data made a powerful case for the existence of substantial school effects.

Detailed observation of the schools and the collection of a large range of material upon pupils' attitudes to school, teachers' perceptions of pupils, within-school organizational factors and school resource levels revealed a number of factors within the school that were associated with more 'effective' regimes. These included a high proportion of pupils in authority positions (as in the Rutter study), low levels of institutional control, positive academic expectations, low levels of coercive punishment, high levels of pupil involvement, small overall size, more favourable teacher-pupil ratios and more tolerant attitudes to the enforcing of certain rules regarding 'dress, manners and morals'.

Crucially, our observations revealed differences between the schools in the ways that they attempted to mobilize pupils towards the acceptance of their goals, differences that were associated with their effectiveness. Such differences seemed to fall within the parameters of one or other of two major strategies, 'coercion' or 'incorporation'. Five more effective schools that took part in the research appeared to be utilizing the incorporative strategy to a greater (three schools) or lesser (two schools) extent. The major components of this strategy were two-fold: the incorporation of pupils into the organization of the school and the incorporation of their parents into support of the school. Pupils were incorporated within the classroom by encouraging them to take an active and participative role in lessons and by letting them intervene verbally without the teacher's explicit directions. Pupils in schools which utilized this strategy were also far more likely to be allowed and encouraged to work in groups than their counterparts in schools utilizing the coercive strategy. Outside formal lesson time, attempts were made to incorporate pupils into the life of the school by utilizing other strategies. One of these was the use of numbers of pupil prefects and monitors, from all parts of the school ability range, whose role was largely one of supervision of other pupils in the absence of staff members. Such a practice appeared to have the effect of inhibiting the growth of anti-school pupil cultures because of its effects in creating senior pupils who were generally supportive of the school. It also had the latent and symbolic function of providing pupils with a sense of having some control over their within-school lives; the removal of these symbols also gave the school a further sanction it could use against its deviants. Attempts to incorporate pupils were paralleled by attempts to enlist the support of their parents, by the establishment of close, informal or semi-formal relations between teachers and parents, the encouraging of informal visits by parents to the school and the frequent and full provision of information to parents that concerned pupil progress and governor and staff decisions.

Another means of incorporation into the values and norms of the school was the development of interpersonal rather than impersonal relationships between teachers and pupils. Basically, teachers in these incorporative schools attempted to 'tie' pupils into the value systems of the school and of adult society by means of developing 'good' personal relationships with them. In effect, the judgement was made in these schools that internalization of teacher values was more likely to occur if pupils saw teachers as 'significant others' deserving of respect. Good relationships were consequent upon minimal use of overt institutional control (so that pupil behaviour was relatively unconstrained), low rates of physical punishment, a tolerance of a limited amount of 'acting out' (such as by smoking or gum chewing, for example), a pragmatic hesitancy to enforce rules which may have provoked rebellion and an attempt to reward good behaviour rather than punish bad behaviour. Within this school ethos, instances of pupil 'deviance' evoked therapeutic rather than coercive responses from within the school.

In contrast, schools which utilized the 'coercive' strategy to a greater or lesser extent (three ineffective schools) made no attempt to incorporate pupils into the authority structure of the school. Furthermore, these schools made no attempt to incorporate the support of parents, because the teachers believed that no support would be forthcoming, and they exhibited high levels of institutional control, strict rule enforcement, high rates of physical punishment and very little tolerance of any 'acting out'. The idea, as in the incorporative schools, of establishing some kind of 'truce' with pupils in these schools was anathema, since the teachers perceived that the pupils would necessarily abuse such an arrangement. Pupil deviance was expeditiously punished, which, within the overall social context of these schools, was entirely understandable; therapeutic concern would have had little effect because pupils would have had little or no respect for the teacher-therapist.

The most likely explanation of the choice of different strategies was to be found in the differences (in the two groups of schools) in the teachers' perceptions of their intakes. In schools which adopted a 'coercive' strategy, there was a consistent tendency to overestimate the proportion of pupils whose background could be said to be 'socially deprived' - in one such school, teachers thought such children accounted for 70 per cent of their intake, while in one of the incorporative schools teachers put the proportion at only 10 per cent - and a consistent tendency to underestimate their pupils' ability. In these coercive schools, teachers regarded pupils as being in need of 'character training' and 'control', which stemmed from a deficiency in primary socialization, a deficiency which the school attempted to make good by a form of custodialism. Such perceptions were germane seeds for the creation of a school ethos of coercion.

In addition to research on secondary school processes, the characteristics of effective *primary* school organizations that are associated with high performance in cognitive areas such as reading and writing and in non-cognitive areas such as low truancy levels have been identified (Mortimore *et al.*, 1988). Mortimore's research identifies a number of schools, effective in both academic and social areas, that possessed the following characteristics:

1 Purposeful leadership of the staff by the head. This occurs where the head understands the school's needs, is actively involved in the school but is good at sharing power with the staff. He or she does not exert total control over teachers but consults them, especially in decision-making such as spending plans and curriculum guidelines.
2 Involvement of the deputy head. Where the deputy was usually involved in policy decisions, pupil progress increased.
3 Involvement of teachers. In successful schools, the teachers

were involved in curriculum planning and played a major role in developing their own curriculum guidelines. As with the deputy head, teacher involvement in decisions concerning which classes they were to teach was important. Similarly, consultation with teachers about decisions on spending was important.

4 Consistency among teachers. Continuity of staffing had positive effects but pupils also performed better when the approach to teaching was consistent.
5 A structured day. Children performed better when their school day was structured in some way. In effective schools, pupils' work was organized by the teacher, who ensured there was plenty for them to do yet allowed them some freedom within the structure. Negative effects were noted when children were given unlimited responsibility for a long list of tasks.
6 Intellectually challenging teaching. Not surprisingly, pupil progress was greater where teachers were stimulating and enthusiastic. The incidence of 'higher order' questions and statements was seen to be vital - that is, where teachers frequently made children use powers of problem-solving.
7 A work-centred environment. This was characterized by a high level of pupil industry, with children enjoying their work and being eager to start new tasks. The noise level was low, and movement around the class was usually work-related and not excessive.
8 A limited focus within sessions. Children progressed when teachers devoted their energies to one particular subject area and sometimes two. Pupil progress was marred when three or more subjects were running concurrently in the classroom.
9 Maximum communication between teachers and pupils. Children performed better the more communication they had with their teacher about the content of their work. Most teachers devoted most of their time to individuals, so each child could expect only a small number of contacts a day. Teachers who used opportunities to talk to the whole class by, for example, reading a story or asking a question were more effective.
10 Thorough record-keeping. The value of monitoring pupil progress was important in the head's role, but it was also an important aspect of teachers' planning and assessment.
11 Parental involvement. Schools with an informal open-door policy which encouraged parents to get involved in reading at home, helping in the classroom and on educational visits tended to be more effective.

12 A positive climate. An effective school has a positive ethos. Overall, the atmosphere was more pleasant in the effective schools for a variety of reasons.

While there are some clear differences between the three British studies in their respective findings, the degree of communality in the findings on the factors associated with organizational effectiveness is quite impressive. However, it is of course important not to over-emphasize the extent of the agreement between the various British studies and between these British studies and the international literature. Rutter *et al.* (1979), for example, find that high levels of staff turnover are associated with secondary school *effectiveness*, a completely counter-intuitive finding that is not in agreement with Reynolds's (1976, 1982) findings of an association between high levels of staff turnover and *ineffectiveness*. Similarly, the consistent American findings on the link between frequent monitoring of pupil progress and academic *effectiveness* is not in agreement with the findings of Mortimore *et al.* (1988) that pupil monitoring which involves frequent testing of children is a characteristic of *ineffective* schools.

In addition to the three studies outlined above, which all provide data on a comprehensive range of school and classroom processes, there are a number of further studies which offer data on a more limited range of aspects. A clutch of studies on difficult or deviant pupils have appeared in the last few years, with Maxwell (1987) suggesting high levels of suspension from school arise from schools where staff groups do not believe in their capacity to affect this problem. McManus (1987) related school suspension rates and school organizational policies on pastoral care, showing that an incorporative, relationship-based approach minimized pupil problems. McLean (1987) also suggested that a preventive, child-centred approach minimized pupil disruption, and Gray and Nicholl (1982), in their study of two secondary schools in disadvantaged communities, generally replicate the findings of Rutter and those of Reynolds on effective schools' rule enforcement policy.

To conclude this section on those factors associated with school effectiveness, it is important to point out the existence of a further large body of knowledge which exists to inform debate, namely the reports generated by the British national school inspectorate, HMI. HMI's publications based upon visits to individual schools may leave much to be desired in terms of their validity, since HMI tends to assess schools' levels of effectiveness by comparison with national standards, not in the context of the schools' local communities and catchment areas (Gray and Hannon, 1986). However, HMI has in recent years attempted to make assessments of the organizational factors that promote school effectiveness *across* the school cases which its inspectors have visited, which are reported in documents ranging from the original *Ten Good Schools* study (Department of Education and Science, 1977) to the more recent observations on schools that promote good behaviour (Department of Education and Science, 1987) and to a major study of secondary school practice based on a sample of 185 schools (Department of Education and Science, 1988). The latter's summary of the characteristics of an effective school is interesting when compared to the academic research reviewed above:

> The report sets out the characteristics of effective schools. These were schools well-led by heads with the capacity to stimulate others and who had a breadth of vision about education together with practical ability to translate this into classroom practice for their pupils. They were supported in this by others who had clearly delegated responsibilities.
>
> In such schools effective communication and confident relationships enabled teachers to contribute to the formulation and implementation of school policies. Effective schools had clear goals and objectives which were often written down for staff, pupils, parents and governors - the production of these goals and objectives had been the result of discussion by all staff.
>
> Effective schools felt it important to help all pupils to reach the highest academic standards of which they were capable. Most lessons in these schools took place in an atmosphere which was relaxed but orderly and firm, with good relationships and clear encouragement to pupils to express their views and develop their ideas in talking with each other and with the teachers.
>
> Effective schools fostered their pupils' personal and social development. They had well qualified staff with an appropriate blend of experience and expertise who were well deployed within the school. Strengths in this respect were developed through, for example, participation in in-service training. (DES Press Release, 26 July 1988)

THE FUTURE OF SCHOOL EFFECTIVENESS RESEARCH IN BRITAIN

Detailed prescriptions of the research agenda that remains to be tackled are available elsewhere (Rutter, 1983; Reynolds and Reid, 1985; Gray, 1982) and elsewhere in this volume in the chapters by Murphy and Mortimore. There is space only to consider the more urgent needs here, in terms of the development of the knowledge base on effective organizational practices.

Clearly the issues concerning the size of school effects, their consistency over time, their consistency across different kinds of school output, their consistency for different types of pupil and the applicability of findings across international settings need further elucidation through research.

We need research undertaken in more typical samples of schools (since early British work has been exclusively urban, has been undertaken either in London or in South Wales and has been based in highly disadvantaged communities) to see if the same factors are associated with effectiveness in different social and geographical areas. Larger sample sizes (like Mortimore's fifty schools rather than Reynolds's eight or Rutter's twelve) are also needed. More studies of primary school effectiveness are also needed, particularly since the literature on school effectiveness from the Netherlands and the United States reviewed in this volume shows a heavy concentration upon research in elementary schools.

Some British studies, particularly those from the Centre for Policy Studies

(Cox and Marks, 1983, 1985), have been highly defective in their measurements of pupil intakes into schools, which may have led to invalid assumptions being made about schools or systems of education being more effective simply because full allowance had not been made for the intake quality of their pupils. Analyses based only on measures of home background (as with Cox and Marks above) or on limited measures of background and ability (as with Rutter *et al.*, 1979) are unlikely to be adequate. What is needed in the future is multiple indicators of intake, covering a range of pupil academic and social factors, as in the study by Mortimore *et al.* (1988).

'Means-on-means' analyses, where school averages for all pupils are used, as in Reynolds's (1976, 1982) work, make it impossible to analyse the school experience of different groups of pupils and also lower explanatory variance. Individual pupil level data rather than group data are now widely agreed to be necessary, both on intake and at outcome (Aitken and Longford, 1986), to permit the appropriate use of multi-level techniques of analysis, which can nest pupils within classrooms and classrooms within schools and the schools within the context of outside-school factors.

Further work is required into the school processes that are associated with effectiveness. We are still not completely sure *which* processes are associated with effectiveness, and also *how* the school organizational factors have their effects - through their effects upon pupil self-concepts or by direct modelling, for example? We need to know what *creates* the organizational factors, which may require a degree of historical study since there are those who insist that what makes an effective school is in part the history of being an effective school. We need to know also whether the effective organizational factors are equally effective with very different types of teacher personality or teachers with different educational philosophies, or by contrast whether the person makes any difference to the effectiveness of the methods. Simply, the 'person-method' interaction and the 'person-method' fit are both areas that will undoubtedly repay further investigation. Most important of all, we need to investigate *which* of the school organizational features are the most important and which factors (like the headteacher, perhaps) may determine other factors. No existing British studies have attempted to do this.

Areas that have been neglected by the existing body of British research need future attention. The leadership or management style of the headteacher is seriously neglected in both the British secondary school studies, since in both cases the researchers felt that it was politically impossible in the mid to late 1970s to give this factor the attention it potentially deserved. The content of the curriculum, the books and materials used, its relevance to children's culture and the world view the curriculum imparts have also received minimal attention, no doubt because of the difficulty of classifying and measuring curriculum 'knowledge' (Wilcox, 1985) and no doubt also because of the destruction of the utility of Bernstein's attempted classification (King, 1983) of curriculum and organization. The interesting finding of Ramsay *et al.* (1982) concerning the distinctive curriculum processes that existed within effective schools remains unexplored in Britain, as it does too (as shown by the literature reviews in this volume) in the Netherlands and the United States.

The classroom environments or instructional processes of effective school organizations have also not been studied in detail in either of the secondary school studies (although the Mortimore study advances our knowledge of primary classrooms), an omission which hampers the integration of the bodies of knowledge on effective schooling and effective instruction. The pastoral or welfare aspects of education and the within-school practice and ethos of care and guidance are also not areas that have received sufficient attention.

Our last serious omission in terms of areas to be studied is the actual administration, management and decision taking process within schools, an area where school effectiveness work would clearly benefit from a closer knowledge of the literature on management and decision-taking in non-school organizations. In part because of the neglect of the headteacher's role in the two secondary studies, we are still unclear about the precise nature of the leadership to be found in effective school organizations, although the portrait to be found in the recent study by Mortimore *et al.* (1988) of the effective headteacher as at the same time both a purposive leader and concerned to involve staff in the running of the school takes our knowledge some considerable way further. What is the departmental or middle management structure of an effective school organization, or the relations with outside supportive agencies, or the appraisal process, or the school self-evaluation processes in use? What is the actual mechanics of the administration in terms of *behaviours* as well as reified organizational *structure*? In these key areas - very important for practitioners or policy-makers who might want to make a direct attempt to change school practice - school effectiveness work is still deficient in knowledge.

To improve our understanding of the complex interaction of persons, methods and processes that generate an effective school we need to undertake greater use of case study and qualitative methods that will enable richer descriptions of processes to be made. This is particularly important if the school effectiveness work is to be made more accessible to practitioner and policy-maker communities in Britain, since the rich description of practice that they may need is currently absent.

The 'contexting' of a school's effectiveness, in terms of an appreciation of how 'what works' may vary according to the circumstances in which individual schools may exist, is another topic of great importance. We have no analysis in Britain equivalent to that in the United States of Brookover *et al.* (1979), who studied how effective schools in different types of catchment area were somewhat different in their organizational characteristics and in their 'phasing' of how they developed to become effective. Nor have we been able to participate in Britain in the 'cutting edge' debates about sensitivity to context that are a central feature of discourse in the field in the United States (Hallinger and Murphy, 1986; Wimpelberg *et al.*, 1989). The British tendency to study homogeneous, socially disadvantaged samples of schools has its costs.

The above list is of course not an exhaustive one. The theories of the 'middle range' variety that can move the field away from the level of simple empiricism are absent. Some variables may have been too easily dismissed from use because of out-of-date assessments of their usefulness; an example would be the neglect of school resources that followed the generally negative findings as to their salience in the 1970s and 1980s but which may now be inappropriate if the differentiation between schools in terms of their resource levels has increased markedly. Social outcomes from schools, which may be independent of academic outcomes, clearly need further attention, even though British school effectiveness work has conceptualized and measured to a greater extent within this area than work from any other nation. Such outcomes may partially determine, as well as being partially determined by, the academic outcomes of schooling. Finally, the effects of variation in outside-school factors, such as the British local education authorities, has not been adequately developed after promising initial work (Gray and Jesson, 1987; Woodhouse and Goldstein, 1988; Cuttance, Chapter 4 in this volume; Willms, 1987), no doubt because of the difficulties of further investigation into such politically sensitive issues and in part no doubt because of the tendency of British research to 'cut off' schools from their surrounding environments, which developed as a reaction to the earlier highly prevalent overestimates of the effects of environments upon school performance. All these, and many other, areas await our attention.

SCHOOL EFFECTIVENESS RESEARCH AND SCHOOL IMPROVEMENT PRACTICE

In the United States, a recent survey by the US General Accounting Office (1989) found that over half the school districts were using elements of what can loosely be called 'effective schools research knowledge', and the United States has seen numerous projects which have aimed to test out the usefulness of the knowledge base in generating school improvement (e.g. McCormack-Larkin, 1985). The literature on school effectiveness can also be increasingly seen in the writing of leading school improvement researchers such as Fullan (1991), and indeed in Canada there is an innovatory project in the Halton School Board that is designed to put school effectiveness knowledge into improvement practice (Stoll and Fink, 1990). In Israel, school effectiveness projects have generated impressive gains in student achievement scores (Bashi and Zass, 1989).

In Britain, things are very different indeed, and the take-up of school effectiveness knowledge by practitioners within the educational system and within schools has been very limited indeed, with the exception of the former Inner London Education Authority 'Inspectors Based in Schools' initiative of direct provision of effectiveness knowledge to schools. In part, this may be because school effectiveness research in Britain is heavily academically dominated, unlike in the United States, for example, where practitioners have undertaken some of the research and where the school effectiveness 'movement' was pioneered by the black American school board superintendent and practitioner, Ron Edmonds.

In part, though, it is probably the actual character of the British research itself that has contributed to poor levels of implementation by practitioners or policy-makers. There are high levels of abstraction and a lack of specific detail in some of the concepts utilized in the research, like 'academic press' or 'balanced control'. The school effectiveness research is weak on issues of management and organization and weak - as we noted earlier - on the 'technology' of schooling.

The research is quite strong on school environments or climates but weak on the organizational arrangements that are associated with effective school environments.

The knowledge base of British school effectiveness research is also not strong on teachers' focal concerns of the curriculum and the actual instructional practices that are utilized within classrooms, as we noted above. The studies are about the *end result* of being an effective school and do not outline *how* to get to the destination of 'effectiveness'. Indeed, the entire school effectiveness enterprise has usually seemed to involve looking at effective schools to see what they have that ineffective schools do not have, even though for school improvement programmes to be effective we may need to know what exists in the ineffective school that is absent from the effective institution. Even the school effectiveness processes may be a *result* of effectiveness rather than merely a *cause*, as in the relationship between high academic expectations and academic success, for example.

The limited effects of school effectiveness work in terms of take-up into programmes of school improvement probably also exist because the school improvement knowledge base (popular with practitioners) has virtually diametrically opposed intellectual characteristics. The school improvement paradigm in Britain probably began with the teacher-researcher movement (Elliott, 1977, 1981), moved on to encompass school self-evaluation and review (Clift and Nuttall, 1987) and later attempted to ensure that the review process was linked to an improvement policy (as with the report *Improving Secondary Schools* by Hargreaves, (1984), the GRIDS scheme of McMahon *et al.* (1984), the International School Improvement Project of Bollen and Hopkins (1987) and others).

Overall, though, this British school improvement effort in total has continued to be concerned more with individual teachers than with the organization of their schools, has rarely empirically evaluated the effect of changes in the schools, has often indeed been more concerned with the journey of undertaking school improvement than with reaching any particular destination and has often celebrated practitioner knowledge whether it is itself a valid improvement strategy or not, leading to a futile reinvention of the wheel in each project. The sociology of education has been particularly good at the latter (for example Woods and Pollard, 1987). The past lack of 'mesh' between the school effectiveness and school improvement literatures and research communities, seen for example in numerous disparaging comments about school effectiveness work by the school improvers Holly and Hopkins in Reid *et al.* (1987), can be argued to have damaged the knowledge base of school improvement work and to have again reduced the potential practitioner impact of school effectiveness work (see Reynolds, 1988 for elaboration of this theme).

The disciplinary isolation of the two communities of school effectiveness researchers and school improvement practitioners has probably also been responsible for the disappointing effects that have been generated when school effectiveness researchers have directly *themselves* tried to influence school practice through programmes of school improvement. Rutter and his colleagues (Maughan *et al.*, 1990; Ouston and Maughan, 1991) attempted major and lengthy interventions with three of the schools that formed the basis of their earlier school effectiveness research, using their findings in a direct attempt to improve practice. Of the three schools involved, only two showed some improvements and even these were in what the researchers called 'restricted' areas. By comparison with some other schools which changed rapidly because of the appointment of a new headteacher, 'change at these schools was less wide ranging, affecting only one or two other of our main outcome measures or being focussed primarily on particular segments of the pupil intakes' (Maughan *et al.*, 1990, p. 207).

In Wales, we tried a rather different consultancy-based method of bringing the results of school effectiveness work to schools, in which the school staff owned the change process, which was exclusively 'bottom-up' in orientation. This too had disappointing results in the short term (Reynolds, 1987). More recently there are occasional examples of the successful translation of school effectiveness work into school improvement programmes, as in the case where teachers attending in-service training in school effectiveness research as school 'change agents' generated over four major organizational changes per person, over 80 per cent of which had survived in a six-year follow-up study (see Reynolds *et al.*, 1989, for an outline of the project's results and philosophy). This study also showed that the schools which changed their organizational functioning also changed their pupil academic and social outcomes markedly, when compared to a group of non-participating control schools. This 'Trojan horse' method of bringing the effectiveness knowledge base to schools may be one worth serious consideration. Its success, though, simply points up the failure of the other attempts to link effectiveness research and improvement practice.

CONCLUSIONS

This survey of the achievements and limitations of British school effectiveness research clearly gives us a mixed picture of the rewards of our efforts. On the one hand, the body of knowledge generated by school effectiveness research is quite substantial and some of the findings concerning effective processes may be quite robust. On the other hand, the translation of findings into school improvement programmes and into practice has been poor, with school improvement as a discipline following a separate set of emphases.

The pity of this situation is that the disciplines of school effectiveness and school improvement need each other intellectually. For school effectiveness researchers, school improvement programmes are the ultimate empirical test of whether effective school variables are causal, and the experiments of nature that take place when schools change, or are changed, can provide a valuable set of data. For school improvement practitioners, school effectiveness research can provide an increasingly sensitive description of good practice, especially useful as school effectiveness becomes more and more sensitive to the context of the school and the precise portions of the ability range that improvers are interested in. Both communities, and bodies of knowledge, have much to learn from each other and one hopes that in the 1990s they will realize this.

ACKNOWLEDGEMENT

This is an expanded, rewritten and updated version of a paper originally published in Reynolds, D., Creemers, B.P.M. and Peters, T. (eds) (1989) *School Effectiveness and Improvement*. Groningen: RION; Cardiff: University of Wales.

REFERENCES

Acton, T.A. (1980) 'Educational criteria of success: some problems in the work of Rutter, Maughan, Mortimore and Ouston', *Educational Research*, **22** (3), 163-73.

Aitken, M. and Longford, N. (1986) 'Statistical modelling issues in school effectiveness studies', *Journal of the Royal Statistical Society, Series A*, **149** (1), 1-43.

Anderson, C.A. (1982) 'The search for school climate: a review of the research', *Review of Educational Research*, **52** (3), 368-420.

Ball, S.J. (1981) *Beachside Comprehensive*. Cambridge: Cambridge University Press.

Bashi, J. and Zass, S. (1989) 'An outcome based school improvement programme', in Reynolds, D., Creemers, B. and Peters, T. (eds) *School Effectiveness and Improvement*. Groningen: RION.

Bollen, R. and Hopkins, D. (1987) *School Based Research: Towards a Praxis*. Leuven, Belgium: ACCO Publishing.

Bowles, S. and Gintis, H. (1976) *Schooling in Capitalist America*. London: Routledge & Kegan Paul.

Bourdieu, P. and Passeron, J.C. (1977) *Reproduction: in Education, Society and Culture*. London: Sage.

Brimer, A., Madaus, G.F., Chapman, B., Kellaghan, T. and Wood, R. (1978) *Sources of Difference in School Achievement*. Slough: NFER.

Brookover, W.B., Beady, C., Flood, P., Schweitzer, J. and Wisenbaker, J. (1979) *School Social Systems and Student Achievement*. New York: Praeger.

Burgess, R.G. (1983) *Experiencing Comprehensive Education: A Study of Bishop Macgregor School*. London: Methuen.

Clift, P. and Nuttall, D. (eds) (1987) *Studies in School Self Evaluation*. Lewes: Falmer Press.

Coleman, J.S. *et al.* (1966) *Equality of Educational Opportunity*. Washington, DC: US Government Printing Office.

Cox, C. and Marks, J. (1983) *Standards in English Schools: First Report*. London: National Council for Educational Standards.

Cox, C. and Marks, J. (1985) *Standards in English Schools: Second Report*. London: National Council for Educational Standards.

Davie, R. *et al.* (1972) *From Birth to Seven*. London: Longmans.

Department of Education and Science (1967) *Children and Their Primary Schools*. London: HMSO. (The Plowden Report)

Department of Education and Science (1977) *Ten Good Schools: A Secondary School Enquiry*. London: DES.

Department of Education and Science (1983) *School Standards and Spending: Statistical Analysis*. London: DES.

Department of Education and Science (1984) *School Standards and Spending: Statistical Analysis. A Further Appreciation*. London: DES.

Department of Education and Science (1987) *Education Observed 5 - Good Behaviour and Discipline in Schools*. London: DES.

Department of Education and Science (1988) *Secondary Schools: An Appraisal by HMI*. London: DES.

Elliott, J. (1977) 'Evaluating in-service activities from above or below?', *Insight*, November.

Elliott, J. (1981) *School Accountability*. London: Grant McIntyre.

Fitz-Gibbon, C.T. (1985) 'A-level results in comprehensive schools - the COMBSE project year 1', *Oxford Review of Education*, **11** (1), 43-58.

Fitz-Gibbon, C.T., Tymms, P.B. and Hazlewood, R.D. (1990) 'Performance indicators and information systems', in Reynolds, D., Creemers, B.P.M. and Peters, T. (eds) *School Effectiveness and Improvement*. Groningen: RION.

Fogelman, K. (1978) 'The effectiveness of schooling', in Armytage, W.H.G. and Peel, J. (eds) *Perimeters of Social Repair*. London: Academic Press.

Fogelman, K. (ed.) (1983) *Growing up in Great Britain*. London: Macmillan.

Fullan, M. (1991) *The New Meaning of Educational Change*. London: Cassell.

Galloway, D. (1983). 'Disruptive pupils and effective pastoral care', *School Organisation*, **13**, 245-54.

Gath, D. *et al.* (1977) *Child Guidance and Delinquency in a London Borough*. London: Oxford University Press.

General Accounting Office (1989). *Effective Schools Programmes: Their Extent and Characteristics*. Gaithersberg, MD: General Accounting Office.

Goldstein, H. (1987) *Multilevel Models in Educational and Social Research*. London: Oxford University Press.

Goldstein, H. (1980) 'Critical notice - Fifteen Thousand Hours by Rutter *et al.*,' *Journal of Child Psychology and Psychiatry*, **21** (4), 364-6.

Gray, J. (1981) 'A competitive edge: examination results and the probable limits of secondary school effectiveness', *Educational Review*, **33** (1), 25-35.

Gray, J. (1982) 'Towards effective schools: problems and progress in British research', *British Educational Research Journal*, **7** (1), 59-69.

Gray, J. and Hannon, V. (1986) 'HMI's interpretations of schools examination results', *Journal of Education Policy*, **1** (1).

Gray, J. and Jesson, D. (1987) 'Examination results and local authority league tables', in Harrison, A. and Gretton, J. (eds) *Education and Training, UK, 1987*, pp. 33-41.

Gray, J. and Nicholl, A. (1982) 'Comparing examination results in two social priority comprehensives: four plausible hypotheses', *School Organisation*, **2** (3), 255-72.

Gray, J., Jesson, D. and Jones, B. (1984) 'Predicting differences in examination results between local education authorities: does school organisation matter?', *Oxford Review of Education*, **10** (1), 45-68.

Gray, J., Jesson, D. and Jones, B. (1986) 'The search for a fairer way of comparing schools' examination results', *Research Papers in Education*, **1** (2), 91-122.

Gray, J., Jesson, D. and Sime, N. (1990) 'Estimating differences in the examination performances of secondary schools in six LEAs: a multilevel approach to school effectiveness', *Oxford Review of Education*, **16** (2), 137-58.

Gray, J. McPherson, A. and Raffe, D. (1983) *Reconstructions of Secondary Education*. London: Routledge & Kegan Paul.

Hallinger, P. and Murphy, J. (1986) 'The social context of effective schools', *American Journal of Education*, **94**, 328-55.

Hargreaves, D.H. (1967) *Social Relations in a Secondary School*. London: Routledge & Kegan Paul.

Hargreaves, D. (1984) *Improving Secondary Schools*. (Report of the Committee on the Curriculum and Organisation of Secondary Schools). London: ILEA.

Hoy, W., Tarter, C.J. and Kottkamp, R.B. (1991) *Open Schools, Healthy Schools*. London: Sage.

Jencks, C. *et al.* (1971) *Inequality*. London: Allen Lane.

King, R. (1983) *The Sociology of School Organisation*. London: Methuen.

Lacey, C. (1970) *Hightown Grammar*. Manchester: Manchester University Press.

McCormack-Larkin, M. (1985) 'Ingredients of a successful school effectiveness project', *Educational Leadership*, March, 31-7.

McLean, A. (1987) 'After the ball: school processes in low exclusion rate schools', *School Organisation*, **7** (3), 303-10.

McMahon, A., Bolam, R., Abbot, R. and Holly, P. (1984) *Guidelines for Review and Development in Schools (Primary and Secondary Handbook)*. York: Longman/Schools Council.

McManus, M. (1987) 'Suspension and exclusion from high school - the association with catchment and school variables', *School Organisation*, **7** (3), 261-71.

McPherson, A. and Willms, D. (1987) 'Equalisation and improvement: some effects of comprehensive reorganisation in Scotland', Paper presented to the Annual Meeting of the American Educational Research Association, May.

Maughan, B., Ouston, J., Pickles, A. and Rutter, M. (1990) 'Can schools change? - 1. Outcomes at six London secondary schools', *School Effectiveness and Improvement*, **1** (3), 188-210.

Maxwell, W.S. (1987) 'Teachers' attitudes towards disruptive behaviour in secondary schools', *Educational Review*, **39** (3), 203-16.

Mortimore, P., Sammons, P., Ecob, R., Stoll, L. and Lewis, D. (1988) *School Matters: The Junior Years*. Salisbury: Open Books.

Musgrove, F. (1981) *School and the Social Order*. Chichester: John Wiley.

Nuttall, D. *et al.* (1989) 'Differential school effectiveness', *International Journal of Educational Research*, **13** (7), 769-76.

Ouston, J. and Maughan, B. (1991) 'Can schools change? - 2', *School Effectiveness and School Improvement*, **2** (1), 3-13.

Power, M.J. *et al.* (1967) 'Delinquent schools?', *New Society*, **10**, 542-3.

Power, M.J., Benn, R.T. and Morris, J.N. (1972) 'Neighbourhood, school and juveniles before the courts', *British Journal of Criminology*, **12**, 111-32.

Purkey, S. and Smith, M. (1983) 'Effective schools: a review', *Elementary School Journal*, **83**, 427-52.

Ramsay, P.D.K., Sneddon, D.G., Grenfell, J. and Ford, T. (1982) 'Successful vs unsuccessful schools: a south Auckland study', *Australia and New Zealand Journal of Sociology*, **19** (1).

Reid, K., Hopkins, D. and Holly, P. (1987) *Towards the Effective School*. Oxford: Blackwell.

Reynolds, D. (1976) 'The delinquent school', in Woods, P. (ed.) *The Process of Schooling*. London: Routledge & Kegan Paul.

Reynolds, D. (1982) 'The search for effective schools', *School Organisation*, **2** (3), 215-37.

Reynolds, D. (ed.) (1985) *Studying School Effectiveness*. Lewes: Falmer Press.

Reynolds, D. (1987) 'The consultant sociologist: a method for linking sociology of education and teachers', in Woods, P. and Pollard, A. (eds) *Sociology and Teaching*. London: Croom Helm.

Reynolds, D. (1988) 'British school improvement research: the contribution of qualitative studies', *International Journal of Qualitative Studies in Education*, **1** (2), 143-54.

Reynolds, D. and Reid, K. (1985) 'The second stage: towards a reconceptualisation of theory and methodology in school effectiveness research', in Reynolds, D. (ed.) *Studying School Effectiveness*. Lewes: Falmer Press.

Reynolds, D. and Sullivan, M. (1979) 'Bringing schools back in', in Barton, L. (ed.) *Schools, Pupils and Deviance*. Driffield: Nafferton.

Reynolds, D., Sullivan, M. and Murgatroyd, S.J. (1987) *The Comprehensive Experiment*. Lewes: Falmer Press.

Reynolds, D., Phillips, D. and Davie, R. (1989) 'An effective school improvement programme based on school effectiveness research', *International Journal of Educational Research*, **13** (7), 801-14.

Rutter, M. (1980) *Changing Youth in a Changing Society*. Oxford: Nuffield Provincial Hospital Trust.

Rutter, M. (1983) 'School effects on pupil progress - findings and policy implications', *Child Development*, **54** (1), 1-29.

Rutter, M., Maughan, B., Mortimore, P. and Ouston, J. (1979) *Fifteen Thousand Hours: Secondary Schools and Their Effects on Children*. Wells: Open Books.

Smith, D. and Tomlinson, S. (1989) *The School Effect*. London: Policy Studies Institute.

Steedman, J. (1980) *Progress in Secondary Schools*. London: National Children's Bureau.

Steedman, J. (1983) *Examination Results in Selective and Non-Selective Schools*. London: National Children's Bureau.

Stoll, L. and Fink, D. (1990) 'An effective schools project: the Halton approach', in Reynolds, D., Creemers, B.P.M. and Peters, T. (eds) *School Effectiveness and Improvement*. Groningen: RION.

Tizard, B., Blatchford, P., Burke, J., Farquhar, C. and Plevis, I. (1988) *Young Children at School in the Inner City*. Hove: Lawrence Erlbaum.

Wilcox, B. (1985) 'Conceptualising curriculum differences for studies of secondary school effectiveness', in Reynolds, D. (ed.) *Studying School Effectiveness*. Lewes: Falmer Press.

Willms, D. (1985) 'The Balance thesis - contectual effects of ability on pupils' "O" grade examination results', *Oxford Review of Education*, **11** (1), 33-41.

Willms, J.D. (1986) 'Social class segregation and its relationship to pupils' examination results in Scotland', *American Sociological Review*, **51**, 224-41.

Willms, J.D. (1987) 'Differences between Scottish educational authorities in their examination attainment', *Oxford Review of Education*, **13** (2), 211-37.

Willms, J.D. and Cuttance, P. (1985) 'School effects in Scottish secondary schools', *British Journal of Sociology of Education*, **6** (3), 289-306.

Willms, D. and Raudenbush, S. (1989) 'A longitudinal hierarchical linear model for estimating school effects and their stability', *Journal of Educational Measurement*, **26**, 209-32.

Wimpelberg, R., Teddlie, C. and Stringfield, S. (1989) 'Sensitivity to context: the past and future of effective schools research', *Educational Administration Quarterly*, **25**, 82-107.

Woodhouse, G. and Goldstein, H. (1988) 'Educational performance indicators and LEA league tables', *Oxford Review of Education*, **14**, 301-20.

Woods, P. and Pollard, A. (eds) (1987) *Sociology and Teaching*. London: Croom Helm.

Chapter 2

An Interpretive Review of US Research and Practice Dealing with Unusually Effective Schools

Daniel U. Levine

Early in 1990, Larry Lezotte and I completed a relatively comprehensive review of research and related analysis bearing on the characteristics and creation of unusually effective schools that have higher achievement than most schools enrolling socioeconomically similar student populations. Nearly all the material we reviewed was drawn from the massive base of writing on this topic that has accumulated in the United States during the past 25 years. Many of my observations in this paper constitute a summary of major sections from the resulting monograph (Levine and Lezotte, 1990) published by the National Center for Effective Schools Research and Development at the University of Wisconsin, Madison.

CONCLUSIONS REGARDING IDENTIFICATION AND ASSESSMENT OF SCHOOLS WITH UNUSUALLY HIGH ACHIEVEMENT

The criteria and analytic methods for classifying a school or schools as effective or ineffective have been topics of considerable debate and research. Studies of school effectiveness can and have used various norm-referenced and criterion-referenced tests and sub-tests assessing academic achievement in reading, maths and other subjects (combined or separated by subject, aggregated or separated across grade levels), measures of attendance and disciplinary patterns, affective variables such as student satisfaction, and a host of other output criteria. In addition, effectiveness defined in terms of academic achievement can and has been assessed in accordance with the current standing of a school or schools compared with others, patterns of recent improvement or non-improvement, rate of gain in outcome measures, performance above or below prediction based on students' background characteristics (the 'outlier model'), and disaggregation to determine whether differing groups of students perform at comparable levels. Our review of the diverse literature involving achievement criteria of effectiveness led to the following conclusions.

1 Differing achievement criteria of effectiveness and data-analysis methods frequently lead to conflicting conclusions about whether a school is effective or ineffective. Thus it is best to be cautious regarding conclusions drawn from school effectiveness research.

Researchers who have carefully examined the data in school effectiveness studies have generally concluded that many schools identified as particularly successful according to a particular measure, such as reading scores or subscores at a particular grade, do not stand out as unusually successful with respect to other grade levels, other subject areas or alternative performance measures (norm-referenced or criterion-referenced) in the same subject or a related subject area (Rowan *et al.*, 1983; Frederick and Clauset, 1985; Levine and Stephenson, 1987; Homiston, 1988; Brousseau, 1989; Tate *et al.* 1989).

Various researchers also report that identification of a given school or schools as effective depends on methodological variations, such as the socioeconomic measures used to control for students' background, and the way data are constructed (e.g. mean achievement versus percentage of students above a criterion level) and disaggregated (no or minimal difference between working-class and middle-class students versus high absolute level of the total group (Lark *et al.*, 1984; Frederick and Clauset, 1985; Zirkel and Greenwood, 1987; Homiston, 1988)). In addition, control for students' social class has frequently been inadequate, multiple regression approaches used to identify outliers have often resulted in designation of a school as effective or ineffective based on only slight achievement differentials, differing data analysis methods frequently produce differing conclusions, invalid conclusions regarding the utility of a particular school characteristic have sometimes been drawn from data on one item embedded in a correlated set of questionnaire items, and conclusions concerning correlates of effectiveness have sometimes been drawn (usually unknowingly) from data on one or two idiosyncratic schools which may report incorrect or misleading data in a sample of fifty, one hundred or more schools (Gastright, 1977; Rowan *et al.*, 1983; Levine and Stephenson, 1987; Brousseau, 1989; Huff *et al.*, 1989; Tate *et al.*, 1989).

2 Both researchers and practitioners should be careful to specify meaningful achievement criteria and to address analytic issues involved in identifying unusually effective schools and in planning, implementing and assessing efforts to make a school or group of schools more effective.

One of the most distressing results of methodological uncertainties such as those enumerated above has been a tendency to draw conclusions regarding school effectiveness correlates and practices from data regarding student performance on low-level learning tasks that are most easily taught and tested by teachers and are most easily memorized and regurgitated by students. This tendency is particularly evident in the many studies which depend wholly or largely on such outcome criteria as: (a) primary-grades test scores, which generally and perhaps necessarily are very limited in assessing independent learning, conceptual application, thinking and other higher-order tasks and skills (Heibert, 1988); (b) scores aggregated across grade levels so that poor performance on higher-order tasks and skills is masked by acceptable performance on low-order skills at lower grades; and (c) scores aggregated across tests and subtests, so that high performance on mechanical skills such as punctuation, spelling and mathematical computation disguises unacceptable performance on fundamental reading and maths skills such as comprehension of text and problem-solving (Levine and Stephenson, 1987; Brousseau, 1989).

Utilization of achievement criteria which allow for identification or designation of unusual effectiveness based on low-level learning is particularly pernicious because it can and does result in stress on correlates and practices that can negatively affect students' later performance. For example, because mechanical skills such as spelling and simple computation may be taught successfully through drill and seatwork, studies that classify schools as effective or improving based mostly on testing of mechanical skills may conclude or suggest that more stress should be placed on teacher presentation of material and passive seatwork even though much other research indicates that more active student learning is required for meaningful long-range performance (Peterson, 1988; Presseisen, 1988; Porter, 1989; Jones and Idol, 1991). This tendency appears to be particularly worrisome with respect to low-achieving disadvantaged students, for whom instruction already places a great emphasis on low-level drill and repetition in regular classes, Chapter 1, special education, bilingual education, and other remedial learning settings (Cazden, 1985; Allington *et al.*, 1986; Allington, 1990).

Given the dysfunctional and counter-productive consequences which can result from selection of inadequate achievement criteria of effectiveness and faulty analytic methods, I believe that researchers and practitioners should utilize the following guidelines to the extent possible in the future:

(a) Performance on higher-order learning should be separated from and treated as ultimately more important than mechanical skills. Examples of utilization of this guideline include: emphasis on reading comprehension and maths problem-solving sections of standardized tests, rather than language mechanics and maths computation; introduction of and emphasis on newly developed assessment instruments focusing on higher-order learning and thinking skills (Guthrie, 1987; Cooper, 1989; Ivens and Koslin, 1989); and insistence that tests utilized should be within most students' independent reading range so that one can obtain a meaningful measure of their levels of performance and functional learning strengths and weaknesses.

(b) Performance in the upper-elementary grades should be stressed more than test scores in the primary grades. Of course, there are some schools which enrol only primary students, usually in grades K-2 or K-3. In this situation, additional caution should be exercised in identifying effective and ineffective schools or assessing the impact of improvement efforts.

(c) Analysis and interpretation should give explicit attention to testing phenomena and conditions likely to generate invalid identification and conclusions regarding unusually effective or ineffective schools. Among the most frequent sources of invalid identification or conclusions are the following: failure to examine the validity and accuracy of unusually high gains reported at some schools (Armor, 1976); failure to take account of spurious effects of retaining a significant number of students in one or more grades (Gottfredson *et al.*, 1988; Walker and Levine, 1988); and failure to take account of floor (i.e. guessing) and ceiling effects in assessing the difference between pre- and post-scores.

(d) Whenever possible, make use of both norm-referenced and criterion-referenced tests. The advantages and disadvantages of each type of test have been widely discussed in recent years. For example, norm-referenced tests assess skills that may not have been emphasized in the classroom, and frequently do not provide adequate data for identifying objectives and skills that require further emphasis (Ivens, 1988; Haney and Madaus, 1989). On the other hand, norm-referenced tests frequently provide the only available indicators of whether school or student performance is adequate compared with other groups of schools or students. Conversely, criterion-referenced mastery tests frequently are superior to normed tests in determining whether performance is adequate and/or improving on the skills emphasized in instruction (Lezotte, 1986; Brousseau, 1989).

(e) If possible, use multiple measures of students' social and economic background to control for social class influences on achievement. The most frequently used US indicator, i.e. students' subsidized lunch status, sometimes is of relatively little use, in part because some principals are much more active than others in reporting students' status and designating students to receive assistance. In addition, many low-income students are from single-adult homes in which the parent ranks misleadingly high on educational measures of status. Some research suggests that use of multiple indicators of socioeconomic status (SES) and related home-environment variables provides a better control for student background than do unidimensional indicators such as family income level or eligibility for federally subsidized lunch. For example, one study of achievement in big cities found that measures of socioeconomic disorganization (e.g. percentage of vacant housing, percentage of adult females separated or divorced) and occupation (e.g. percentage of employed persons classified as labourers) in neighbourhoods served by elementary schools sometimes provided a much better prediction of school reading level than did the most commonly used indicator portraying student eligibility for subsidized lunch (Levine *et al.*, 1979).

Data on students' racial/ethnic background are also useful and important in determining whether a school or group of schools is unusually effective. Researchers are not certain whether the entire achievement differential between high-achieving non-minority groups and low-achieving minority groups (e.g. black, Mexican American, Native American) is due to social class differences, in part because social class is difficult to measure and may have different achievement dynamics for differing students or group of students. If some minorities are additionally disadvantaged over and beyond the effects of SES, data on racial/ethnic composition can help control for this difference in assessing school effectiveness. Even if there were no such differential, moreover, data on racial/ethnic composition might still help in assessing social class differentials that have not been captured by available SES measures.

(f) Except in special circumstances, assessment of a given school's effectiveness should be in accordance with data disaggregated by student SES and race/ethnicity. Advocacy of disaggregation by social class and race/ethnicity has played a key part in research and school improvement efforts carried on by Edmonds (1978), Brookover (1985), Shoemaker (1984), Lezotte (1986) and other prominent individuals associated with the effective schools movement. Their central ideas in advocating this position have included a concern that failure to disaggregate can result in identification of schools as effective even though their working-class students and/or minority students have unacceptably low performance, and a belief that calling attention to achievement discrepancies by social class and race/ethnicity can both point the way towards needed changes and begin to build in accountability for initiating such change (Lezotte and Bancroft, 1985a; LeMahieu, 1988).

(g) Gender differentials and interactions should be examined in determining whether a given school or group of schools is effective or is becoming more effective. This guideline is desirable partly because the average achievement of females has tended to lag behind average male achievement in science and maths and partly because performance in these subjects is becoming increasingly important for subsequent success in the educational system and the economy.

EFFECTIVE SCHOOLS CORRELATES

After examining and re-examining numerous large- and small-scale studies of unusually effective schools as well as related literatures (e.g. on organizational theory and school improvement in general), we (Levine and Lezotte, 1990) identified their characteristics (or 'correlates') as shown in Figure 2.1. We tried to word the characteristics in terminology which has more immediate and practical implications than most earlier formulations, and we have somewhat expanded

Productive school climate and culture
- Orderly environment
- Staff commitment to a shared and articulated mission focused on achievement
- Problem-solving orientation
- Staff cohesion, collaboration, consensus, communications and collegiality
- Staff input into decision-making
- School-wide emphasis on recognizing positive performance

Focus on student acquisition of central learning skills
- Maximum availability and use of time for learning
- Emphasis on mastery of central learning skills

Appropriate monitoring of student progress

Practice-oriented staff development at the school site

Outstanding leadership
- Vigorous selection and replacement of teachers
- Maverick orientation and buffering
- Frequent, personal monitoring of school activities, and sense-making
- High expenditure of time and energy for school improvement actions
- Support for teachers
- Acquisition of resources
- Superior instructional leadership
- Availability and effective utilization of instructional support personnel

Salient parent involvement

Effective instructional arrangements and implementation
- Successful grouping and related organizational arrangements
- Appropriate pacing and alignment
- Active/enriched learning
- Effective teaching practices
- Emphasis on higher-order learning in assessing instructional outcomes
- Co-ordination in curriculum and instruction
- Easy availability of abundant, appropriate instructional materials
- Classroom adaptation
- Stealing time for reading, language and maths

High operationalized expectations and requirements for students

Other possible correlates
- Student sense of efficacy/futility
- Multi-cultural instruction and sensitivity
- Personal development of students
- Rigorous and equitable student promotions policies and practices

Figure 2.1 *Characteristics of unusually effective schools*
Source: Levine and Lezotte (1990)

most traditional listings to include additional headings and subheadings which we believe have relatively solid support in the literature as well as from experience in the field. For example, we concluded that the characteristic designating 'high expectations' for students should be redefined to refer to 'high *operationalized* expectations *and* requirements', with the focus centring on how teachers and administrators *act* to ensure that students receive adequate support and encouragement to satisfy high expectations. The reader should note that most of the research in the United States deals with elementary and intermediate schools. Although such research generally has relevance for secondary schools, implications may differ somewhat because of their greater complexity and size.

Throughout our analysis, we emphasized that the correlates constitute a *set* of characteristics identifying considerations *all or most of which must be addressed* if a school is to be unusually effective in producing student achievement. For example, the staff may well have high expectations for students and may establish a productive climate, but achievement is not likely to be high in the absence of effective arrangements for delivering instruction. Similarly, focus on student acquisition of central learning skills will have little impact unless the staff insist on high expectations and requirements. (Our use of the term 'central learning skills' refers to a manageable number of key cognitive skills, rather than a host of mechanical skills frequently taught through page-by-page coverage of text.)

We were surprised at the extent of support apparent in the literature for several of the correlates and sub-correlates identified in Figure 2.1. For example, the sub-correlate describing 'active/enriched learning' is identified in numerous descriptions of unusually effective schools, but this characteristic has not generally been highlighted in most previous formulations, perhaps in part because differing authors have used varied terminology in drawing attention to one or another aspect of the same general underlying phenomenon.

Other correlates and sub-correlates for which support in the literature seemed considerably more widespread than we expected included those dealing with the presence and importance of building-level instructional support personnel to assist the headteacher and staff in implementing effective instruction, the tendency for leaders of unusually effective schools to take vigorous action in selecting and, sometimes, replacing teachers, and leadership behaviours focused on acquisition of resources for the school.

An additional correlate of effectiveness that seemed to grow in prominence as we reviewed various studies is related to the widely remarked tendency for headteachers of unusually effective schools to be 'maverick' risk-takers who practise 'creative insubordination' as they 'buffer' their school from negative external influence. What struck us as we reviewed descriptions of outstanding headteachers was that their risk-taking frequently seemed to extend as much or more to internal as to external relationships. That is, they seem to be as willing to risk 'organizational maintenance' objectives as they are to ignore or reject unproductive external regulations and policies. Examples of internal risk-taking involve such matters as insistence that teachers follow school-wide policies that benefit the entire school even if doing so disturbs seniority arrangements in the building or otherwise discomforts some staff, and stress on transferring out of non-contributing teachers. In other words, headteachers of unusually effective schools do not allow organizational maintenance goals to subvert productivity goals. At the same time, they appear to be skilled in providing a supportive environment for teachers and in motivating staff to perform at a high level. Thus they do not neglect or discount maintenance considerations, but they also do not sacrifice academic effectiveness to maintain internal harmony.

CREATING EFFECTIVE SCHOOLS

Before the 1980s, most unusually effective schools attained this status basically on their own with little or no external assistance or participation in an effective schools 'project'. A portrayal of developments frequently present at these rare schools has been provided by Stringfield and Teddlie (1987) as follows:

> **Step 1.** An instructional leader or leadership group, ideally though not necessarily including the principal, emerges or, more often, arrives. This [person or group has] ... a vision for what the school and its students could become. Though [the leaders] may not consciously know it in the beginning, they are prepared to work very long hours for years to achieve their vision....
>
> **Step 2.** [The principal chooses] new teachers and aides with great care ... [looking] for 'spark' or 'energy' ... [rather than] years of teaching experience or advanced degrees.
>
> **Step 3.** Either alone or with the aid of their staff the instructional leader(s) conduct an accurate instructional audit of the school.
>
> **Step 4.** In areas where multiple resources are available, effective principals become increasingly active in targeting career development for some, occasionally all, staff.
>
> **Step 5.** The level of principal awareness of research on teacher effectiveness varied ... from moderate to non-existent. But all exercised the common sense notion that hard work leads to success.... Teachers who do not meet reasonable instructional standards are put on probation, provided assistance, then either exhibit improvement, transfer to another school/district, or are fired.
>
> **Step 6.** A uniform homework policy ... [and] a minimum daily homework expectation [often are established].
>
> **Step 7.** Special programs such as Chapter 1 and Special Education are thoughtfully coordinated with the regular program.
>
> (Stringfield and Teddlie, 1987, pp. 11-13)

Many schools that have participated in effective schools projects or similar school improvement efforts have failed to register substantial and lasting gains in student achievement or other major indicators reflecting student performance. On the other hand, many other schools have improved substantially while participating in such efforts (McCormack-Larkin and Kritek, 1982; Clark and McCarthy, 1983; Eubanks and Levine, 1983; Taylor, 1984; Gauthier *et al.*, 1985; Lezotte and Bancroft, 1985a; Everson *et al.*, 1986; Nagel, 1986; Butler, 1989; Groom, 1989; Murphy and Waynant, 1989). The remainder of this section will review some of the most important guidelines and lessons that have emerged from experience at schools participating in effectiveness improvement projects.

1 Substantial staff development time must be provided for participating schools preferably at least in part during the regular teacher work day. In agreement with research indicating that teachers' acquisition and successful utilization of new or improved instructional approaches requires considerable time and practice extending to coaching and practice at the classroom level, staff development must be an integral and ongoing activity in projects to make schools more effective. The lengthy period of time required to provide teachers with significantly more effective methods for improving students' comprehension skills has been underlined by Kurth and Stromberg (1984), who worked with a small group of teachers to promote more independent reading in a suburban elementary school and found that success depended on 'continuous, almost Herculean' staff development efforts.

2 Staff engaged in effective schools projects must not wait very long before beginning to address issues involving improvement of instruction. Schools should place some stress on general climate, academic press, orderly environment and related effectiveness correlates that almost always need some attention and sometimes should be treated as the highest priority on which other improvements are dependent. Unfortunately, some schools participating in effective schools projects tend to become fixated on climate, parent involvement or other correlates which do not directly involve instruction (Pecheone and Shoemaker, 1984; Lezotte and Bancroft, 1985b; Azumi, 1987; Lezotte and Taylor, 1989), perhaps in part because instructional issues are more difficult to address, involve fundamental intra-school differences in philosophy and values, and/or tend to require more resources than do climate improvements (Benore, 1989).

3 Schools embarking on an effective schools project must avoid getting bogged down in elaborate schemes to train all staff in the details of a particular instructional technique or approach at the beginning of the project. This guideline is of great importance for three reasons. Firstly, significant attention must be given to the larger effective schools framework and set of correlates during the critical first stages of a project. Secondly, intensive training in a new instructional approach frequently will preoccupy the staff and drain their mental and physical energy. Thirdly, imposition of a particular instructional approach, such as a specific lesson-delivery sequence or co-operative student learning, early in a project frequently results in mindless implementation that tends to discredit the concept of instructional reform. Thus considerable time and effort during the first year should be devoted to general awareness and to key effective schools correlates involving expectations and requirements for students, grouping arrangements, alignment of curriculum, instruction, testing, availability of adequate instructional materials, and other prerequisites for success in implementing instructional techniques.

4 Improvement goals must be sharply focused to avoid teacher and school overload. One of the most common reasons why effective schools projects fail is because they try to do too much in too short a time (Lezotte and Bancroft, 1985b; Henderson and Lezotte, 1988). This is particularly the case when staff development, curriculum development and other resources are limited (as they almost always are).

One common example of counter-productive overload involves school improvement projects in which the staff of inner-city elementary schools are expected to improve instruction in reading, language, arts, maths, science and social studies, all in one year (Levine, 1985). Overload of teachers participating in effective schools projects is but one small subset of a widespread US and perhaps international tendency to expect teachers to improve all aspects of instruction within a very short period of time. Thus success in an effective schools project sometimes may depend on bringing about an 'organized abandonment' of numerous existing activities which are fragmented and incoherent.

5 The success of components dealing with instruction depends substantially on identifying and overcoming obstacles to effective implementation of whatever arrangements and programmes are selected and utilized. Inevitably, existing and proposed arrangements and programmes for delivering instruction will pose particular obstacles associated with their implementation in a school or classroom. For example, the absence of mastery learning arrangements frequently results in neglect of the problems of low achievers, but introduction of fully fledged mastery learning requires substantial training, technical assistance, teacher planning time and other resources (Levine, 1985). Similarly, homogeneous grouping in secondary schools will generally detract from the learning of low achievers unless steps are taken to maintain high expectations, provide skilled and motivated teachers, and otherwise bolster learning opportunities, while heterogeneous grouping will tend to reduce the learning of high achievers unless decisive steps are taken to counteract this tendency.

6 Significant technical assistance must be made available to schools participating in effective schools projects. Primarily in the form of specialized personnel, technical assistance is critically important in helping schools to assess their current levels of effectiveness and to initiate and carry out significant changes in educational programming and delivery. Depending on the nature, scope, history, stage and origins of a given effective schools project, technical assistance may involve state department of education or central office specialists, other external consultants, and/or in-school staff or organizational development personnel.

For example, Pecheone and Shoemaker (1984), Shoemaker (1986) and Kelly (1989) have described substantial specialized assistance made available by the Connecticut, Maine and New York State Departments of Education; Groom (1989) portrays a successful big-city project in which three full-time effective schools staff and other external resources as well as a full-time instructional specialist at each school are available to eighteen elementary schools; Kopple's (1985) assessment of school improvement efforts in Philadelphia concluded that a facilitator must be present in the school at least one day a week for several years; and Murphy and Waynant (1989) describe somewhat similar arrangements for a project involving the predominantly black elementary schools in a large suburban district.

7 Effective schools projects should be 'data-driven' in the sense that appropriate information should be collected and utilized to guide participants in preparing

and carrying out plans for improvement. As pointed out in the preceding section, staff attention in effective schools projects should include a focus on discrepancies between advantaged and disadvantaged students in acquiring key learning skills, particularly those involving higher order learning. School-level analysis of such data not only provides a basis for designing pertinent improvement efforts, but, equally importantly, calls attention to the educational outcomes to which school and district personnel attribute priority importance (Lezotte and Bancroft, 1985a). Examples of effective schools projects in which appropriate data played a central part in shaping effective implementation have been provided in Murphy and Waynant's (1989) description of a large suburban project, Benore's (1989) analysis of a multi-district project in Michigan, descriptions by Gauthier (1982), Shoemaker (1982, 1984) and their colleagues working at the state level in Connecticut, and Azumi's (1987) description of an elementary-school project in Newark.

8 Effective schools projects must avoid reliance on bureaucratic implementation stressing forms and checklists as well as mandated components rigidly applied in participating schools and classrooms. Among the best established findings of research dealing with significant school improvement efforts are the conclusions that: scope must be allowed for adapting a proposed change in curriculum or instruction in the context of participating schools and classrooms; assistance should be provided through the efforts of informed individuals as contrasted with bureaucratic checklists and regulations; and identification and resolution of practical problems in implementation depend on participants' personal knowledge and understanding of complex realities more than impersonal control mechanisms that are convenient for high-level decision-makers (Fullan, 1982; Taylor, 1984; Cox *et al.*, 1987; Henshaw *et al.*, 1987; Wimpelberg, 1987; Guba and Lincoln, 1989). 'Technoholic' approaches (Vaill, 1989) that attempt to impose improvement through comprehensive, linear programming and supervision are no more likely to work well in schools than in other types of organizations.

9 Effective schools projects should seek out and consider using materials, methods and approaches that have been successful in schools and projects elsewhere. Improving school effectiveness is a difficult undertaking which the staff of a participating school or project cannot be expected to implement successfully entirely on their own initiative. Approaches developed elsewhere can seldom if ever be transported successfully without considerable adaptation, but prospects for success in effective schools projects are greatly enhanced when participants judiciously consider and adapt appropriate approaches developed and successfully implemented in other locations (Lezotte and Bancroft, 1985b; Heim *et al.*, 1989).

10 The success of an effective schools project depends on a judicious mixture of autonomy among participating faculties and a measure of directiveness from the central office, a kind of 'directed autonomy'. Flexibility and independence in making decisions about the implementation of instruction and other aspects of education have been identified as correlates of effectiveness at both the school

and classroom levels. On the other hand, except in the case of isolated maverick schools that have become effective largely on their own, success also requires considerable direction and support from central leadership. This conclusion is compatible with those of researchers who have studied innovation in general and found that it is most likely to be successful when it combines elements of 'bottom-up' planning and decision-making with 'top-down' stimuli and support in setting directions and guiding the change process (Huberman and Miles, 1982; Hackman and Walton, 1986; Hall and Hord, 1987; McLaughlin, 1987; Pajak and Glickman, 1989).

DIRECTIONS FOR EFFECTIVE SCHOOLS RESEARCH AND PRACTICE

The preceding brief discussion of the characteristics and creation of unusually effective schools has identified a number of implications arising from US research dealing with school effectiveness and related topics. In this section I will discuss several of the research-related issues that have large, general implications in studying school effectiveness and working to enhance it.

1 Whenever possible, research on the characteristics of unusually effective schools should begin with multivariate analysis to identify a limited set of clear outliers among a large group of schools, and proceed to case studies that examine possible differences between unusually effective and ineffective schools. A number of multivariate studies (e.g. Kijai, 1988; Brousseau, 1989) have primarily used linear analysis and reported that few if any school characteristics are related to effectiveness. That is, schools which rank somewhat high in leadership, climate, expectations or other correlates do not have consistently higher achievement than schools that rank somewhat low. This is not surprising in that much of the variance in achievement in a large group of schools is associated with student SES and other hard-to-measure extraneous factors.

This analytical problem can be overcome to some extent by identifying those relatively few schools that are clearly and consistently effective or ineffective after controlling for SES and determining whether they differ on proposed correlates. Equally importantly, this approach encompasses a (justified) presumption that the correlates are *prerequisites* for unusual effectiveness: ranking relatively high on one correlate will not have much impact unless a school also ranks relatively high on other key correlates. Extending the research into case study analysis of the clear outliers can then not only allow for identification of those correlates which distinguish unusually effective and ineffective schools, but can help identify 'new' correlates and formulations not previously examined. Indeed, much of the most valuable knowledge of school effectiveness in the United States has emerged from just this type of research (e.g. Hallinger and Murphy, 1986; Stringfield and Teddlie, 1988; Teddlie *et al.*, 1989).

2 Case study research is also required to disentangle and understand the dynamics of variables that are or should be part of a scale in multivariate analysis. In order to avoid washing out variables in a set of correlated variables in a multivariate analysis of effectiveness, researchers can and indeed must

create scales encompassing those that are highly intercorrelated. Particularly if analysis is based on a theoretically justified model, scales can then provide useful information concerning the possible sources of unusual effectiveness.

For example, a recent study (Heck *et al.*, 1990) of outlier schools in California organized variables into an eighteen-item scale assessing School Instructional Organization (e.g. headteacher behaviours involving identification of in-service needs, co-ordination of the instructional programme across grade levels, and evaluation of curricular programmes). After controlling for information on student background and school climate and governance, the study found that Instructional Organization apparently has independent effects on climate and achievement. However, although findings from the study are instructive, it would be a mistake to conclude that each of the eighteen intercorrelated instructional organization variables is universally or even frequently an important determinant of effectiveness. Without additional information, it is difficult to conclude that any given variable in an intercorrelated set is operationally important. To conclude that a particular instructional organization variable, such as 'identifies in-service needs', 'makes regular visits to the classroom' or 'uses test results for program improvement', is a central consideration in improving effectiveness requires some form of case study analysis at schools which rank high or low in effectiveness.

3 Effective schools research in the future must devote much more systematic attention to considerations involving emphasis on or neglect of active/enriched learning and higher-order skills in implementing and assessing instruction. As noted in Figure 2.1, our review of the literature (Levine and Lezotte, 1990) concluded that emphases on mastery of central learning skills, active/enriched learning, and higher-order learning in assessment (or similar constructs) are important correlates of unusual effectiveness. Unfortunately, the importance of these correlates has frequently been masked by deficiencies in defining and measuring effectiveness. In particular, studies which categorize schools as effective when students achieve well on low-order skills in the lower grades may not identify and support such correlates because they will not contribute to measured effectiveness. Indeed, the opposite emphasis - on teacher presentation and testing of mechanical skills - is more likely to be associated with effectiveness. Not until students move into upper grades and encounter more advanced subject matter in which success is dependent on higher order functioning do the counter-productive consequences of thus misdefining effectiveness become readily apparent. In the meantime, tendencies to stress correlates of low-level 'effectiveness' (e.g. over-testing of students, over-emphasis on direct instruction in small skills) may well be reinforced through participation in misguided effective school projects based on misguided research and analysis. Much of this negative cycle has been captured in Porter's (1990) characterization of mathematics instruction which places:

> too much attention on computation skills and not enough on conceptual understanding and the ability to solve novel problems. . . . The curriculum as taught is largely the curriculum one finds in popular textbooks and in the bulk of assessment

> practices. It is the curriculum typically emphasized as a part of the so-called effective schools movement . . . [implemented within state and district frameworks that] typically specify minimum standards for what should be taught, standards that also take a heavy skills orientation.
>
> (Porter, 1990, p.v. 16)

4 How one formulates effective schools correlates will determine whether they will be supported by research and whether they will be useful guides for improving practice. Although the preceding generalization is an obvious truism, it has not been adequately addressed and recognized in effective schools research and practice. Perhaps I can communicate this point best with a few examples.

Both researchers and practitioners in the United States have disagreed among themselves concerning the role and meaning of parent and community involvement as an effective schools correlate. Some formulations have used terminology such as 'high parent involvement' on the grounds that several studies support this correlate and involvement of parents clearly can be helpful in working to improve effectiveness. Other analysts omit this correlate, usually after pointing to research indicating no difference between more and less effective schools. After reviewing numerous descriptions of unusually effective schools, Lezotte and I decided to include the correlate 'salient parent involvement' because so many of these descriptions highlighted one or another aspect of parent or community participation in working to improve student achievement (Levine and Lezotte, 1990).

What is 'salient parent involvement'? I cannot offer any relatively concrete definition since we deliberately used an ambiguous phrase calling attention to the context-dependent value of any particular aspect of involvement and the wide range of appropriate involvement activities that may be desirable at a given school. The point I want to emphasize in this chapter is that more concrete terminology could be misleading and counter-productive because it might encourage researchers and practitioners to fixate on one aspect, such as frequent school visits or high expressed support for school change, when other aspects may be more important or have greater potential value at a particular school or group of schools.

Similarly with respect to monitoring of student progress, some formulations have cited 'frequent' monitoring but some studies have found little support for this correlate, and in the field advocacy of frequent monitoring sometimes reinforces over-testing of narrow, mechanical skills. After reviewing descriptions of unusually effective schools, we identified 'appropriate monitoring of student progress' as a correlate of effectiveness, but I can't tell you exactly what this means in terms of specific prescriptions for practice and I don't know how to remedy this gap in our knowledge other than through continuing research designed to define our understanding of 'appropriate monitoring' in the future.

A third example involves grouping of students. As mentioned above, either homogeneous or heterogeneous grouping can have deleterious consequences unless something is done to counteract their disadvantages. From this point of view, grouping clearly has important implications for school effectiveness. Yet most correlate formulations have not included any characteristic dealing with grouping, perhaps because the large body of research on this topic has been complex and internally conflicting and because grouping is a very contentious issue at the school site. (There are important reasons to minimize or eliminate homogeneous grouping and tracking to the extent possible, but this conclusion cannot be drawn simply from clear research findings.)

One frequent result has been to omit consideration of grouping in conducting achievement improvement projects, despite its central importance in determining effectiveness. After reviewing descriptions of unusually effective schools, Lezotte and I formulated the subcorrelate 'Successful grouping and related organizational arrangements' (Figure 2.1) and listed numerous examples, particularly focusing on introduction of workable arrangements to help low achievers. We hope that this formulation will help to point future research towards examination of such arrangements and also will be useful in helping practitioners consider what to change and improve in their schools.

5 Effective schools research should do more to delineate the interplay and interrelationships between central-level and school-site decisions and actions in generating unusual effectiveness. As noted above, success in working to improve effectiveness across a group of schools depends on a mixture of autonomy among participating schools and appropriate directiveness and support from central-office decision-makers. In my own experience, some effective schools projects have been either severely compromised or virtually destroyed in districts where central administrators maintained the facade and terminology associated with a project but diverted participants' attention to other topics temporarily spotlighted in the latest educational journals and magazines. Other projects fail because schools are left alone to ignore key correlates of effectiveness.

Research on district responsibilities in contributing to school effectiveness has been limited, but results tend to confirm the central importance of district leadership and support. For example, Murphy and Hallinger (1986) studied superintendents of twelve unusually effective school districts in California and concluded that they were 'actively involved' and 'influential' in developing both district and school goals, in procedures for actually selecting staff (particularly new administrators), in supervising and evaluating headteachers, establishing and regularly monitoring a 'district wide instructional and curricular focus', and ensuring consistency in 'technical core' operations such as functioning of categorically funded programmes and use of standardized teacher evaluation procedures.

Much of the responsibility of central leadership in implementing effective schools projects revolves around provision and/or assurance of adequate resources to allow for successful implementation of mandated system-wide policies and practices (Stevens, 1988). 'Mandating improvement without providing needed resources', as recently was concluded in an evaluation of school-based reform efforts in New York City, 'only encourages staff cynicism and inaction' (Kelley and Willner, 1988, p. 67). Central responsibility frequently centres on the need to make sure that changes are manageable for teachers with respect to considerations such as record-keeping, class size, daily student load responsibilities, and time for staff development and individual and collaborative planning. When central decision-makers abdicate their responsibilities for providing sufficient resources to implement their mandates, the result is likely to be an outcome variously described by informed observers with terminology such as 'nonimplementation' (Brieschke, 1987), 'illusory' implementation (Popkewitz *et al.*, 1982), 'cosmetic' reform (Orlich, 1989), 'symbolic' implementation (Mann, 1989), 'phantom' implementation (Pogrow, 1983) and 'hallucinatory' implementation (Levine and Lezotte, 1990).

In addition to delineating connections between allocation of resources and unusual effectiveness at the building level, research should help us learn more about the ways in which the functioning as well as the absence of central policies and practices supports or detracts from effectiveness. Allington (1990) has described examples of this interplay as follows:

> The importance of discovering the district plan or plans is best demonstrated [in studies indicating that] when the district plan produced four separate and incompatible commercial reading/language arts materials, most teachers offered an incoherent array of instructional tasks drawn from these materials. When the district plan mandated a different and incompatible curricular approach to reading in remedial or special education, teachers followed that mandate. . . . On the other hand, when district plans called for coherent and collaborative approaches . . . teachers offered the same. When districts included literature in their reading curriculum and made appropriate materials available, teachers used them. When books were unavailable, but workbooks and Xerox machines were available, teachers filled up the day with low-level paper/pencil tasks.
>
> (Allington, 1990, p. 1.12)

6 In examining connections between effective teaching and school-level effectiveness, effective schools research should take account of distinctions between principles of effective instruction and prescriptions for teacher behaviour. Effective schools research in the USA has been relatively sparse in identifying and explicating relationships between teaching practices and school characteristics that may interact to generate unusual effectiveness (Levine and Lezotte, 1990). Difficulties in linking these two areas of research have undoubtedly been due in part to the perplexing problem researchers encounter in trying to define and reach generalizable conclusions regarding effective teaching (Gage and Needels, 1989) and to the fact that teachers in a school may rank relatively high with respect to presumably desirable practices such as positive reinforcement for correct responses, but the school may be inadequate with respect to numerous other correlates. In addition, there has been a tendency to define effective teaching in terms of relatively prescriptive practices (e.g. three-second wait time, six- or seven-step lesson sequence) which may have positive or negative effects depending on flexibility in implementation and on student's achievement levels, type of content taught and many other contextual considerations.

Recent analysis by Porter (1990) has called attention to fundamental differences between detailed, micro-level 'prescriptions for teaching' and 'principles of good teaching [which] are general guidelines and predispositions that point teachers in productive directions'. After citing teacher emphasis on ensuring that 'each student knows what is to be learned' as a principle of good teaching, Porter points out that it is much more difficult to determine whether teachers are implementing such principles than whether they are following specific behavioural prescriptions (Porter, 1990, p. v. 9). Effective schools researchers can benefit from recognition of this distinction, which may help them avoid futile diversions that search for unlikely relationships between highly specific and mechanical teaching behaviours on the one hand and substantial gains in student achievement on the other.

Research to date has identified several principles of effective instruction (i.e. 'good teaching') that appear to be identified with school effectiveness. For example, unusually effective schools appear to emphasize 'maximum availability and use of time for learning', 'mastery of central learning skills' and 'active/enriched learning' (Levine and Lezotte, 1990; see Figure 2.1). A recent synthesis by Blum *et al.* (1990) of research on 'effective schooling' identifies many more such principles which may be associated with unusual effectiveness at the school level. For example, under the heading 'Effective questioning techniques are used to build basic and higher-level skills', Blum *et al.* conclude that effective teachers 'make use of classroom questions as a part of interactive teaching and to monitor student understanding', and that questions are 'structured so as to focus students' attention on key elements in the lesson' (Blum *et al.*, 1990, p. 10). Future research exploring relationships between classroom instruction and school outcomes probably would do well to define effective instructional practices at about this level of generality.

CONCLUDING OBSERVATIONS

As noted in several ways in the preceding discussion, research and practice dealing with unusually effective schools have been somewhat bedevilled by neglect of higher-order learning in assessing effectiveness and its correlates. Such neglect has contributed to an unfortunate though not entirely unjustified rejection in some quarters of effective schools research and of frequently unproductive school improvement approaches based simplistically on its findings. This consequence has been particularly unfortunate inasmuch as plentiful support for stressing higher-order learning in identifying and creating effective schools has been present, if perhaps a little below the surface, in much of the literature.

Tendencies to neglect higher-order learning have constituted a major problem not just in effective schools research and practice but in larger domains concerned with teaching, learning and schooling. In part because research has focused on narrow teaching behaviours and objectives which are easiest to assess and implement, much was learned about how to teach small, mechanical skills but relatively little about organizing and operating classrooms and schools to deliver effective instruction focused on higher-order skills. From this point of view, effective schools research mirrors and confronts much the same problem as research on teaching and school effects in general.

Contemplating such developments, Doyle (1990) recently called for a fundamental reorientation in overall analytic perspectives regarding improvement of teaching and learning. Reiterating his earlier conclusions (Doyle, 1983) involving the difficulties of teaching for meaning in actual classrooms, he advocated stress on 'adventuresome teaching and learning' that is as relevant for the effective schools movement as for social scientists and educators who approach the issues from other perspectives:

> We have now reached a fundamental dilemma in teaching and especially the teaching of disadvantaged students. Cognitive and curricular research increasingly supports higher-order thinking as essential for achievement in all content areas. Yet classroom studies consistently point to the difficulties of enacting tasks involving such thinking in classroom environments. . . . My own sense is that meaning is vulnerable in classrooms and that learning how to construct and enact a classroom curriculum for meaning is a fundamental engineering problem in the field today.
>
> (Doyle, 1990, p. 10.12)

I cannot here attempt to provide a comprehensive analysis of the implications of this challenge to reorient schools towards a focus on thinking and meaning, but I do want to stress that meeting it will be likely to require pervasive improvement in school organization and functioning as well as curriculum and instruction. Regarding curriculum and instruction, teachers will require a great deal of 'special training in teaching a reduced curriculum in depth, with emphasis on cognitive modeling of strategies, sustained teacher-student discourse designed to produce conceptual understanding of and critical thinking about content, and follow through to a level of integration and application of learning that corresponds to the intended outcomes' (Brophy, 1990, p. 9.12). Regarding school organization and functioning, requirements will include practice-oriented staff development at the school site, superior leadership, supportive administration and resources, instructional support personnel, co-ordination of instruction across classrooms and grade levels, improvements in grouping and related organizational arrangements, and other effective schools correlates listed in Figure 2.1 (Levine, 1988; Levine and Cooper, 1991). The challenge involved in reforming schools for the purpose of enhancing higher-order learning will constitute a formidable agenda for effective schools research and practice in the 1990s.

REFERENCES

Allington, R.L. (1990) 'Effective literacy instruction for at-risk children', in Knapp, M.S. and Shields, P.M. (eds) *Better Schooling for the Children of Poverty: Alternatives to Conventional Wisdom*. Washington, DC: US Department of Education, Office of Planning, Budget and Evaluation.

Allington, R.L., Stuetzel, H., Shake, M. and Lamarche, S. (1986) 'What is remedial reading? A descriptive study', *Reading Research and Instruction*, **26** (1), 15-28.

Armor, D. *et al.* (1976) *Analysis of the School Preferred Reading Program in Selected Los Angeles Minority Schools*. Santa Monica, CA: Rand Corporation.

Azumi, J.E. (1987) 'Effective schools characteristics, school improvement and school outcomes: what are the relationships?', Paper delivered at the annual meeting of the American Educational Research Association, Washington, DC, April.

Benore, L. (1989) 'Middle cities in Michigan', in Lezotte, L.W. and Taylor, B.A. (eds) *Case Studies in Effective Schools Research*. Okemos, MI: National Center for Effective Schools Research and Development.

Blum, R.E., Butler, J.A. and Cotton, K. (1990) *Effective Schooling Practices: A Research Synthesis 1990 Update*. Portland, OR: Northwest Regional Educational Laboratory.

Brieschke, P.A. (1987) 'A study of the implementation of regulatory policy in the urban elementary school', in Noblit, G.W. and Pink, W.T. (eds) *Schooling in Social Context: Qualitative Studies*, pp. 119-43. Norwood, NJ: Ablex.

Brookover, W.B. (1985) 'Can we make schools effective for minority students?', *Journal of Negro Education*, **54** (3), 257-68.

Brophy, J.E. (1990) 'Effective schooling for disadvantaged students', in Knapp, M.S. and Shields, M.S. (eds) *Better Schooling for the Children of Poverty: Alternatives to Conventional Wisdom*. Washington, DC: US Department of Education Office of Planning, Budget and Evaluation.

Brousseau, B.A. (1989) *A Test of Five Correlates from Effective Schools Research Using Hierarchical Linear Modeling*. Unpublished PhD dissertation, Michigan State University, Lansing.

Butler, J.A. (1989) *Success for All Students*. Portland, OR: Northwest Regional Educational Laboratory.

Cazden, C.B. (1985) 'Effectiveness of instructional features in bilingual education classrooms', Paper delivered at the annual meeting of the American Educational Research Association, Chicago, April.

Clark, T.A. and McCarthy, D.P. (1983) 'School improvement in New York: the evolution of a project', *Educational Research*, **12** (4), 17-24.

Cooper, E.J. (1989) 'Toward a new mainstream of instruction for American schools', *Journal of Negro Education*, **58** (1), 102-16.

Cox, P.L., French, L.C. and Loucks-Horsley, S. (1987) *Letting the Principal off the Hotseat: Configuring Leadership and Support for School Improvement*. Andover, MA: The Regional Laboratory for Educational Improvement of the Northeast and Islands.

Doyle, W.A. (1983) 'Academic work', *Review of Educational Research*, **53**, 159-99.

Doyle, W.A. (1990) 'Class tasks: the core of learning from teaching', in Knapp, M.S. and Shields, P.M. (eds) *Better Schooling for the Children of Poverty: Alternatives to Conventional Wisdom*. Washington, DC: US Department of Education Office of Planning, Budget and Evaluation.

Edmonds, R. (1978) 'A discussion of the literature and issues related to effective schooling', Paper prepared for the National Conference on Urban Education, CENREL, St Louis, MO.

Eubanks, E.E. and Levine, D.U. (1983) 'A first look at effective schools projects in New York City and Milwaukee,' *Phi Delta Kappan*, **64** (10), 697-702.

Everson, S.T., Scollay, S.J., Fabert, B. and Garcia, M. (1986) 'An effective schools program and its results: initial district, school, teacher, and student outcomes in a participating district', *Journal of Research and Development in Education,* **19** (3), 35-49.

Frederick, J.M. and Clauset, K.H. (1985) 'A comparison of the major algorithms for measuring school effectiveness', Paper delivered at the annual meeting of the American Educational Research Association, Chicago, April.

Fullan, M. (1982) *The Meaning of Educational Change.* New York: Teachers College Press.

Gage, N.L. and Needels, M.C. (1989) 'Process-product research on teaching: a review of criticisms', *Elementary School Journal,* **89** (3), 253-300.

Gastright, J.F. (1977) 'Some empirical evidence on the compatibility of school unit residuals based on achievement and non-achievement variables', Paper delivered at the annual meeting of the American Educational Research Association, New York, April.

Gauthier, W.J. Jr (1982) 'Connecticut perspectives on instructionally effective schools', Paper delivered at the annual meeting of the American Educational Research Association, New York, March.

Gauthier, W.J. Jr, Pecheone, R.L. and Shoemaker, J. (1985) 'Schools can become more effective', *Journal of Negro Education,* **54** (3), 388-408.

Gottfredson, D.C., Hybl, L.G., Gottfredson, G.D. and Castaneda, R.P. (1988) *School Climate Assessment Instruments: A Review.* Baltimore, MD: The Johns Hopkins University Center for Social Organization of Schools.

Groom, B. (1989) 'Striving towards excellence in the performance of students - an effective school project', *Effective School Report,* **7** (2), 8.

Guba, E.G. and Lincoln, Y.S. (1989) *Fourth Generation Evaluation.* Newbury Park, CA: Sage.

Guthrie, J.T. (1987) *Indicators of Reading Education.* CRPE Research Report Series RR-005. New Brunswick, NJ: Rutgers Center for Policy Research in Education.

Hackman, J.R. and Walton, R.E. (1986) 'Leading groups in organizations', in Goodman, P.S. (ed.) *Designing Effective Work Groups,* pp. 72-119. San Francisco: Jossey-Bass.

Hall, G.E. and Hord, S.M. (1987) *Change in Schools.* Albany: State University of New York Press.

Hallinger, P. and Murphy, J. (1986) 'The social context of effective schools', *American Journal of Education,* **94** (3), 328-54.

Haney, W. and Madaus, G. (1989) 'Searching for alternatives to standardized tests: whys, whats, and whithers', *Phi Delta Kappan,* **70** (9), 683-7.

Heck, R.H., Larsen, T.J. and Marcoulides, G.A. (1990) 'Instructional leadership and school achievement: validation of a causal model', Paper delivered at the annual meeting of the American Educational Research Association, Boston, April.

Heibert, E.H. (1988) 'The role of literacy experiences in early childhood programs', *Elementary School Journal,* **89** (2), 161-71.

Heim, M.O., Flowers, D. and Anderson, P. (1989) 'School improvement in Beary County schools', in Lezotte, L.W. and Taylor, B.O. (eds) *Case Studies in Effective Schools Research.* Okemos, MI: National Center for Effective Schools Research and Development.

Henderson, A. and Lezotte, L. (1988) 'SBI and effective schools: a perfect match', *NETWORK for Public Schools,* **13** (5), 1, 3-5.

Henshaw, J., Wilson, C. and Morefield, J. (1987) 'Seeing clearly: the school as the unit of change', in Goodlad, J.I. (ed.) *The Ecology of School Renewal*, pp. 134-51. Chicago: University of Chicago Press.

Homiston, D. (1988) 'Identifying effective schools by both quantitative and qualitative methods', Paper delivered at the annual meeting of the American Educational Research Association, New Orleans, April.

Huberman, A.M. and Miles, M.B. (1982) *Innovation Up Close: A Field Study in 12 School Settings*. Andover, MA: The Network.

Huff, K., Serlin, R., Schneider, S. and Foley, E. (1989) 'A comparative analysis of achievement gains and related school characteristics', Paper delivered at the annual meeting of the American Educational Association, San Francisco, March.

Ivens, S.H. (1988) 'High stakes tests and the assessment of comprehension', *Teaching Thinking and Problem Solving*, **10** (5), 7-11.

Ivens, S.H. and Koslin, B.L. (1989) 'An important technology for assessing comprehension', Paper delivered at a meeting of the Urban Coalition for Effective Schooling, San Francisco, February.

Jones, B.F. and Idol, L. (eds) (1991) *Dimensions of Thinking and Cognitive Instruction*. Hillsdale, NJ: Erlbaum.

Kelley, T. and Willner, R. (1988) *Small Change: The Comprehensive School Improvement Program*. Albany, NY: The Educational Priorities Panel.

Kelly, T.F. (1989) 'What's new in effective schools research', Paper prepared for the BOCES III-Suffolk, New York Effective Schools Consortium.

Kijai, J. (1988) 'Discriminating Ability of the School Effectiveness Correlates', Paper delivered at the annual meeting of the American Educational Research Association, New Orleans, April.

Kopple, H. (1985) 'Replicating success', Paper delivered at the annual meeting of the American Educational Research Association, New York, April.

Kurth, R.J. and Stromberg, L.J. (1984) 'Improving the teaching of reading in elementary schools', Paper delivered at the annual meeting of the American Educational Research Association, New Orleans, April.

Lark, H.N., Blust, R.S. and Coldiron, J.R. (1984) 'An investigation of the variation in student scores for effective and ineffective schools', Paper delivered at the annual meeting of the American Educational Research Association, New Orleans, April.

LeMahieu, P.G. (1988) 'Shedding light on things that matter: toward an agenda of research on minority achievement', in Hathaway, W.E. and Kushman, J.W. (eds) *Rising to the Challenge of Differential School Performance among Student Ethnic Groups*, pp. 1-13. Portland, OR: Portland State University/Portland Public Schools.

Levine, D.U. (1985) 'A mini-description of initially-unsuccessful attempts to introduce outcomes-based instruction', *Outcomes*, **4** (2), 15-19.

Levine, D.U. (1988) 'Teaching thinking to at-risk students: generalizations and speculation', in Preisseisen, B.Z. (ed.) *At-Risk Students and Thinking: Perspectives from Research*, pp. 117-37. Washington, DC: NEA.

Levine, D.U. and Cooper, E.J. (1991) 'The change process and its implications in teaching thinking', in Idol, L. and Jones, B.F. (eds) *Educational Values and Cognitive Instruction: Implications for Reform*. Hillsdale, NJ: Erlbaum.

Levine, D.U. and Lezotte, L.W. (1990) *Unusually Effective Schools: A Review and*

Analysis of Research and Practice. Madison, WI: National Center for Effective Schools Research and Development.

Levine, D.U. and Stephenson, R.S. (1987) 'Are effective or meritorious schools meretricious?' *The Urban Review*, **19** (1), 25-34.

Levine, D.U. *et al.* (1979) 'Concentrated poverty and reading achievement in seven big cities', *The Urban Review*, **11** (2), 63-80.

Lezotte, L.W. (1986) 'School effectiveness: reflections and future directions', Paper delivered at the annual meeting of the American Educational Research Association, San Francisco, April.

Lezotte, L.W. and Bancroft, B,A. (1985a) 'Growing use of the effective schools model for school improvement', *Educational Leadership*, **42** (6), 23-7.

Lezotte, L.W. and Bancroft, B.A. (1985b) 'School improvement based on effective schools research: a promising approach for economically disadvantaged and minority students', *Journal of Negro Education*, **54** (3), 301-12.

Lezotte, L.W. and Taylor, B.A. (eds) (1989) *Case Studies in Effective Schools Research*. Okemos, MI: National Center for Effective Schools Research and Development.

McCormack-Larkin, M. and Kritek, W.J. (1982) 'Milwaukee's project RISE', *Educational Leadership*, **40** (3), 16-21.

McLaughlin, M.M. (1987) 'Learning from experience: lessons from policy administration', *Educational Evaluation and Policy Analysis*, **9** (2), 171-8.

Mann, D. (1989) 'Conditional deregulation', Unpublished paper, Teachers College, Columbia University.

Murphy, J. and Hallinger, P. (1986) 'The superintendent as instructional leader: findings from effective school districts', *Journal of Educational Administration*, **22** (2), 213-36.

Murphy, J.A. and Waynant, L.F. (1989) 'Reaching for excellence and equity in Prince George's County public schools', in Lezotte, L.W. and Taylor, B.O. (eds) *Case Studies in Effective Schools Research*. Okemos, MI: National Center for Effective Schools Research and Development.

Nagel, T. (1986) 'A longitudinal study of systematic efforts to raise standardized achievement test scores using factors from school effectiveness research', Paper delivered at the annual meeting of the American Educational Research Association, San Francisco, 1986.

Orlich, D.C. (1989) 'Educational reforms: mistakes, misconceptions, miscues', *Phi Delta Kappan*, **70** (7), 512-17.

Pajak, E.F. and Glickman, C.D. (1989) 'Dimensions of school district improvement', *Educational Leadership*, **46** (8), 61-4.

Pecheone, R. and Shoemaker, J. (1984) *An Evaluation of the School Effectiveness Program in Connecticut*. Hartford: Connecticut State Department of Education.

Peterson, P.L. (1988) 'Teaching for higher order thinking in mathematics: the challenge for the next decade', in Grouws, D.A., Cooney, T.J. and Jones, D. (eds) *Effective Mathematics Teaching*, pp. 2-26. Reston, VA: National Council of Teachers of Mathematics.

Pogrow, S. (1983) *Education in the Computer Age*. Beverly Hills, CA: Sage.

Pogrow, S. (1988) 'Teaching thinking to at-risk elementary students', *Educational Leadership*, **45** (7), 79-85.

Popkewitz, T.S., Tabachnik, R.T. and Wehlage, G. (1982) *The Myth of Educational Reform*. Madison, WI: University of Wisconsin Press.

Porter, A.C. (1989) 'A curriculum out of balance', *Educational Researcher*, **18** (5), 9-15.

Porter, A.C. (1990) 'Good teaching of worthwhile mathematics to disadvantaged students', in Knapp, M.S. and Shields, P.M. (eds) *Better Schooling for the Children of Poverty: Alternatives to Conventional Wisdom*. Washington, DC: US Department of Education Office of Planning, Budget, and Education.

Presseisen, B.Z. (ed.) (1988) *At-Risk Students and Thinking: Perspectives from Research*. Washington, DC: NEA.

Rowan, B., Bossert, S.L. and Dwyer, D. (1983) 'Research on effective schools: a cautionary note'. *Educational Researcher*, **12** (4), 24-31.

Shoemaker, J. (1982) 'Effective schools: putting the research to the ultimate test', *Pre-Post-Press*, **7** (2), 1.

Shoemaker, J. (1984) *Research-Based School Improvement Practices*. Hartford: Connecticut State Department of Education.

Shoemaker, J. (1986) 'Developing effectiveness in the district, school and classroom', *Equity and Choice*, **2** (Winter), 1-8.

Stevens, F.I. (1988) 'How do you make an elephant move? Project intervention', in Hathway, W.E. and Kushman, J.W. (eds) *Rising to the Challenge of Differential School Performance among Student Ethnic Groups*, pp. 63-85. Portland, OR: Portland State University/Portland Public Schools.

Stringfield, S. and Teddlie, C. (1987) 'A time to summarize: six years and three phases of the Louisiana School Effectiveness Study', Paper delivered at the annual meeting of the American Educational Research Association, Washington, DC, April.

Stringfield, S. and Teddlie, C. (1988) 'A time to summarize: the Louisiana School Effectiveness Study', *Educational Leadership*, **46** (2), 43-9.

Tate, R.L., Piotrowski, W. and Im, S.H. (1989) 'School comparisons with hierarchical linear models', Paper delivered at the annual meeting of the American Educational Research Association, San Francisco, March.

Taylor, B.A.O. (1984) *Implementing What Works: Elementary Principals and School Improvement Programs*. Unpublished PhD dissertation, Northwestern University, Evanston, IL.

Teddlie, C., Kirby, P.C. and Stringfield, S. (1989) 'Effective versus ineffective schools: observable differences in the classroom. *American Journal of Education*, **97** (3), 221-36.

Vaill, P. (1989) *Managing as a Peforming Art*. San Francisco: Jossey-Bass.

Walker, J. and Levine, D.U. (1988) 'The inherent impact of non-promoted students on reading scores in a big city elementary school', *The Urban Review*, **20** (4), 247-52.

Wimpelberg, R. (1987) 'The dilemma of instructional leadership and a central role for central office', in Greenfield, W. (ed.) *Instructional Leadership*, pp. 100-17. Boston, MA: Allyn & Bacon.

Zirkel, P.A. and Greenwood, S.C. (1987) 'Effective schools and effective principals: effective research?' *Teachers College Record*, **89** (2), 255-67.

Chapter 3

School Effectiveness, Effective Instruction and School Improvement in the Netherlands

Bert P.M. Creemers

INTRODUCTION

Until recently, the research basis for school effectiveness has not been very strong. What findings we can observe in one country we cannot find in another, so we clearly need more comparative research between countries based on a sound reconceptualization of ideas and theories of school effectiveness. If we have a proven theory about school effectiveness, our basis for school improvement can therefore become more stable. However, educational practice cannot wait for research results! So, even on the basis of existing knowledge, we should try to generate school and instructional improvement and thereby contribute to our knowledge base about school and instructional effectiveness. This can be achieved by rigorous evaluation procedures based upon classic quasi-experimental designs and upon analysis of the results of school improvement in terms of goals and means. In this chapter I will elaborate on these ideas, based on the experience gained in the Netherlands. In the first section I will give a review of developments in school effectiveness and school improvement in the Netherlands in the past few years, based on country reports made for the meetings of the International Congress for School Effectiveness and Improvement (Creemers and Lugthart, 1989; Creemers and Knuver, 1989). In the next section, I will argue that instructional effectiveness is not just an important component of school effectiveness, but is the starting and central point for school improvement. We have to look, then, for factors in terms of instruction which separately or together contribute to effectiveness. School effectiveness factors can in fact be seen as conditions for instructional effectiveness. In the final section I shall draw some conclusions for future research and improvement based upon the results and experiments in these fields in the Netherlands.

AN OVERVIEW OF SCHOOL EFFECTIVENESS AND SCHOOL IMPROVEMENT IN THE NETHERLANDS

The structure and organization of the Dutch educational system is characterized by centralized planning and policy-making and decentralized execution (Creemers and Terlouw, 1984). The Department of Education prescribes (by means of legislation) the structure and final achievement levels of the various school types. The curriculum (content, methods, etc.) is more or less free. Activities for the improvement of education are undertaken by individual schools and supported by local, regional and national agencies. At the national level there are an institute for curriculum development, an institute for educational testing and an institute for educational research that co-ordinates research carried out by research institutes connected with the universities.

In recent years a number of substantial changes in the educational system have demanded much attention, in the first place a change in primary education, namely the integration of kindergarten and elementary schools with primary schools (age group four to twelve). In addition developments are going on in secondary education. The lower level of secondary education in the Netherlands has not yet been integrated within one type of secondary school for all pupils. This means that a segmented system still exists, with separate schools for lower vocational and lower, intermediate and higher general education. After a number of steps towards integration, such as the integrated first form, the extended integrated first form, comprehensive school experiments and school development projects, a new change in legislation has been introduced, namely basic education. In this change in secondary education the goals of delaying choice of vocational education and of equality of opportunities are combined with a general raising of the level of education by means of a compulsory basic curriculum for all pupils of school age. These goals are given concrete form in demands for final achievement levels of all pupils.

Another important government measure is the educational priorities programme. This policy implies that schools with a large number of disadvantaged pupils can get extra teaching staff. In addition, on a regional level in areas with a great number of disadvantaged pupils, schools can obtain extra facilities for the support of their own programmes of educational priorities by co-operating with regional agencies in education and welfare. The schools are free to decide how to use the extra staff and facilities.

On the part of the policy-makers, there has been little attention so far to the evaluation of policy measures. Measures were taken mainly on the basis of political convictions and there was little interest in the effects of these measures. Therefore information is lacking about a large number of changes in the Dutch educational system and about school improvement projects, and certainly about their effects on the functioning and achievement of pupils. Attention to the effects of education and information about effective schools and school characteristics in the Netherlands can be found primarily in the area of research. This situation is changing: in the past few years and in educational policy-making and educational practice more attention has been given to school improvement based on ideas about school effectiveness. The background to this increasing attention to school improvement based on school effectiveness research can be found in experiences in the past.

School Improvement Projects

In the 1960s and 1970s school improvement projects started in a number of big cities. These projects aimed at increasing the opportunities of certain culturally disadvantaged groups. The majority of the projects aimed at both change and integration by means of developing and implementing new programmes and influencing the social environment and the relation between parents and schools. Two strategies can be found in these projects. In the project Education and Social Environment in Rotterdam a kind of research development-dissemination approach can be found, and in the Amsterdam Innovation Project a more 'bottom-up' approach, in which schools and teachers themselves were to develop educational strategies and curriculum material, was used. In the Amsterdam Innovation Project, evaluation was just a minor part of the programme and was limited to process variables, the satisfaction of teachers and the school climate. In the Education and Social Environment project, evaluation took place with regard to the effects of the developed programmes. From this evaluation it appeared that, although it was established that educational characteristics could easily be influenced, the ultimate goal of the project (pupil achievement equal to or higher than the national norm) was not achieved (Slavenburg, 1986). It appeared, however, that the more structured programmes had more positive effects than the less structured. But these effects appeared only with tests connected with the programme and not with general standardized tests.

The reasons for these disappointing results are debatable. One reason could be that the aspiration level of the developers was not high enough. They stated their own objectives for the programmes and did not develop the programmes according to the national objectives, formulated in the national tests. Another reason could be the insufficient implementation of the programmes in educational practice (see, for instance, Slavenburg and Peters, 1989; Creemers, 1990). Van Tilborg (1987) and Leseman (1990) demonstrated the limited possibilities of projects such as the Education and Social Environment project to minimize the effects of social environment. Leseman in his rigorous analysis of the results of the project demonstrates that the disappointing outcomes have to be attributed to the relatively structured character of the differences in cognitive and linguistic competences of children entering the educational system and to the quality of the projects, which apparently were not utilized for their compensatory and equalizing goals. He proposes a quite questionable alternative approach, less tightly connected to the school curriculum, aiming at fostering, training and elaborating so-called thinking skills. Furthermore, there are strong treatments by sub-group interaction effects. The evaluation of the effects of the programme seems to indicate that group-specific socio-historical factors, like extreme poverty, determine the extent to which social intervention programmes may have success. The ecological and cultural contexts offered by home and peer group are major vehicles mediating the positive effects into long-term outcomes (Leseman, 1990, pp. 365-405).

Large-scale Innovation Projects

As stated above, the large-scale innovation projects aimed at changing the structure of the Dutch educational system in the 1970s. The innovation of the basic school and the middle school were not accompanied by evaluation of the educational outcomes. Research was directed to school improvement processes and factors. With regard to the innovation of the new basic school it was possible to draw some conclusions about the effectiveness of these programmes, based on the combining of different datasets. The innovation of primary education, which intended to combine the kindergarten and grades one to six of the former primary education into a new 'basic school' from grades one to eight, was less questionable in the Netherlands, although this project was also directed to changing goals of primary education. The points of departure for this new basic education were to be:

- enhancing educational development of pupils from four to twelve years of age;
- enhancing individualization and differentiation;
- taking into account the identity of pupils;
- development of social, emotional, verbal and manual creativity;
- improvement of the diagnostic and remedial functioning of education;
- improvement of education for disadvantaged pupils.

It was considered that an important instrument to achieve these goals was the development of the school curriculum. This curriculum should be developed by the team of teachers for the whole school. The curriculum should be an operationalization of the aims of the educational reform. Implementation of this curriculum was expected to lead to the achievement of pupils, in accordance with the aims of the innovation. In the evaluation of the development of primary education, strong emphasis was given to the evaluation and results of the curriculum development. Van der Werf (1988) reports on the results. Curricula are not elaborate and only contain summaries of the teaching/learning material which is being used. Table 3.1 shows that the curricula are being used only to give information to other parties (parents, inspectorates, and so on).

The second, somewhat less important, way of using curricula is in the evaluation of the achievement of pupils. The curricula are also being used in support of teaching. The least important way of use is in the evaluation of teaching. The most important finding is that there is no direct relationship between the various ways of using the school curriculum and the learning outcomes. The correlation between the use of the curriculum for evaluation of support and student achievement is shown in Table 3.2. As this table shows, there is no relationship between the different uses of the school curriculum and learning outcomes. The

Table 3.1 *Use of school curricula*

Curriculum use	*Mean*	*Standard deviation*
Support of teaching	37	21
Control of instruction	15	21
Evaluation of learning outcomes	50	21
Information material	58	30

Source: Van der Werf (1988, p. 72).

Table 3.2 *Correlations between use of school curriculum and learning outcomes*

	Learning outcomes	
Predictors	*Mean*	*Standard deviation*
1. Use for evaluation	−0.05	−0.02
2. Use in support	−0.07	−0.02
3. Interaction 1 and 2	−0.07	−0.08

Source: Van der Werf (1988, p. 85).

closing conclusion is that school curricula do not matter. This is quite a negative conclusion, since it takes a lot of time and money to develop them. So school improvement with an emphasis on curriculum development and using that school curriculum does not succeed in influencing the educational process in the classroom and the achievement of pupils. The reason for this is that the innovational goals for primary education were too global: the goals should have been given a concrete form in learning methods and textbooks. The connection between achievement, innovation in general and curriculum innovation in particular is too weak. The conclusion and recommendations of Van der Werf are that, in the future, more use should be made of empirical evidence on school effectiveness, teacher effectiveness and factors related to educational productivity.

Doubts about the aims of educational innovation and the outcomes of pupils in primary education are also the subject of Hoeben's (1989) research. Hoeben investigated the hypothesis that there is a discrepancy between educational innovation, which is focused on process-variables in schools, such as curriculum development, and school effectiveness, which aims at higher results in pupils achievement. He investigated this hypothesis in a sample of schools involved in educational innovation towards a new 'basic school' (for primary education). The progress in this innovation is measured by: (1) development in innovation of the school curriculum; (2) differentiation and individualization; (3) professional development of the teaching staff; (4) not only the organizational but also the educational integration of kindergarten and the traditional primary school; and (5) broadening the teaching content. Based on the scores of 290 schools, Table 3.3 presents the proportions of variance in schools' achievement scores, explained by different sources.

Table 3.3 *Proportions of variance in schools' achievement scores, successively explained by SES, instructional variables, innovation progress and educational leadership*

Step	*Variable*	*R-square*	*Change*
1.	Modal SES	0.199	0.199
2.	Mastery level	0.239	0.040
3.	Pupil evaluation	0.253	0.015
4/5.	Implementation of curriculum	0.264	0.010
6.	Instructional time	0.267	0.003
7.	Progress in innovation	0.268	0.001
8.	Educational leadership	0.268	0.000

Source: Hoeben (1989, p. 162).

In explaining variance in the achievement scores the socioeconomic status of pupils is most important. Variables at the instructional level contribute somewhat but others connected with innovation, like progress in it, have no influence at all. The same holds for educational leadership. The last conclusion is in accordance with some other results of school effectiveness studies in continental Europe (Mortimore *et al.*, 1988; Brandsma and Knuver, 1989). Other variables, such as instructional time, do not contribute much to the explanation of the variance, probably as a result of the way they were measured.

The innovatory programmes of the 1970s and 1980s, directed at innovation in primary and secondary education, were not directed at improving the achievement and results of pupils in general. But even in the case of improving the education of disadvantaged groups (one of the aims of the innovation in primary education) the results were negative (see, for example, the results of differentiation within classes and schools promoted by innovatory programmes as evaluated by Reezigt and Weide (1989)).

Educational Improvement Based on School Effectiveness

Partly caused by the disappointing results of compensatory programmes in the innovation of the educational system, from 1985 onwards more attention was given to educational effectiveness in educational innovation and programme development.

In a large-scale innovation programme, the educational priority programme that aimed to enhance educational opportunities for the disadvantaged, more attention was given to educational outcomes. A large-scale project is in progress to evaluate the outcomes of this educational priority programme. From the first publications of this project, it can be concluded that a small amount of variance between schools could be found and explained. Only high expectations, aspirations and structured lessons seem to have an impact on the average recommendation for a secondary school type. In other areas, like basic education (an innovation directed to integrate primary and secondary education), more attention can be established for educational outcomes and for factors contributing to educational effectiveness. Advisory boards draw attention to the findings of school effectiveness research (Adviesraad, 1988 a, b) and these factors are also a part of the programme for evaluation of the innovation in primary and secondary education (Tesser and Van der Werf, 1989; Peschar, 1988). Although more autonomy is given to schools in the decision-making for the allocation of specific budgets (the budget allocated to a school is dependent on the number of pupils and the proportion of low socioeconomic status and ethnic minority pupils), attention is also given to educational outcomes. In vocational education and university education part of the budget is allocated based on results in terms of students' outcomes from the schools and universities. In 1990 a committee of the Dutch Teachers' Union stated in an advisory note, 'Towards a more business-like school', that autonomous schools should pay attention to educational outcomes and active ways to reach them. Although the ideas behind this report can be criticized (it is more 'business-like' and directed towards simple school marketing), it is important to note that more attention is being given to processes within schools that can contribute to the growth of the knowledge and skills of students. However, as we can see from educational research in the Netherlands, educational policy and practice should be careful when implementing research results based on the mainstream of effective schools research in the United States. Educational researchers should also be cautious not to provide unjustified recommendations for educational practice based on these research results.

As stated before (Creemers and Scheerens, 1989; Creemers, 1990; Scheerens, 1989), the knowledge base for school improvement based on school effectiveness research is not very substantive in the Netherlands (for an overview see Creemers and Lugthart, 1989; Creemers and Knuver, 1989). From 1980 onwards there has been a growing stream of research in which relationships between school characteristics and results at the pupil level have been explored. Mostly correlational procedures have been used, but these correlation techniques do not produce a clear picture of the contribution of school effectiveness factors to educational outcomes (Stoel, 1980; Van Marwijk Kooij-von Baumhauer, 1984). In replication studies most of the correlations found in earlier studies were not explicated again (Knuver, 1987). Important studies with respect to the improvement of primary education were the studies of Meijnen (1984, 1986) and Van der Wolf (1984). Meijnen showed that children with disadvantaged backgrounds appeared to be more sensitive to variations in the curriculum than children from the higher occupational groups. After the schools were grouped into four types on the basis of a cluster analysis, pupils in traditional subject-matter oriented schools appeared to achieve beneath their intelligence level, and in pupil oriented schools the pupils achieved even more beneath their level, but in the 'cultural integrative' type of school the pupils achieved above their intelligence level. This type of school is characterized by a fair amount of attention to educational objectives, a moderate amount of differentiation, systematic organization of lessons and attempts to bridge the gap between school and home environment. The study of Van der Wolf showed that the affection/'well being' oriented type of schools had the highest rate of school drop-out. The achievement oriented schools had the lowest rate of school drop-out, referred more to higher forms of secondary education and had less referrals to special forms of education. On the other hand, more pupils had to repeat a class. It is a pity that in this last study no relationship with learning achievement could be determined because data from a number of schools were lacking and the control for intake was not very convincing.

In this first series of research projects, a number of studies were orientated to replicate in Dutch education the results of American studies. In the Dutch situation, however, the American research results do not appear to be confirmed. A first attempt to replicate the American research into effective schools is the study by Vermeulen (1987). Vermeulen investigated the relationship between five school characteristics and the effectiveness of schools among school leaders and teachers of twenty-two educational priority schools in Rotterdam. By means of translating instruments used in American research that measured school characteristics (Schweitzer, 1984) and the CITO primary school final achievement test, he tried to verify the model of five effective school characteristics for the Dutch situation. Of the five, only the characteristic of 'an orderly atmosphere aimed at the stimulation of learning' could be reliably measured and proved to have a relation with the average learning achievement. Because of the unreliable measurements the only conclusion that can be drawn is that the questionnaires are not suited for the Dutch situation.

In a study by Brandsma and Stoel (1986) of school leaders in secondary education, educational leadership, school management aspects and individual school leader characteristics (e.g. age) were investigated. With the aid of stepwise multiple regression analyses, the influence of these characteristics on the percentage of graduates, moving-on, moving-up and moving-down, repeaters, re-examinations, truants, premature school leavers and absenteeism was established. For each independent variable different relations with the school leader characteristics were found. The factors of educational leadership seem the most important, among them the percentage of time that school leaders spend on educational matters and the evaluation of pupil achievement. School management aspects and individual school leader characteristics are of less importance.

Van de Grift (1987a, b) made a study into relations between the educational leadership of primary school leaders and average pupil achievement. The instrument developed for measuring self-perceptions of educational leadership proved to contain reasonably reliable scales for various aspects of this leadership. The relations between these various aspects of educational leadership and average pupil achievement were on the whole negative, non-existent or at any rate non-linear. Van de Grift interprets these outcomes as an indication that school leaders react to pupil achievements instead of being able to influence these achievements. However, the lack of control for aptitude and socioeconomic status of pupils renders these conclusions debatable.

A third example of research that is being done at present and in which (in the preparatory phase) no relations were found between effective school characteristics and school output (in the form of the percentage of pupils moving on to the various forms of secondary education) is the study by Van der Hoeven-van Doornum and Jungbluth (1987). They designed instruments for measuring team consensus, school leadership, innovation-orientation and achievement-orientation. Here also the reliability of the instruments appeared problematic and almost no relation with the effect measure was found.

The studies mentioned show a number of flaws which could provide an explanation for the effectiveness characteristics found in foreign research not being found in these Dutch studies. One of these flaws concerns aggregating output variables to the school level and not using the multi-level character of research into school effectiveness characteristics in doing this. After the development of project techniques, like VARCL and HLM, the school effectiveness research was improved.

One of the first studies using this kind of analysis was done in primary education with data collected in two grades of 250 primary schools (Brandsma and Knuver, 1988). In this study 8 per cent of the variance in language and about 12 per cent of the variance in arithmetic could be connected to differences between schools. Part of this variance could be explained by some school and class organizational factors, like frequent evaluation. In a study of Van der Hoeven-van Doornum and Jungbluth (1987) the effect of aspiration levels set by teachers for the students on learning achievement was investigated. The effect of school and teaching factors on learning achievement appeared to be small. Higher aspiration levels, however, tended to lead to higher test scores for children. Seven per cent of the variance in test scores could be explained by the aspiration level of the teacher as a direct or interaction effect. In secondary education Bosker and Van der Velden (1989) and Bosker (1990) found that cohesive schools (i.e. democratic in decision-making, a strong relationship with parents, etc.) with a positive school climate were effective in terms of effectiveness and school career. In the evaluation of the educational priority programme Tesser and Van der Werf (1989) report on the first findings. A small amount of variance between schools could be found and explained. Only high expectations and structured lessons seem to have an impact on the average recommendation for the secondary school type. In Amsterdam a project is in progress in which an attempt is made to use effective school factors in improving 'black' schools (schools with a high percentage of children from ethnic minority groups). The project is directed towards the school principals (educational leadership), the material presented (the quality and quantity of material), team performance (involvement, co-operation) and the teaching climate (secure and pleasant). The available data are about the measures used, the influence of the composition of classes (percentage of white versus percentage of black ethnic minority children) and the effects of these factors on measures for achievement and disruption. At this moment no data are available about the results of the programme (Van der Wolf, 1990).

Scheerens and Creemers (1989) have presented an overview of the results of Dutch studies. In general the twelve research projects involved in this review do not support the five factor model of school effectiveness. The studies show positive results for individual factors (but not consistently in all studies), such as orderly climate (Stoel, 1986; Vermeulen, 1987), high expectations (Van Marwijk Kooij-von Baumhauer, 1984; Tesser and Van der Werf, 1989), frequent evaluation (Van der Hoeven-van Doornum and Jungbluth, 1987; Brandsma and Knuver, 1988), direct instruction (Van der Wolf, 1984) and achievement orientation (Bosker and Hofman, 1987; Tesser and Van der Werf, 1989; M.J. De Jong, 1989; R. De Jong, 1989). These results are comparable with the results of the project Education and Social Environment and the preliminary results of the educational priority programme (for reviews see Scheerens, 1989; Scheerens and Creemers, 1989; Creemers and Lugthart, 1989; Creemers and Knuver, 1989) (see also Table 3.4). A remarkable conclusion of Dutch school effectiveness research is that instructional leadership does not contribute to school effectiveness. In a re-analysis of data sets from other - mostly American - research Van de Grift points at the over-optimistic conclusions in these other studies and also presents Dutch data that show the absence of a strong relationship between leadership and effectiveness (Van de Grift, 1990).

Table 3.4 *School effectiveness factors supported by Dutch studies (total 12)*

Factor	*Number of studies*
Orderly climate	3
High expectations	2
Frequent evaluation	4
Direct instruction	2
Achievement orientation	3

Source: Creemers (1990).

Conclusions Based on School Effectiveness Research and School Improvement in the Netherlands

If we combine the experiences in the past, the experiences of practitioners in school improvement and the research in school effectiveness, we can summarize and draw some conclusions.

1 Large-scale school reforms with an emphasis on process variables, changing the school curriculum and content, but not on pupil achievement, do not contribute much to the increase of growth in the knowledge and skills of pupils. In the evaluation of large-scale reform programmes, a correlation could not be determined between the innovatory instruments and pupils' achievement. Programmes such as those developed in the project Education and Social Environment can contribute to an improvement in the achievements of disadvantaged pupils, but do not succeed if they are not congruent with objectives on national and norm-referenced tests. If not, then they are effective only with respect to their own objectives, and that is not enough. Too much self-directedness should be avoided by promoting the congruence between the programme goals and the content of norm-referenced tests. Another possibility is putting more emphasis on transfer goals: transfer of what is learned in the programme into new situations, such as the testing situation, by a norm-referenced test.

2 A well structured programme can be effective, because the performance on an earlier task in the project Education and Social Environment was a good predictor of the performance on a new task.

3 Measurement of whether or not a school improvement programme is implemented correctly and whether teachers are willing to carry out the programme as intended is mostly too weak. It merely consists of counting the activities of a programme as carried out by the teacher. But outcomes can be influenced in a lot of other ways, as research on the educational productivity of teaching and effectiveness has shown.

4 Secondary analyses of school improvement pointed out that

instructional variables could be more important for student achievement than the innovation process and school effectiveness factors, such as educational leadership. The same holds for the so-called 'school effectiveness factors' in Dutch research.

5 A few factors probably can be effective. It seems that an emphasis on basic skills, evaluation and feedback can contribute to school effectiveness, but this should be realized in a consistent continuous way connected with classroom instruction. So it would be premature to develop school improvement programmes based on only a single set of school effectiveness factors. In programmes like the project Education and Social Environment, the five 'effective school factors' did not explain variance, so it seems that through programme development and implementation the influence of these kinds of variables could be diminished.

6 Educational reform in the past shows - in a somewhat negative way - the importance of programmes being directed at pupils' achievement. Programme development and implementation can contribute to effectiveness but should take into account the standards set by norm-referenced tests and the multiple ways to raise educational productivity or the level of the outcomes. School effectiveness research as well as the results of large- and small-scale educational reforms point at the instructional process.

COMPONENTS OF EFFECTIVE INSTRUCTION

In the previous section I concluded that some school effectiveness variables are of importance, but that on the whole more attention should be paid to the variables within the classroom or to the different components of the instructional process. Even the disappointing results of programmes like Education and Social Environment indicate that better results could be achieved through putting more emphasis on such components. These experiences with educational reform and school effectiveness research can be combined with conclusions of educational research on the components of the instructional process. In this section I will give an overview of some research results about these components: curriculum, grouping of pupils, instructional behaviour of teachers and instructional approaches. The greater part of this research is based on meta-analyses.

The Curriculum

As we have seen in the previous paragraph, the school curriculum does not have any influence at all on the achievement of pupils. Here curriculum means the curriculum for the class, which consists of textbooks, handbooks for the teachers, and teaching and learning material. If an adequate implementation strategy is used, teachers seem to make use of these kinds of textbooks and programmes (see the results of the project Education and Social Environment), although teachers indicate that they mostly use about 30 per cent of the curriculum material. Even then, it is not known whether the curriculum material is used properly, as intended by its developers. Probably this is one of the reasons why, in Dutch research projects which compared the different textbooks for language, arithmetic and English as a second language, no significant differences could be found in terms of achievement of pupils. Not the textbook itself, but the way it is used by the teacher, seems to be important. Nevertheless, based on research, some characteristics of the curriculum material proved to be important. These are the following:

- a restricted set of objectives should be formulated and ordered hierarchically, so that it is clear which objective the pupils should reach before they can start mastering another objective;
- the content of the curriculum material should be ordered along the lines of the objectives - the structure of the content should be clear and should correspond with the hierarchical order of the objectives;
- one aspect of structuring the content is to make use of advanced organizers, in which the objectives of a learning task and the way it is structured are given;
- the evaluation of pupils' learning is important - this can be done in different ways, such as through questions in textbooks and evaluation after completing tasks;
- Corrective feedback based on evaluation is needed.

Several of these characteristics of learning material are also components of teaching behaviour. In fact, in the classroom situation it is impossible to make a difference between the curriculum material and the way it is used by the teacher. But Van den Akker (1988) shows in his research that a structured curriculum provides more time for instruction instead of organizing, and also more time for learning for pupils.

Pupils in the Classroom

Reezigt and Weide (1989) report a research project on the effects of differentiation and individualization in Dutch primary schools. They found that in Dutch primary schools there are different forms of heterogeneous grouping, in addition to whole-group instruction. Forms of grouping based on the time allowed for learning are less frequent in Dutch primary schools. It is remarkable that pure forms of differentiation are hard to find. In fact, teachers use different forms of differentiation in their own way - for example, they do or do not use evaluation instruments, they do or do not give corrective feedback and do or do not give further explanation. In short, differentiation and individualization are given concrete form by the teacher. Moreover, most teachers do not use forms of differentiation and individualization strictly: for the whole instruction process they make changes within a subject and between subjects. Because of this it is very difficult to determine the effects of differentiation and individualization. Reezigt and Weide were unable to draw straight conclusions in favour of specific, well-defined ways of differentiation in primary schools. In fact their research shows no differences at all in educational practice between different forms of differentiation and whole class instruction.

Based on meta-analyses by Kulik and Kulik (1989) and Slavin (1987), it can be said that heterogeneous grouping has a small positive effect on pupils' learning. Mastery learning (criticized by Slavin) has a stronger positive effect. Co-operative learning, in which heterogeneous groups work together to achieve a common objective, has a slight positive effect.

Again, we can conclude that the forms of organization of a classroom can contribute to effective instruction, but the effect is strongly related to teacher behaviour. In fact the teacher is the organizer of the classroom and the teaching-learning process. The way teachers differentiate depends also on the curriculum material. One of the reasons for the disappointing results with different forms of differentiation is, according to Reezigt and Weide, that no curriculum material, such as textbooks and evaluation material, was available and so teachers did not differentiate properly.

Teaching Behaviour

Based on research and experiences in educational reform as described above, we can conclude that the teacher is the key component in the instructional process. A lot of research on the effectiveness of teaching behaviour has been carried out in the past. Research has shown that teacher behaviour in its turn is influenced by a lot of other components of instruction (as we have seen, the classroom curriculum and ways of differentiation determine teacher behaviour to a greater or lesser extent).

Based on empirical research in the past it is possible to give a list of components of teaching behaviour that are effective. According to Brophy and Good (1986) the findings of research on teaching behaviour (not all based on meta-analyses) can be summarized as follows.

1 Academic learning time is an important variable, which can especially be influenced by management behaviour of teachers. This academic learning or student-engaged time can be enlarged, but academic learning time is an empty vessel that has to be filled with learning, which is induced by teaching.

2 Opportunity to learn is the other side of the same coin. If we can make use of academic learning time by providing as much learning material as possible in a proper way, then the learning of pupils will be promoted.

3 If teachers expect pupils to learn, and emphasize academic learning, this will influence their own behaviour and the behaviour of pupils.

4 In providing information, effective characteristics are structuring of the content, using advance organizers,

hierarchical ordering of objectives and content used to reach these objectives, some redundancy in providing information, and clarity of presentation (enthusiasm of teachers did not prove to be very effective).

5 With respect to the questioning behaviour of teachers, the use of higher-order questions, the clarity of the questions and the wait time (time between stating the question and asking for a response) are important.

6 Even more important is the teachers' reaction to the responses. In fact, by correcting the answers, immediate feedback is given during the classroom instruction. In recent Dutch research by Westerhof (1989) these components were the only ones that contributed significantly.

7 Seatwork assignments can be effective, if they are clearly defined, combined with corrective feedback and so on. The same holds for homework, which can enlarge the academic learning time (but it has to be enhanced learning).

Next to teaching behaviour, and somewhat corresponding to it, there is the management behaviour of teachers. This behaviour also contributes to creating a quiet learning situation in which pupils can learn. Time provided for learning is an especially important device teachers have at their disposal to improve pupils' learning.

Instructional Strategy

One of the findings of research on teaching was that specific teaching behaviour, such as questioning, does not provide great differences in pupils' achievement, and that the value of a specific behaviour is not very high, but that a combination of characteristics of teaching behaviour, for example questioning and wait time, increases the explained variance in pupils' learning. So it is probably a more extended set of behaviours within an instructional strategy that will incorporate effective components.

After looking at different teaching behaviours, an attempt was made to combine those that are effective. One of these approaches was called 'active, direct, effective teaching instruction' (Rosenshine, 1987). According to Rosenshine the following activities of teachers during instruction are important components.

- structure the learning experience;
- proceed in small steps but at a rapid pace;
- give detailed and more redundant instructions and explanations;
- have a high frequency of questions and overt, active practice;
- provide feedback and corrections, particularly in the initial stages of learning new material;
- have a success rate of 80 per cent or higher in initial learning;

- divide seatwork assignments into smaller segments or devise ways to provide frequent monitoring;
- provide for continuous student practice (overlearning) so that they have a success rate of 90-100 per cent and become rapid, confident and firm.

From the above, it is obvious that direct instruction contains effective teaching factors, especially structuring, questioning behaviour, feedback and corrective measures. Direct instruction depends completely on teaching behaviour but its success is also influenced by curriculum material and grouping procedures. These components of instruction facilitate direct teaching.

Aside from active effective instruction, mastery learning can be viewed as an instructional approach. It is not just a way to organize students within the classroom but also a way of teaching. The advantage of this is that an explicit idea is developed about pupils' learning, such as ability (time that is required for mastering a specific task), motivation, perseverance and the time allowed for learning. The quality of instruction can also influence the pupils' achievement. Mostly the quality of instruction is not very well developed and is only used as a device for the grouping of students within the classroom. As we have seen in the project Education and Social Environment, in which a mastery learning model was used, it provides an important contribution to the achievement of pupils within the programme. Although less obviously than in active effective instruction that combines different teacher behaviours, mastery learning depends strongly on the way teachers carry it out. Probably that is an important reason for the somewhat negative results of the Education and Social Environment project. Anderson and Block (1987) pointed to the fact that the success of mastery learning depends to a great extent on the curriculum material and especially on the teacher.

Conclusions Based on Research on Effective Instruction

Based on research on the different components of the instructional process, it can be concluded that - aside from any conclusions about the individual components - they refer to each other (see Figure 3.1). So curriculum material is important but the way teachers use it is responsible for the results. A combination should be made of the different components and the characteristics that prove to be effective. The point of departure for such a combination of components and effective characteristics is a basic idea about how students' learning takes place. The starting point for that could be a model for school learning as developed by Carroll (1989) - or others - which points at an important variable for student learning: the time available for learning. So, we can look at the components to see to what extent and in what way they create time for learning. After that, what happens within this time should be taken into account. These are important qualitative components of the instructional process. Again this provides a place for the interrelationship between such components as instructional material, grouping, teaching behaviour and instructional approaches.

Instructional strategies:
- direct teaching
- mastery learning

Curriculum:
- restricted set of objectives
- emphasis on basic skills
- cognitive learning and transfer
- structuring of the content
- advance organizers
- evaluation and feedback

Grouping within classroom:
- mastery learning
- heterogeneous grouping
- co-operative learning

Teacher behaviour:
- management of the class(room) (orderly and quiet atmosphere, time for learning)
- high expectations
- restricted set of objectives
- emphasis on cognitive learning
- structuring content/lessons
- clarity of explanation
- redundancy
- high-order question/wait time
- structuring seating and homework
- evaluation and corrective feedback

Figure 3.1 *Factors contributing to effective instruction*

Integration of School and Instructional Effectiveness

In the previous paragraphs we looked for factors that contribute to educational productivity and effectiveness. Research has revealed a lot of factors in the area of instruction that prove to be effective. Separately these factors contribute but their effect is enlarged if they are combined with other effective factors. The reality in education is that mostly there exists no consistency or congruence within classroom instruction and between classroom, school, national policy and home environment.

Attention to instructional effectiveness at the school level is important because it encourages teachers to be effective. At the school level (sometimes by means of the school effectiveness factors) a situation can be created in which effective instruction is supported, stimulated or even elicited. This can be achieved by means of organizing a quiet and orderly atmosphere in the school, and by the development of a school curriculum in which evaluation, feedback and a restricted set of objectives are emphasized - in short, factors that proved to be effective at the level of the instructional process in the classroom. These components and factors at the school level do not create the instructional process, but are conditional for the performance of teachers and pupils (see Figure 3.2). We can look at other components around the school that can contribute to effective instruction within classrooms, like school boards at the district level or even at a national level - at the school board level by hiring competent headteachers and teachers. At the national level final goals are set for education and an evaluation and monitoring system is imposed for the self-evaluation of schools, which can contribute to effective instruction within schools and within the classroom. National testing systems and curriculum development can also contribute in their own ways. One can expect that again all these factors, if they are congruent and coherent, together contribute to a greater extent to school effectiveness and educational productivity than each of them, even if they are effective, separately does.

Again the national and school level can support the instructional level where ultimately learning takes place and outcomes are achieved. Everything in education has to tune in on that process/product. Hypothetically this can be summarized in a model for educational outcomes (see Figure 3.3). As we have seen in this chapter, ultimately the teacher is of most importance. If teachers are so

EFFECTIVE FACTORS AT SCHOOL LEVEL

curriculum
- restricted set of objectives
- emphasis on basic skills
- structure of the content
- evaluation and feedback policy
- grouping of students within and between classes (same policy in all classes and for all curriculum subjects)

school organization
- quiet and orderly atmosphere
- structure of education through grades
- good team work/coherence in team
- educational leadership (?)

school board
- hiring teachers and principals according to the school policy

BROADER EDUCATIONAL LEVEL

parents
- supporting the school and the school's policy

national level
- educational policy supporting and 'guiding' education within schools (including curriculum development evaluation testing system, research)
- teacher pre-service and inservice training

Figure 3.2 *Effective factors at school level and in a broader educational context*

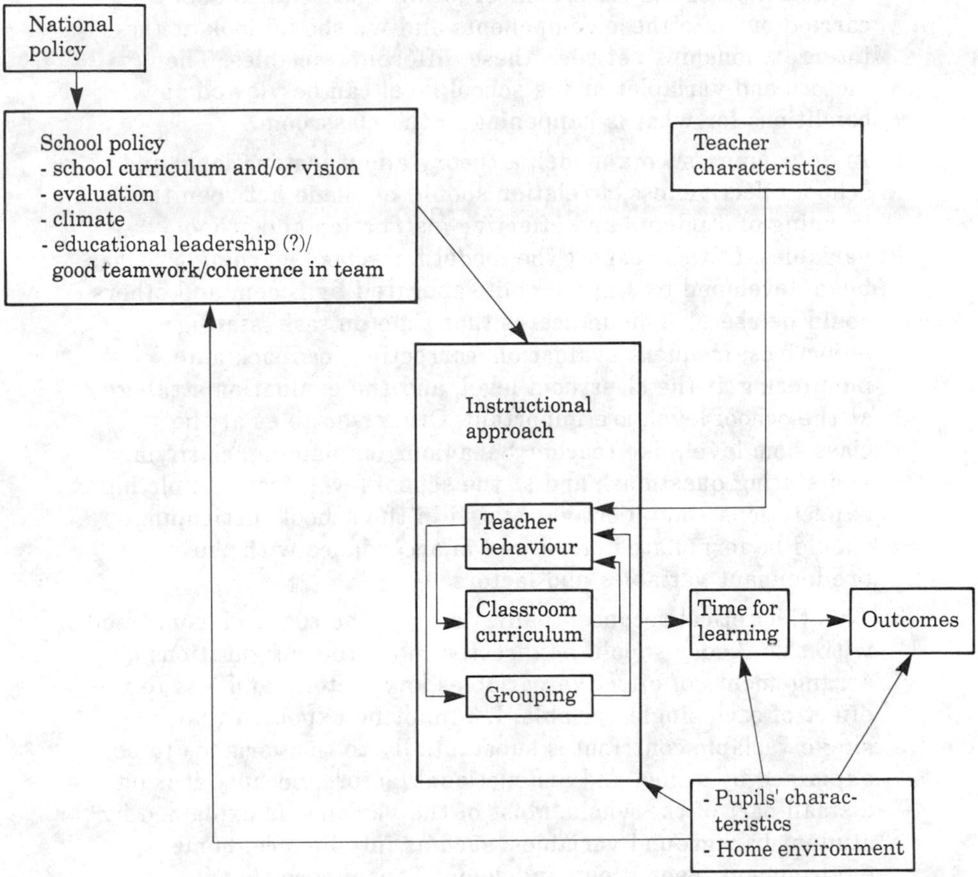

Figure 3.3 *A model of educational outcomes*

important in the instructional process and responsible more or less for the outcomes of education then they should receive the means, training, support and material to fulfil their task in a self-confident, competent, professional way.

CONCLUSIONS BASED ON SCHOOL EFFECTIVENESS AND SCHOOL IMPROVEMENT IN THE NETHERLANDS: DIRECTIONS FOR FUTURE SCHOOL EFFECTIVENESS AND SCHOOL IMPROVEMENT

1 We need a theoretical reconceptualization of the idea of school effectiveness. In research we have found strong support for school effectiveness factors on the school level, but even more on the instructional level, so it is likely that explanatory factors can be found on the instructional level. At the instructional level we can make a distinction between material (textbooks, methods), the behaviour of students and teachers and the

organization of the classroom. A lot of research has been carried out into these components and we should look at the interrelationships between these different variables. The factors and variables at the school level can be viewed as conditions for what is happening in the classroom.

2 In developing such a model, a theory about instructional and school effectiveness, a relation should be made between the learning of students and effective instruction and school variables. In this respect the model for school learning that has been developed by Carroll and elaborated by Bloom and others could be useful. This indicates that time on task, stating objectives, frequent evaluation, corrective feedback and monitoring at the classroom level, and the evaluation strategy at the school level, are important. Other variables at the classroom level, like teacher behaviour (explaining, clarifying and stating questions), and at the school level, for example high expectations and objectives stated in the school curriculum, should be formulated or viewed in accordance with these predominant variables and factors.

3 This theoretical reconceptualization and the research connected with this theory should be directed more to configurations or arrangements of effective variables and factors, and less to the effect of each single variable. It cannot be expected that one single variable contributes substantially to the variance to be explained by school and instructional factors, because it is only a small part of the whole. Most of the variance is explained by student background variables, such as intelligence, home environment, peer group and so on. That means that in developing statistical techniques, we ought to look at techniques that can combine multi-level techniques and causal analyses, in which we can combine single variables.

4 In the reconceptualization of a theory and in research more attention should be given to the context factors for school effectiveness and educational productivity, which is the reason why some factors that can explain variance in American research do not hold in Dutch research. The re-analysis of IEA datasets (Scheerens *et al.*, 1989) showed that cultural differences between countries probably can explain variance, but what is the reason for this? What are these cultural differences? For example, in Sweden through political measures the differences between schools disappear, but within schools the differences between classes still exist. Bosker *et al.* (1990) conclude that in the Netherlands differences within schools are smaller.

5 In connection with the results of evaluation studies like the IEA study in educational effectiveness and improvement, attention

should be given to the question of quality and equity in education as desired goals. We should probably redefine our goals in enhancing educational effectiveness. Educational effectiveness and improvement should be directed to educational quality (for all students). A decline of equity is more a societal problem, and a declining educational equity is embedded in societal and political measures.

6 Educational practitioners and policy-makers cannot wait for the results of educational research. They have their own responsibilities for educational improvement. In school and instructional effectiveness we should be cautious in making recipes: there are many factors and variables that influence, in a holistic way, educational effectiveness and productivity. Educational improvement should always be combined with careful evaluation and collection of data, with the ultimate criterion being the outcome of education in terms of growth of the knowledge and the skills of students. In this way educational improvement and its evaluation can contribute to the enlargement of our knowledge base of what matters in schools and classrooms.

REFERENCES

Adviesraad voor het basisonderwijs, speciaal onderwijs en voortgezet onderwijs (1988a) *Voorrang aan achterstand*. Advies over een integraal beleid ter voorkoming en bestrijding van onderwijsachterstand. Zeist: ARBO.

Adviesraad voor het basisonderwijs, speciaal onderwijs en voortgezet onderwijs (1988b) *Een boog van woorden tot woorden*. Advies over het onderwijs aan leerlingen uit etnische minderheden. Zeist: ARBO.

Anderson, L.W. and Block, J.H. (1987) 'Mastery learning models', in Dunkin, M.J. (ed.) *The International Encyclopedia of Teaching and Teacher Education*. Oxford: Pergamon Press.

Bosker, R.J. (1990) *Extra kansen dankzij de school? Het differentieel effect van schoolkenmerken op schoolloopbanen in het voortgezet onderwijs voor lager versus hoger milieu leerlingen en jongens versus meisjes*. Groningen: RION.

Bosker, R.J. and Hofman, W.H.A. (1987) *Evaluatie van de propadeuse-opleidingen rechtsgeleerdheid en economische wetenschappen te Leeuwarden*. Eindrapport. Groningen: RION.

Bosker, R.J. and Van der Velden, R.K.W. (1989) 'The effects of secondary schools on the educational careers of disadvantaged pupils', in Creemers, B., Peters, T. and Reynolds, D. (eds) *School Effectiveness and School Improvement. Proceedings of the Second International Congress, Rotterdam 1989*. Amsterdam/Lisse: Swets & Zeitlinger.

Bosker, R.J., Kremers, E. and Lugthart, E. (1990) 'School and instruction effects on mathematics achievement', Paper presented at ICSEI 1990, Jerusalem.

Brandsma, H.P. and Knuver, J.W.M. (1988) 'Organisatorische verschillen tussen basisscholen en hun effect op leerprestaties', *Tijdschrift voor Onderwijsresearch*, **13**, 201-12.

Brandsma, H.P. and Knuver, J.W.M. (1989) 'Organisational differences between Dutch primary schools and their effect on pupil achievement', in Reynolds, D., Creemers, B.P.M. and Peters, T. (eds) *School Effectiveness and Improvement: Proceedings of the First International Congress London 1988*. Groningen: RION; Cardiff: University of Wales.

Brandsma, H.P. and Stoel, W.G.R. (1986) *Schoolleiders in het voortgezet onderwijs: een exploratieve studie naar de determinanten en effecten van schoolleiderskenmerken.* Groningen: RION.

Brophy, J.E. and Good, T.L. (1986) 'Teacher behavior and student achievement', in Wittrock, M.C. (ed.) *Handbook of Research on Teaching, 3rd edn.* New York: Macmillan.

Carroll, J.B. (1989) 'The Carroll model, a 25-year retrospective and prospective view', *Educational Researcher*, **18**, 26-31.

Creemers, B.P.M. (1990) 'School effectiveness and effective instruction: the need for a further relationship', Paper presented at ICSEI 1990, Jerusalem.

Creemers, B.P.M. and Knuver, J.W.M. (1989) 'The Netherlands', in Creemers, B., Peters, T. and Reynolds, D. (eds) *School Effectiveness and School Improvement: Proceedings of the Second International Congress Rotterdam 1989*. Amsterdam/Lisse: Swets & Zeitlinger.

Creemers, B.P.M. and Lugthart, E. (1989) 'The Netherlands', in Reynolds, D., Creemers, B.P.M. and Peters, T. (eds) *School Effectiveness and Improvement: Proceedings of the First International Congress London 1988*. Groningen: RION; Cardiff: University of Wales.

Creemers, B.P.M. and Scheerens, J. (1989) 'Developments in school effectiveness research', *International Journal of Educational Research*, **13**, 691-707.

Creemers, B.P.M. and Terlouw, C. (1984) 'Onderwijsevaluatie in Nederland, een review', *INFO*, **15**, 126-50.

De Jong, M.J. (1989) 'Educational climate and achievement in Dutch schools', in Reynolds, D., Creemers, B.P.M. and Peters, T. (eds) *School Effectiveness and Improvement: Proceedings of the First International Congress London 1988*. Groningen: RION; Cardiff: University of Wales.

De Jong, R. (1989) *Probleemoplossen binnen het vak Techniek, kenmerken en effecten van een onderwijsleerprogramma voor lbo- en middenscholen.* Groningen: RION.

Hoeben, W.Th.J.G. (1989) 'Educational innovation or school effectiveness: a dilemma?', in Creemers, B., Peters, T. and Reynolds, D. (eds) *School Effectiveness and School Improvement: Proceedings of the Second International Congress Rotterdam 1989*. Amsterdam/Lisse: Swets & Zeitlinger.

Knuver, A. (1987) *Schoolkenmerken en leerling functioneren: een replicatie-onderzoek.* Groningen: Rijksuniversiteit.

Kulik, J.A. and Kulik, C.C. (1989) 'Meta-analysis in education', *International Journal of Educational Research*, **13**, 223-340.

Leseman, P.P.M. (1990) *Structurele en pedagogische determinanten van schoolloopbanen: verslag van een longitudinaal onderzoek naar de invloed van het gezin op de schoolprestaties.* Rotterdam: Rotterdamse Schooladviesdienst, project Onderwijs en Sociaal Milieu.

Meijnen, G.W. (1984) *Van zes tot twaalf: een longitudinaal onderzoek naar de milieu- en schooleffecten van loopbanen in het lager onderwijs*. The Hague: SVO.

Meijnen, G.W. (1986) 'Ongelijke onderwijskansen en effectieve scholen', in van der Wolf, J.C. and Hox, J.J. (eds) *Kwaliteit van het onderwijs in het geding.* Lisse: Swets & Zeitlinger.

Mortimore, P. *et al.* (1988) *School Matters. The Junior Years*. Wells: Open Books.

Peschar, J.L. (1988) *Evaluatie van de basisvorming: kader voor het uitvoeringsplan*. The Hague: SVO.

Reezigt. G.J. and Weide, M.G. (1989) *Effecten van differentiatie: resultaten survey-onderzoek*. Groningen: RION.

Rosenshine, B. (1987) 'Direct instruction', in Dunkin, M.J. (ed.) *The International Encyclopaedia of Teaching and Teacher Education*. Oxford: Pergamon Press.

Scheerens, J. (1989) *Wat maakt scholen effectief?: samenvattingen en analyses van onderzoeksresultaten*. 's-Gravenhage: SVO.

Scheerens, J. and Creemers, B.P.M. (1989) 'Towards a more comprehensive conceptualization of school effectiveness', in Creemers, B., Peters, T. and Reynolds, D. (eds) *School Effectiveness and School Improvement: Proceedings of the Second International Congress Rotterdam 1989*. Amsterdam/Lisse: Swets & Zeitlinger.

Scheerens, J., Nanninga, H.C.R. and Pelgrum, W.J.H. (1989) 'Generalizability of instructional and school effectiveness indicators across nations; preliminary results of a secondary analysis of the IEA second mathematics study', in Creemers, B., Peters, T. and Reynolds, D. (eds) *School Effectiveness and School Improvement. Proceedings of the Second International Congress Rotterdam 1989*. Lisse: Swets & Zeitlinger.

Schweitzer, J.H. (1984) *Characteristics of Effective Schools*. AERA paper, New Orleans.

Slavenburg, J. (1986). *Onderwijsstimulering en gezinsactivering*. Groningen, dissertatie.

Slavenburg, J.H. and Peters, T.A. (eds) (1989) *Het project Onderwijs en Sociaal Milieu: een eindbalans*. Rotterdam: Rotterdamse School Advies Dienst.

Slavin, R.E. (1987) 'Ability grouping and student achievement in elementary schools: best evidence synthesis', *Review of Educational Research*, **57**, 293-336.

Stoel, W.G.R. (1980) *De relatie tussen de grootte van scholen in het voortgezet onderwijs en het welbevinden van leerlingen*. Groningen: RION.

Stoel, W.G.R. (1986) *Schoolkenmerken en het gedrag van leerlingen en docenten in het voortgezet onderwijs*. Groningen: RION.

Tesser, P. and van der Werf, M.P.C. (1989) 'Educational priority and school effectiveness', in Creemers, B., Peters, T. and Reynolds, D. (eds) *School Effectiveness and School Improvement: Proceedings of the Second International Congress Rotterdam 1989*. Amsterdam/Lisse: Swets & Zeitlinger.

Van de Grift, W. (1987a) *Implementatie van vernieuwingen: de rol vande schoolleider*. Leiden: dissertatie.

Van de Grift, W. (1987b) 'Zelfpercepties van onderwijskundig leiderschap en gemiddelde leerlingprestaties', in Scheerens, J. and Stoel, W.G.R. (eds) *Effectiviteit van onderwijsorganisaties*. Lisse: Swets & Zeitlinger.

Van de Grift, W. (1990) 'Educational leadership and academic achievement in elementary education', *School Effectiveness and School Improvement*, **1**, 26-41.

Van den Akker, J.J.H. (1988) *Ontwerp en implementatie van natuuronderwijs*. Lisse: Swets & Zeitlinger.

Van der Hoeven-Van Doornum, A.A. and Jungbluth, P. (1987) 'De bijdrage van schoolkenmerken aan schooleffectiviteit', in Scheerens, J. and Stoel, W.G.R. (eds) *Effectiviteit van onderwijsorganisaties*. Lisse: Swets & Zeitlinger.

Van der Velden, R.K.W., Akkermans, D.H.M., van der Heul, H. *et al.* (1989) *De lange arm van het onderwijs: een vergelijkend onderzoek naar de lange-termijn effecten van opleidingen bij MBO en leerlingwezen*. Groningen: RION.

Van der Werf, M.P.C. (1988) *Het schoolwerkplan in het basisonderwijs: ontwikkeling, implementatie en opbrengst*. Groningen: RION.

Van der Wolf, J.C. (1984) *Schooluitval: een empirisch onderzoek naar de samenhang tussen schoolinterne factoren en schooluitval in het regulier onderwijs*. Lisse: Swets & Zeitlinger.

Van der Wolf, J.C. (1990) *Effectief onderwijs op kleurrijke scholen. Tussenstand van het Amsterdamse EGAA-project*. Delft: Eburon.

Van Marwijk Kooij-von Baumhauer, L. (1984) *Scholen verschillen: een verkennend vergelijkend onderzoek naar het intern functioneren van vijfentwintig scholengemeenschappen vwo-havo-mavo*. Groningen: Wolters-Noordhoff.

Van Tilborg, I.A.J. (1987) *De betekenis van het arbeidersgezin voor het leerniveau en de schoolloopbaan van het kind: een voorlopige evaluatie van het project onderwijs en sociaal milieu in de eerste drie jaren van de basisschool*. The Hague: SVO.

Vermeulen, C.J. (1987) 'De effectiviteit van onderwijs bij zeventien Rotterdamse stimuleringsscholen', *Pedagogische Studieen*, **64**, 49-58.

Westerhof, K.J. (1989) *Productivity of Teacher Behaviour: An Empirical Study of Teacher Behaviour and Its Correlation with Learning Gain*, unpublished PhD thesis, University of Groningen.

Chapter 4

Evaluating the Effectiveness of Schools

Peter Cuttance

INTRODUCTION

This chapter discusses three approaches to the assessment of the effectiveness of schools. General issues in the assessment of the effectiveness of schools are discussed before the main methods and models are introduced. Later sections then present an example of the application of the most appropriate of the three methods to data on Scottish schools, and a discussion of the assessment of school effectiveness in the context of national assessment in the Education Act 1988. Although the chapter covers material that is of a technical nature, technical terminology is kept out of the discussion as far as possible. The intention is to give the reader a general overview of the issues without dwelling on the technical details of the complex statistical methods that have been developed for separating the effects that are due to the differences in the pupil intakes to schools from those that are due to the activities of schools themselves.

MEASURING THE OUTCOMES OF SCHOOLING

Although it often seems obvious what the outcomes of schooling are, there is a wide range of divergent views on which of these should be employed in assessing the effectiveness of schooling. By its very nature the concept of effectiveness implies a comparison among schools, either directly or via some external criterion. First, however, it is necessary to set out some terminology that allows us to differentiate between the outcomes of schools and the outcomes of pupils. Although there will nearly always be a parallel outcome in the school domain for each outcome in the pupil domain, it is sometimes easier to discuss particular issues in terms of one or other of these domains. For example, although the average examination attainment of pupils from a given school, a school outcome, is directly calculated from the attainment of the pupils from that school who presented for the examination, i.e. the pupil outcomes, any given school average may reflect a range of distributions of individual pupil attainments within schools with that average.

It is useful to delimit the use of the terms attainment and outcomes and to introduce two further terms that will be useful in distinguishing between schools and pupils. The term *outcome(s)* will be reserved for educational outcomes that refer to schools, while the term *attainment* will be reserved for outcomes that refer to individual pupils. The additional terms of *pupil (background) characteristics* and *intakes* will also be delimited in their usage to pupils and schools, respectively. Thus, school intakes are the school-level counterpart to pupil-level characteristics at the point of pupils' entry into schools. Ideally, all characteristics of the initial status of pupils that are related to subsequent attainment should be taken into account in assessing school effectiveness. The complete set of pupil-level characteristics will be referred to collectively as the background characteristics of the pupils who enter each school. The section below on adjusting school outcomes for their intakes will discuss the rationale for taking account of the variation in intakes across schools. The term intakes will be used as a descriptive term for the characteristics of the pupils entering individual schools.

Before any attempt is made to assess the variation in effectiveness among schools, however, it is necessary to discuss the range of outcomes that are of interest. British secondary school systems, unlike their counterparts in many other countries, have one feature that at some stage plays a dominant role in the life of most pupils that pass through them, the preparation for and presentation for public examinations. The attainment of pupils in these public examinations provides a prominent measure of both pupil and school academic success. Regardless of whether or not one approves of examination outcomes as the basis of assessments of the effectiveness of schools, they are subsequently used in the selection and channelling of pupils in post-school educational and occupational careers, which means that they have real effects on the lives of pupils once they have left school. About three-quarters of all pupils take a public examination in at least one subject before leaving school. In England and Wales these public examinations have been drawn from two examination systems, the General Certificate of Education (GCE) and the Certificate of Secondary Education (CSE). In Scotland, which has a separate education system, there has been much greater homogeneity, with almost all pupils who presented doing so for the Scottish Certificate of Education (SCE), although a small number also presented for examinations offered by English GCE or CSE examination boards.

This structure of public examinations has been replaced by new systems. In Scotland the Standard Grade provides a three-tier system of foundation, general and credit level examinations, while in England and Wales the CSE and GCE examinations have been replaced by the General Certificate of Secondary Education (GCSE) examination. The essential point is that public examinations continue to provide a highly visible and widely used framework for selection into post-school educational and occupational careers. Of course, the situation is much more complex than this. The Technical and Vocational Training Initiative (TVEI) and the substantial amount of education and training that is taking place under the aegis of the Youth Training Scheme (YTS) provide but two indications that the teaching of academic, vocational and life skills, which was previously the sole preserve of schools, cannot be viewed in isolation from other institutions, nor simply from an academic perspective.

Furthermore, the various philosophies of schooling that underlie the British education system give the school a wider mission than that dictated by academic attainment alone. Most individuals would want schools to play a role in the all-round development of young people. This means that the outcomes of schooling have to be seen in a wider perspective. An ILEA report (Hargreaves, 1984) on improving secondary schools listed four domains of pupils' achievement that schools should address:

1 Knowledge acquisition/expression - the capacity to retain propositional knowledge, to select from such knowledge appropriately in response to a specified request, and to do so quickly without reference to sources of information.
2 Knowledge application/problem-solving - the application of knowledge to practical rather than theoretical ends, and in an oral rather than written form.
3 Personal and social skills - the capacity to communicate with others in face-to-face relationships; the ability to co-operate with others in the interests of the group as well as the individual; initiative, self-reliance and the ability to work alone without close supervision; and the skills of leadership.
4 Motivation and commitment - the willingness to accept failure without destructive consequences; the readiness to persevere; the self-confidence to learn in spite of the difficulty of the task.

Although these four domains of pupil achievement may not address all the objectives that parents, pupils and other constituencies might have for schooling, they provide a basis for assessing the relationship between attainment as measured by pupil performance in public examinations and a wider set of outcomes that schools are striving to achieve. The first domain, knowledge acquisition, is probably quite well reflected in pupils' examination performances. Such examinations are primarily of a written nature, and are undertaken in conditions of strict time limits with the requirement that pupils have little additional resources available to them. 'The examinations emphasize knowledge rather than skill; memorisation more than problem solving or investigational capacities; writing rather than speaking or other forms of communication; speed rather than reflection; individual rather than group achievement' (Hargreaves, 1984, p. 2). Public examinations also partially assess the second domain of achievement, knowledge application/problem-solving, but they do so to a lesser extent than for the previous domain. The assessment of this domain is typically more time-consuming and often involves the examination of practical exercises. The third and fourth domains of achievement are not directly assessed by public examinations, although they are indirectly assessed insofar as they interact with attainment in the first two domains. Thus, in assessing the effectiveness of schools on the basis of pupils' performances in public examinations we are at best gaining only a partial picture of the way that schools vary from one to another in terms of their outcomes. The tendency to consider that which is measured as the objective of assessments of schools poses the danger of narrowing of the overall criteria for assessing the effectiveness of schools. It is, therefore, important to emphasize the importance of the link between the curriculum and pupil assessment, and to provide the necessary structures to ensure that it is the former that determines the latter, rather than the reverse.

Torrance (1986) raises several issues related to the use of examination performances as a basis for the evaluation of schools. The thrust of his criticism of the use of school examinations is three-fold: examination scores are designed to discriminate between pupils, rather than schools; examination scores and measures of pupil background characteristics are unreliable; and school evaluation should link directly with school development. The charge that the information available is less than perfect can be disposed of fairly rapidly. Of course, the measures of examination performance and pupil background characteristics are unlikely to be measured with absolute accuracy. However, this does not mean that they are invalid in this context. Although the foregoing has indicated that examination marks do not measure all aspects of pupil attainment, they are probably relatively accurate measures of pupil attainment in the first domain discussed earlier. In fact, the studies that Torrance cites in support of his argument indicate that within examination boards the marks awarded are relatively reliable.

Torrance's main disagreement is with attempts to compare or equate marks across examination boards, or across time. It is true that the problems are greater here, and this indicates that studies of school effectiveness need either to control for the boards at which pupils presented or to analyse their data wholly within board constituencies. Again, it is known that the measures of pupil background characteristics are less than perfect, but if they are collected with some care they are usually fairly reliable. The fact that they are measured with some error does not make them unusable, but merely requires that we take this into account in interpreting the results of the assessment of differences in effectiveness between schools. Provided the errors of measurement of pupil characteristics and attainment are not consistently biased in one direction or the other for individual schools, the estimates of school effectiveness will not be biased by such errors. Since examiners generally do not know which schools their randomly allocated scripts come from, there should be no significant problems for estimating school outcomes, even though the marks for individual pupils are not 100 per cent reliable. However, to the extent to which the marks awarded do contain such errors of measurement, the proportion of the overall pupil-level variation in attainment that can be attributed to schools will be reduced. Measurement error pervades almost all observations in our everyday lives, but it is rarely so debilitating as to make communication and comprehension impossible. Estimates of the effectiveness of schools need not be treated as if they were tablets of scripture, and they can be observed again if there is any reason to suspect that something is odd about them.

Torrance's other two criticisms are less easily cast aside. First, the argument that examinations are designed to discriminate between individual pupils, and not between schools, has a long history in the school effectiveness literature. It dates back to the early critiques of the seventies.[1] However, the argument carries more force in systems in which there is only a weak articulation between curriculum and the tests employed to assess pupil performance, such as that typified by the tests employed in the National Assessment of Educational Progress (NAEP) in the United States. Indeed, in the construction of these tests any items that are sensitive to school contexts are dropped on the grounds that they would unfairly advantage some pupils and disadvantage others. The situation in Britain is, however, quite different. The syllabus for the public examinations in each subject is sufficiently well understood by subject teachers to produce a direct link between the knowledge examined in the examinations and the knowledge that teachers are attempting to convey to their pupils. In terms of the jargon employed in the literature, the examinations are *curriculum sensitive*, not perfectly, but probably to quite a high degree. This feature of the examinations would be enhanced further by the introduction of criterion-referenced examinations, rather than the present norm-referenced examinations.

In criterion-referenced examinations marks are awarded on the basis of some predefined criterion of what constitutes a correct answer, whereas in norm-referenced examinations marks are determined by the sagacity of the pupil's answers relative to those of other pupils. Under a criterion-referenced system there are no predetermined quotas for the numbers of pupils who may receive passes at each level; they could all, for example, obtain marks of 90 per cent, or above. In a norm-referenced system, on the other hand, the examiners usually have some preset proportion whom they will classify as passing the examination, 50 per cent, for example. The Standard Grade which is being introduced to replace the Ordinary Grade examination in Scotland was initially built within a criterion-referenced framework, although various pressures have since reduced its adherence to this ideal.

The criticism that examination marks can be of little relevance in the evaluation of schools rests on the mistaken assumption that they are the sole, or even the main, element in any such evaluation. It also raises the issue of whom such evaluations are of and the purpose for which the evaluation is conducted. No single evaluation strategy is likely to be of equal utility for all possible purposes. Thus, it is important to delimit the purposes for which one might wish to assess the variation among schools in terms of their pupils' examination performances. Clearly, school effectiveness studies have a very limited role to play in staff assessment schemes, and probably no direct role in staff development schemes. Successful school improvement programmes in the USA have, however, included a substantial role for the assessment and monitoring of outcomes. They have been used to provide information on the academic progress of different types of pupils within individual schools, and feedback on the effectiveness of particular improvement strategies. In this context such assessments are not expected to produce a simple estimate or index of effectiveness, but indicators of the effects of particular practices on a range of outcomes. As will be evident in the discussion below, the idea of a single unidimensional index of effectiveness is untenable, because schools are likely to be differentially effective for different types of pupil.

On another level, estimates of the effectiveness of schools provide an indication of whether the variation between schools is important relative to variation between school sectors - grammar and comprehensive, say - and an indication of the magnitude of differences between schools relative to changes in pupil attainment over time. This is important in assessing the priority to be attached to reductions in the disparities in effectiveness between schools relative to efforts to raise the overall level of attainment in the system through the introduction of better teaching practices, environments and technology. If there are only small disparities in effectiveness between schools then there may be only small gains to be obtained from attempts to transfer the practices found in the most effective schools to the less effective schools, provided that such practices can be located and that their effects are reproducible in other contexts. This indicates one of the limitations of studies of schools in an extant system. The variation in the system is constrained by present practices and contexts. It is possible that the introduction of new practices and contexts could have much larger effects than those that would result from a more widespread adoption of the best practices in the current system.

A range of uses for studies of the effectiveness of schooling has now been delimited, but there still remains a set of technical issues that have to be addressed before such studies can be carried out. Ideally, the variation in effectiveness between schools, after adjustment for the background characteristics of their pupil intakes, should be explainable by variation in school process, pedagogy, etc. However, many data sets that contain the requisite pupil-level information on pupil background and attainments do not contain the necessary measures of the school characteristics which are responsible for producing differences in effectiveness among schools. Usually, only studies designed specifically for the task, such as the Rutter study (Rutter *et al.*, 1979) and the Inner London Junior School Project (Mortimore *et al.*, 1988), contain information on both pupil intake characteristics and school characteristics. There are, however, various data sets available which contain the information on both pupil background and attainment that provides a basis for estimating the variation in school outcomes after adjustment for their intakes. The estimates presented below are based on data available for all Scottish secondary schools in the Scottish Educational Data Archive (SEDA). Willms and Cuttance (1985) have previously estimated the effectiveness of a subset of twenty-one schools in one Scottish local authority, and Gray *et al.* (1986) have analysed similar data for forty-one schools drawn from two English local authorities.

ASSESSING EFFECTIVENESS

In this section three models of effectiveness that can be found in the literature are compared. Only one of them is shown to yield valid estimates of effectiveness after taking account of school intakes. The three models are referred to as the standards model, the school-level intake adjusted model and the pupil-level intake adjusted model.

The Standards Model

The standards model (Gray and Hannon, 1986) is the basic league table model that one often finds in the popular press. It is also the model that underlies the reporting of school examination results as required under the 1980 Education Act. This model references the performance of schools against some external norm or standard, usually the average performance of all pupils in the system. The assessment of the performance of individual schools, or sectors (e.g. LEAs), is undertaken by comparing the average performance of pupils in a given school with the average performance of pupils across all schools. Figure 4.1 illustrates this model. The performance of schools is assessed on the basis of where they lie on the continuum from the lowest to the highest level of performance. Those above the centre line are said to be performing above average and those below this line as below average.

This model is fundamentally inadequate as a tool for assessing the effectiveness of schools because of its failure to take account of the intake characteristics of the pupils in schools (Goldstein and Cuttance, 1988). It is incapable of indicating the effectiveness of schools in terms of the gains made by pupils. In order to assess the extent of the gains made by pupils in each school it is necessary to control for the background characteristics and prior attainment of pupils at the point of their entry into the school. However, most measures of attainment that are appropriate at the point of entry to any stage of schooling are generally not also appropriate at the stage at which pupils exit from the stage of schooling. A measure that adequately captures the variation in the skills and knowledge across the range of pupils, say at entry to secondary schooling, is not likely also to be able to capture adequately either the full range or level of skills and knowledge attained at the time the pupil leaves secondary schooling. This is because the types of skills and knowledge that characterize pupils at the various stages of schooling cannot necessarily be viewed as cumulative within a linear hierarchical structure of learning. Thus, it is likely that any single measure that is appropriate at entry to any stage of schooling will also be sensitive to the particular curriculum that the pupil has been exposed to during that

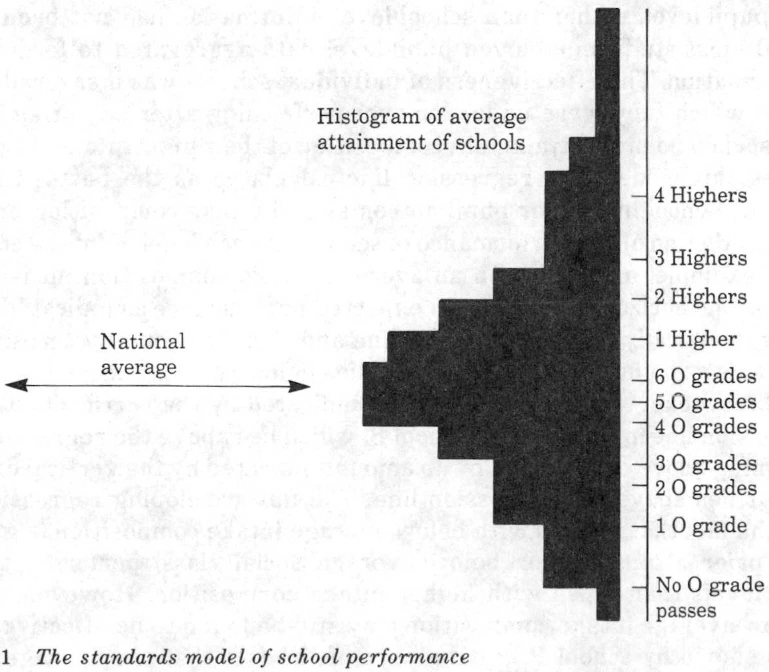

Figure 4.1 *The standards model of school performance*

stage of schooling. For this reason, plus the practical consideration that such prior information on attainment is rarely available for matching with data on pupil attainment for cohorts as they exit from each stage of schooling, it is often necessary to adopt a second best solution to the problem of adjusting for variation in the prior attainment of pupils at the time of their intake to each stage of schooling.

The solution generally adopted is to employ measures of the ascribed characteristics of pupils known to be associated with attainment, such as pupil social class and parental education, and where available to include suitable measures of pupil prior attainment in cognate curriculum areas, to control for variation in the pupil intakes to schools. To emphasize the fact that the prior attainment and current attainment measures are generally scored on different metrics the difference between the two will be referred to as an indication of pupil *progress* rather than of pupil *gains*. Estimates of school effectiveness that are based on these considerations are referred to as *intake-adjusted* estimates. The estimates of variation in school outcomes that are presented later are based on a model which includes measures to control for the social characteristics of pupils in school intakes, but not for the prior attainments of pupils. In order to stress the qualifications that must pertain to these estimates because they are based on a model that does not include a control for prior attainment, they will be referred to simply as (intake) adjusted school outcomes, rather than estimates of school effectiveness.

School-level Intake-Adjusted Models

Until recently the importance of assessing the effectiveness of schools on the basis of pupil-level, rather than school-level, information had not been recognized and most studies employed pupil-level data aggregated to form school-level information. The effectiveness of individual schools was measured by the degree to which they were under- or over-performing after adjusting for the average social and prior attainment composition of their pupil intake. Figure 4.2 illustrates this model. The regression line calculated as the best-fitting line through the school means for pupil outcomes and intake composition provides the best prediction of the performance of schools at each level of intake composition. For example, a school with an average intake composition measured at point X_1 on the horizontal axis has an expected performance as indicated by the line drawn vertically to the regression line and then horizontally across to the outcome axis at point Y_1. School A, which lies below the regression line, is performing below expectation by the amount indicated by the vertical distance to the regression line (p_1). Likewise, school B, which lies above the regression line, is performing above expectation by an amount indicated by the vertical distance (p_2) that it lies above the regression line. The upward-sloping regression line reflects the fact that schools with below average intake composition (e.g. below average prior attainment or below average social class) perform at lower absolute levels than those with higher intake composition. However, schools with below average intake composition may still be found to be effective in this mode, as shown by school B. But because of the fact that the average intake

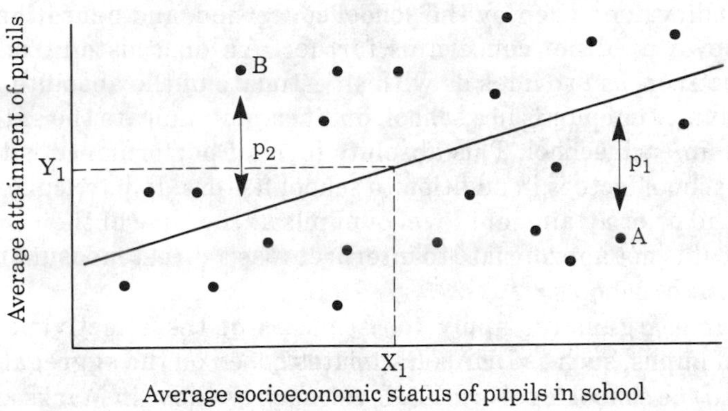

Figure 4.2 *School-level intake-adjusted model*

composition and the average performance of pupils are positively correlated, schools with below average intake composition are more likely to be below the national average in performance.

The school-level standards and intake-adjusted models of effectiveness may lead to contradictory conclusions about the effectiveness of individual schools. Figure 4.3 superimposes the two models on the same axes. Schools above the centre line are performing above the national mean, and hence would be termed above average under the standards model, but those in the shaded area to the right of the vertical axis are performing below expectation in the context of the intake-adjusted model, given the above average composition of their intake. Similarly, schools below the centre are performing below the national average in terms of the standards model, but they are performing above expectation in terms of the intake-adjusted model if they fall within the shaded area, given their intakes.

Clearly, a failure to adjust the measures of effectiveness for the characteristics of pupils at the time of their intake to the school invalidates them as

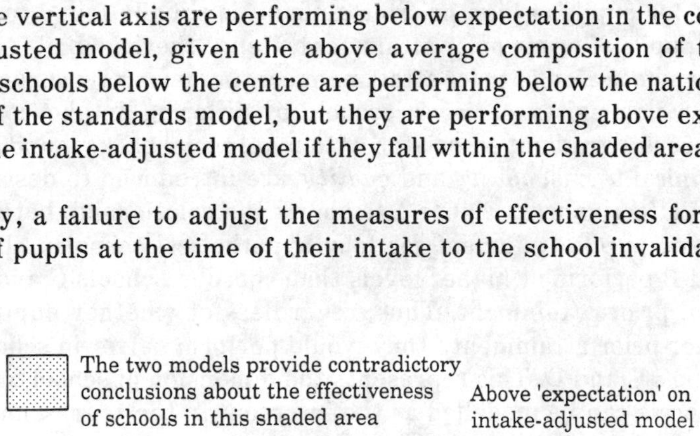

Figure 4.3 *Standards model superimposed on the school-level intake-adjusted model*

measures of the value added by the school concerned, and hence the contradictions just shown need not concern us further. An unadjusted (i.e. standards) model of effectiveness provides us with an estimate of the absolute level of the average attainment of pupils in a school, but it cannot indicate the extent of pupil progress within each school. This absolute level of performance is the product of many non-school factors in addition to school factors. In particular it depends crucially on the prior attainment level of pupils at the time of their intake to the school, and so it is not appropriate to interpret it as a direct measure of the effectiveness *per se* of schools.

These same arguments apply to estimates of the effectiveness of other aggregates of pupils, such as LEAs. Estimates based on the aggregation of pupil information to the school level or LEA level, such as those in Marks and Pomian-Srzednicki (1985), are also inappropriate for assessing the differences in effectiveness among these units because they fail to take account of the variation in the pupil intakes to schools across LEAs, and hence are incapable of indicating the differences between LEAs that are associated with pupil progress in schools.

Pupil-level Intake-Adjusted Models

Thus far the discussion has been in terms of the average performance of pupils in each school, but because there is correlation between ascribed pupil characteristics and individual pupil attainment, pupils of different background characteristics within a school will have *different* levels of attainment. The level of attainment for pupils of high prior attainment is usually found to be higher than that for pupils of lower prior attainment. Hence there is likely to be a gradient in performance along a prior attainment continuum *within* schools, in addition to that which exists *between* schools of differing intake composition. Similarly, there is a gradient associated with pupil social background in schools.

Two technical terms, *equity* and *quality*, are introduced to describe these dimensions of effectiveness. Figure 4.4a shows the relationship between pupil background and pupil attainment for four hypothetical schools. All pupils in schools A and B perform at higher levels than those in schools C and D, for all levels of pupil prior attainment. Thus, regardless of whether pupils were of lower or higher prior attainment,[2] they would perform better in schools A and B than in schools C and D. This represents the dimension of school quality, and in technical terms can be modelled as the intercept in the regression equation for each school.

Within each of the four schools in Figure 4.4a there is a gradient describing the difference in performance between pupils of higher and lower prior attainment. This gradient will be referred to as the *equity differential* within each school, and it is modelled as the slope of the regression line in each school. For analytical purposes, schools which have steep slopes may be designated as *disequalizing*, because in comparison with other schools they promote the attainment of pupils of higher prior attainment to a greater extent than those of lower prior attainment. And schools with flatter slopes may be designated as *equalizing*, because they promote the attainment of pupils of lower prior attainment in comparison with those of higher prior attainment more so than other schools.

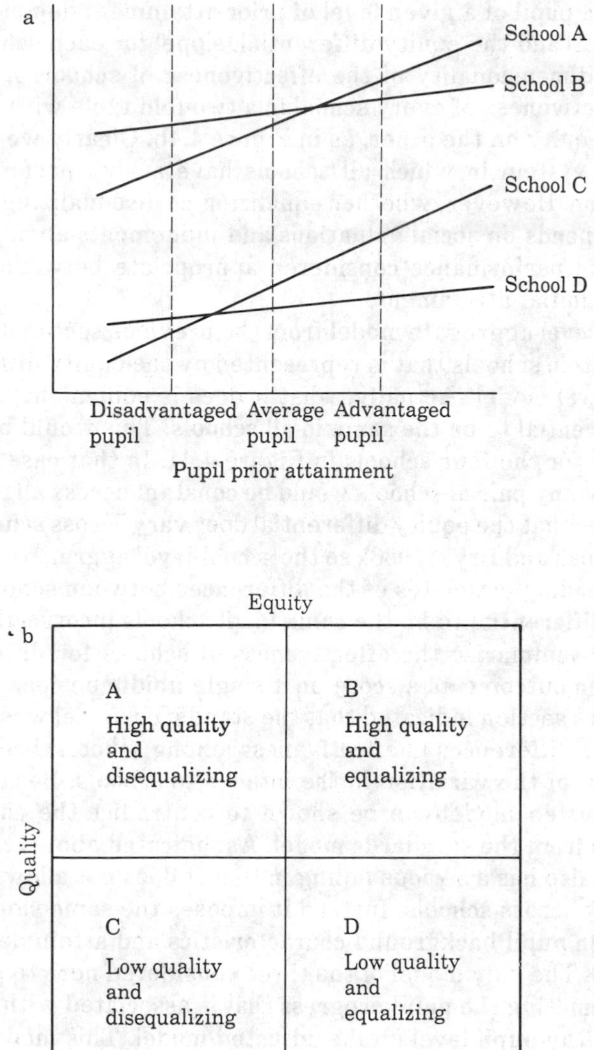

Figure 4.4 *a, Pupil attainment in four schools. b, School quality by equity matrix of the four schools*

This does not mean that pupils from lower prior attainment perform better than those of higher prior attainment in equalizing schools, merely that the differential between the two groups is less in such schools.

The terms socially *advantaged* and socially *disadvantaged* are now introduced to refer to pupils whose prior attainment is above, or below, respectively, that of the nationally average pupil. In Figure 4.4a the regression lines for schools A and B intersect, indicating that pupils of all prior attainment levels do not perform better in school A than in school B, and vice versa. Pupils with lower levels of prior attainment perform better in school B while those with higher levels of prior attainment perform better in school A. The expected performance of a pupil of a given level of prior attainment depends on both the quality (intercept) and the equity differential (slope) for each school. From this analysis of the dimensionality of the effectiveness of schools it is possible to classify the effectiveness of every school in a two-fold table with quality on one dimension and equity on the other, as in Figure 4.4b. Clearly we would wish to move toward a system in which all schools have a high performance on the quality dimension. However, whether equalizing or disequalizing schools are to be preferred depends on social valuations and judgements about the degree of differentiation in performance considered appropriate between pupils at different levels of initial attainment.

The school-level aggregate model from the previous section fails to capture the variation within schools that is represented by the equity differential in the present pupil-level model. Actually, what it does is equivalent to constraining the equity differential to be the same in all schools. This would be represented by parallel lines for the four schools in Figure 4.4a. In that case the difference in attainment for any pair of schools would be constant across all types of pupils. There is evidence that the equity differential does vary across schools (Cuttance, 1988a; Raudenbush and Bryk, 1986), so the school-level aggregate model is likely to provide misleading estimates of the differences between schools. Constraining the equity differential to be the same in all schools incorrectly implies that it is possible to summarize the effectiveness of schools for different types of pupils on a given outcome as a score on a single unidimensional index.

The previous section indicated that the standards model was inappropriate for assessing the differences in effectiveness among schools, because it fails to take any account of the variation in the intakes to schools. Because of this the school-level adjusted model can be shown to contradict the conclusions that would be drawn from the standards model. As indicated above, the school-level adjusted model also has a serious failing in that it does not allow the equity differential to vary across schools. Instead it imposes the same slope for the relationship between pupil background characteristics and attainment on the data for every school. The only model of the three considered here to provide a valid approach to estimating the pupil progress that is associated with schools is that considered last, the pupil-level intake adjusted model. This model is capable of adjusting for the differences in the characteristics of pupils entering schools, and it also allows for differences among schools in the relationship of these pupil characteristics to attainment. The only British studies to have employed this model to assess the variation in effectiveness among schools are Aitkin and Longford (1986), Gray *et al.* (1986), Mortimore *et al.* (1988), and Willms and Cuttance (1985). The studies by Marks and Pomian-Srzednicki (1985), Marks *et al.* (1983) and Gray and Jesson (1987) of the variation in outcomes between LEAs employed the school-level adjusted model which was shown above to be deficient, but the studies of local authority differences reported by Willms (1987) and by Cuttance (1988b) are both based on this pupil-level adjusted model.

The shortcomings of the standards model and the school-level adjusted model carry over to analyses which aim to estimate the variation between any division of schools into sectors. The variation between schools can be thought of as a simple sector model with all schools belonging to one sector, while assigning schools to their LEAs is a sectoring of the system based on the administrative structure of the school system. Other criteria for dividing the system into sectors of particular interest have included selective versus comprehensive sectors (Steedman, 1980, 1983; Gray *et al.*, 1983; McPherson and Willms, 1987), Catholic versus secular schools and sectors based on the period in which schools were founded, the selectivity of schools and the types of community that they serve (Cuttance, 1988b) and public versus private schools (Coleman *et al.*, 1983; Coleman and Hoffer, 1987).[3] The analyses presented below illustrate the application of the pupil-level adjusted outcomes model to the estimation of variation in effectiveness among schools, and to a classification of the system into sectors that jointly describe the degree of selectivity of schools and the types of community that they serve.

DATA AND METHODOLOGY

The data from the 1981 Scottish School Leavers Survey (Burnhill *et al.*, 1984) are employed below to estimate the variation in outcomes between schools and between school sectors. They relate to pupils who left school at the end of the 1979-80 school year. Because the sample is of pupils who left school in that year it is comprised of the members of the entry cohorts for the years 1974-5 (the sixth-year leavers), 1975-6 (the fifth-year leavers), and 1976-7 (the fourth-year leavers). The pupils entered over a three-year period and moved through the system in a staged manner; thus the progress through the system of each entry cohort may have been influenced by particular period specific factors that varied from year to year, in addition to any systematic factors that were present throughout the period.

The data are for a selected sample of these school leavers. The full response data set comprised 23 151 pupils drawn from all 470 schools in the Scottish secondary school system. The target sample had been set at 37 per cent of the population and the achieved sample covered approximately 72 per cent of the target sample (Burnhill, 1984). All schools with more than one pupil represented in the sample were retained, after deleting cases without a complete record of data on their SCE attainment level and social background characteristics. These selections result in an analysis sample of 18 851 pupils and 456 schools.

The information employed in the analyses describes pupils' Scottish Certificate in Education (SCE) fourth-year attainments in English, arithmetic and an overall indicator of attainment across all subjects at the time pupils left school, plus socioeconomic characteristics of their families. The SCE data have been rescaled to give each of the attainment measures a logistic distribution with a mean of zero and unit variance. This means that the SCE awards in English and arithmetic are rescaled so that the overall distribution, inclusive of those who did not enter for the particular subject, are approximately normally distributed. The overall measure of SCE attainment employed in the analyses is one in which passes at O level are given less weight than those at Higher level. This measure is based principally on the number of passes at O grade and Highers, and it also has an approximately normal distribution inclusive of the zero scores for pupils who passed no SCE examinations.

The socioeconomic background data on the pupil's families include the following: a measure of socioeconomic status, the level of educational attainment of the pupil's mother, and the number of children in the family. The socioeconomic status measure is based on a rescaling of the Registrar General's seven-point classification of social class, using weights from the Hope-Goldthorpe classification of socioeconomic status (Willms and Cuttance, 1985).

Details of the statistical model are not discussed here. Readers are referred to Cuttance (1988a), which presents a discussion in the context of the present data, or to Gray *et al.* (1986). Both these discussions present a relatively non-technical overview of the multi-level statistical model as it is applied to the task of estimating variation in effectiveness among schools. Expositions of a more technical nature can be found in Aitken and Longford (1986), Goldstein (1986, 1987) and Raudenbush and Bryk (1986).

THE EXTENT OF VARIATION IN ADJUSTED OUTCOMES AMONG SCHOOLS

Figure 4.5 shows the variation in school outcomes for disadvantaged, average and advantaged pupils for the two fourth-year outcomes and for the overall SCE measure, after adjustment for the social background characteristics of the pupil intakes to schools. The boxplots represented in these figures refer to the estimated school outcomes for the three types of pupil across all schools (the wider boxplots), and for the subset of all schools that were not subject to creaming by selective schools (the narrower boxplots). Each boxplot represents the range of estimates for the adjusted outcomes for disadvantaged, average and advantaged pupils in all schools. The points that underlie each boxplot are the

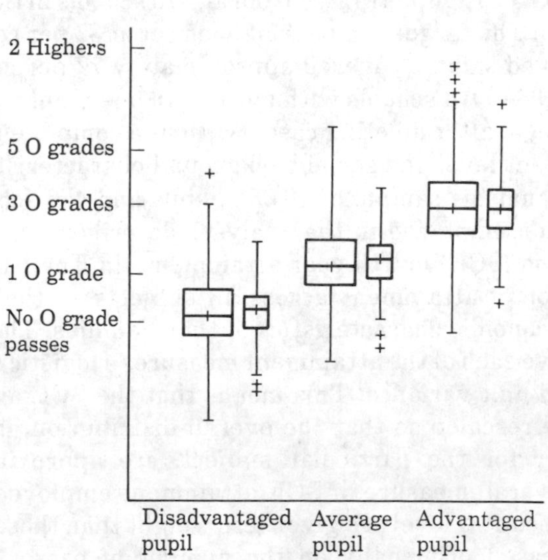

Figure 4.5 *Adjusted estimates of mean attainment. a, Overall SCE measure. b, Fourth-year English. c, Fourth-year arithmetic*

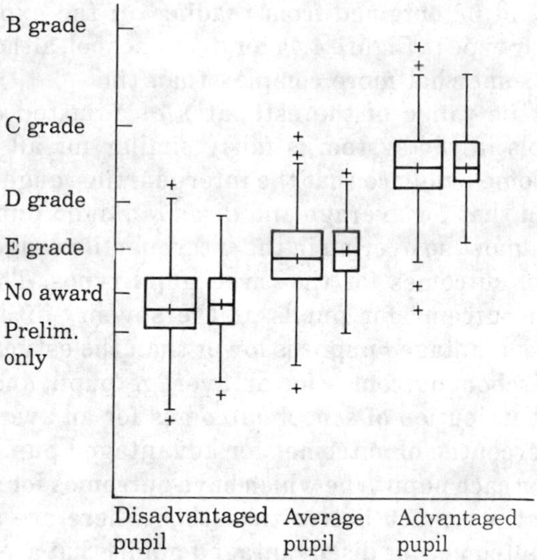

Figure 4.5b

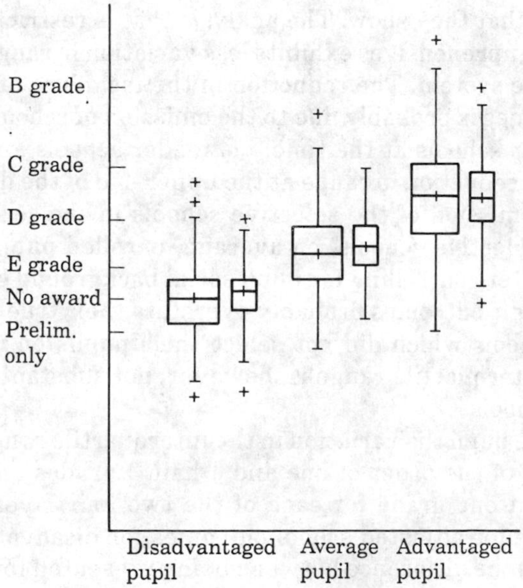

Figure 4.5c

estimates that would be obtained from reading off the expected outcome for pupils of a particular type in Figure 4.4a for every school, although the statistical model required is somewhat more complex than this.

The interquartile range of the estimates of adjusted outcomes that are based on all schools in the system is fairly similar for all three pupil types, although there is some evidence that the interquartile range for an advantaged pupil is larger than that for average and disadvantaged pupils for fourth-year English. There is almost no overlap in the interquartile range of these adjusted estimates of school outcomes for the three pupil types. This means that the estimate of school outcome for pupils at the seventy-fifth percentile of the distribution for disadvantaged pupils is lower than the estimate for the twenty-fifth percentile of school outcomes for an average pupil, and the seventy-fifth percentile of the distribution of school outcomes for an average pupil is below the twenty-fifth percentile of outcomes for advantaged pupils. However, there are some schools for each pupil type which have outcomes for disadvantaged and average pupils that are much better than this. There are a small number of schools that have outcomes for disadvantaged pupils that are above the twenty-fifth percentile level for advantaged pupils, and some schools in which the average pupil attains at a level above the seventy-fifth percentile of the distribution for advantaged pupils. There are few schools with such exceptional outcomes on the two fourth-year measures, but more on the overall SCE measure.

The median level of adjusted school outcomes is very similar for the box-plots based on all 456 schools and those based only on the 162 uncreamed schools. The main difference in the estimates between these two sets of schools is in the range of variation that they show. The analysis that is restricted to the 162 six-year uncreamed comprehensives exhibits less variation in range than that based on all schools in the system. The reduction in the incidence of schools with low estimates of outcomes is probably due to the omission of schools which were not all-through six-year schools at the time, i.e. feeder schools and recently established schools. The reduction in range at the upper end of the distribution is probably due to the omission of the selective schools in the second analysis. We know that these selective schools, on average, enrolled pupils of higher prior attainment even after controlling for pupil social background characteristics, so the estimates of their outcomes probably overstate their true level of outcomes relative to the schools which did not select their pupils on the basis of prior attainment. The interquartile range is, however, not substantially different for the two sets of schools.

For an average pupil the variation in the interquartile range of the adjusted school outcomes is of the order of one and a half O grades on the overall SCE measure, and about one grade for each of the two fourth-year outcomes. The interquartile range for adjusted school outcomes for disadvantaged pupils can be characterized as the difference between being presented for the examination and gaining an E grade mark for the two fourth-year outcomes, and the difference between gaining no O grade passes and one O grade pass on the overall SCE measure. For advantaged pupils the differences are more or less equivalent to a grade difference in the two fourth-year single subject outcomes, and are about two O grades on the overall SCE measure, which is similar to the range of variation associated with the average pupil.

VARIATION IN OUTCOMES AMONG SECTORS

The foregoing analysis has ignored information on school types that can be employed to partition the school system into various sectors. By way of example the analysis presented below classifies schools according to the degree of selectivity of their intakes and according to the type of community which they serve. More detailed analyses based on these characteristics of schools are available in Cuttance (1988b), and the variation associated with other sectors is analysed in Cuttance (1988c, d).

During the evolution of the Scottish school system a variety of types of schools were founded to suit the needs of different communities. The system as it stood when comprehensive reorganization was announced in 1965 consisted of a wide range of different types of institutions, some highly selective, others almost fully comprehensive, some fee-paying, and some of course having to take whichever pupils the selective system rejected as unfit for an advanced secondary education.

After a 1947 government report (SED, 1947) which had strongly suggested that a comprehensive system would be the best system to adopt, but which in the end opted to give the junior/senior secondary system further time to prove itself, some educational authorities fostered the development of the comprehensive model in the form of omnibus schools. These schools were clearly non-selective, in that they accepted all pupils from a given local area, although their intakes were creamed by any selective schools which also drew on the same catchment for their intake. Schools of this type had existed for some time in smaller communities where the population was not large enough to support more than one secondary school. Some of these schools also received pupils from the rural feeder school system in which pupils would receive their initial secondary education in a rural short-course (three-year) school before transferring to a five-year receiver school in a nearby town to complete their schooling. The age of transfer varied between fourteen and sixteen years, depending on local arrangements.

At the time that the pupils in the 1981 leaver cohort embarked on their secondary schooling in the mid-1970s, comprehensive reorganization had been in progress for almost a decade. However, twenty-seven schools in the public sector still had selective intakes, mainly because reforms had been slow to have an impact on the selection of pupils into the public schools that had been the former local authority fee-paying sector and the grant-aided school sector in the four major cities. Thus, the comprehensive schools in the cities were probably still losing the more able and socially advantaged pupils from their catchments to the partially reformed former selective sector. In some cases the reformed former selective schools, like their counterparts from whom they creamed the able pupils, were comprehensive in the sense that they accepted all pupils in their territorial catchment, but they were selective in the sense that they also selectively drew a proportion of their intake from the wider cross-section of all nearby school catchments.

In the mid-1970s, when the cohort of pupils analysed here passed through the system, the selectivity of schools was described by the following typology, which divides the system into eight sectors: (1) all-through six-year comprehensive schools with uncreamed intakes, (2) all-through six-year comprehensive schools with creamed intakes, (3) all-through six-year comprehensive schools with uncreamed intakes, but which were formerly two-, three- or four-year schools, (4) all-through six-year comprehensive schools with creamed intakes but which were formerly two-, three- or four-year schools, (5) selective EA and independent schools, (6) short-course feeder schools, (7) all-through six-year comprehensive schools which also had a selective intake on transfer from the above short-course feeder schools at the end of the second or fourth year of secondary schooling, (8) other schools, a small group of schools not classifiable on any of the above criteria.[4] The comprehensive schools that were established comprehensives before the entry of the present cohort of pupils (sectors 1 and 2 in the above typology) will be referred to as *established* comprehensives and the more recently established comprehensives (sectors 3 and 4) as *transitional* comprehensives.[5]

The analysis presented below classifies schools jointly on the above typology and according to the type of community that they served. The typology of communities employed was based on schools serving rural areas, new towns, small burghs, large burghs and city populations (Cuttance, 1988b).

Figure 4.6 shows the interaction between community type and the selectivity of schools. In the mid-1970s almost all pupils in the cities attended comprehensive schools that were potentially creamed of their more able and socially

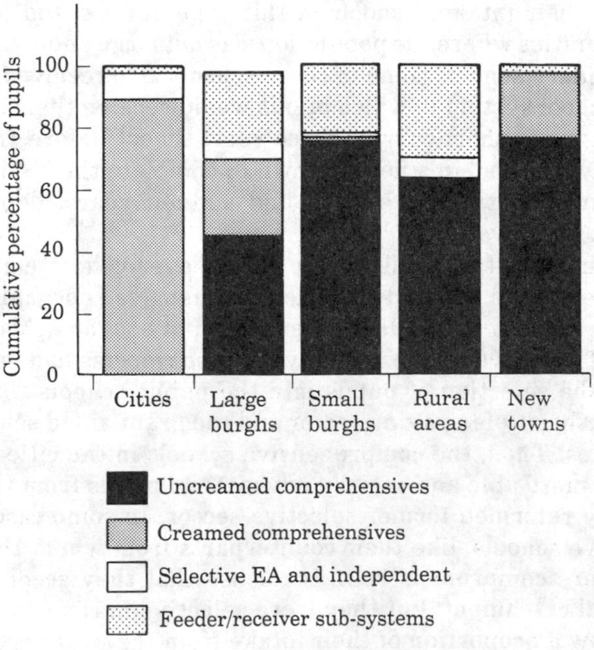

Figure 4.6 *Distribution of pupils within communities by selectivity of schooling*

advantaged pupils, while the majority of pupils in the small burghs, rural areas and new towns attended comprehensive schools that were uncreamed. Figure 4.6 also shows the location of the feeder/receiver system in the burghs and rural areas. As indicated above, this sub-system had evolved specifically to provide post-compulsory schooling for pupils from small burghs and rural areas where post-compulsory classes were too small to be viable.

Although there are thirty-five potential categories of schools in the cross-classification of the typologies based on community type and on school selectivity, many categories contained few pupils in the present data. For example, there were no city comprehensives that were classified as uncreamed, and only one creamed comprehensive rural school. The selective and the feeder/receiver school sectors were designated as groups independent of the type of community in which they were located. The purpose of the latter group of schools is explicitly to serve a catchment which extends across communities, and the whole country may legitimately be regarded as the catchment for the former group. Among the other potential categories of schools, all but six contained fewer than nine schools and were omitted from the analyses. Figure 4.7 presents the findings for schools in the resulting eight categories of schools.

There is a clear pattern across all three outcomes for these eight categories of schools. The median adjusted outcome of schools rises as the categories move from left to right in each figure, with one significant exception. The large burgh creamed comprehensives had higher adjusted outcomes than the uncreamed comprehensives in all communities, including uncreamed comprehensives in large burghs. The combined feeder and receiver sub-system of schools had the lowest median level of adjusted outcomes across all three outcomes. Among the uncreamed comprehensive schools those in the new towns had the highest median on all three outcomes, although they were few in number.

The estimates for the selective sectors cannot be interpreted as measuring the same adjusted outcomes as those for the other sectors. The known pattern of selection based on the prior attainment of pupils in these sectors means that the model overestimates the adjusted outcomes for the selective sectors relative to those for the non-selective sectors. Because information on the prior attainments of pupils is not available in the present data it is not possible to make a direct comparison between the selective and non-selective sectors. However, the difference between these sectors is an indication of the relative advantage that selective schools gain over their non-selective counterparts, after taking account of the social background characteristics of their respective intakes, by virtue of the fact that they are able to select their intakes on the basis of the prior performance of the pupils. Some of this advantage may represent real differences in the effectiveness of selective schools, but it could also be due entirely to the advantaged intakes of the schools in the selective sector. Without a measure of prior attainment it is impossible to determine how much of the difference is simply a result of the higher levels of prior attainment of pupils and how much, if any, is because of the schools themselves.

These problems of the selectivity of intakes are not as much of a concern when comparing the adjusted outcomes of the various comprehensive sectors, although it is the case that the adjusted outcomes of the city schools, which are

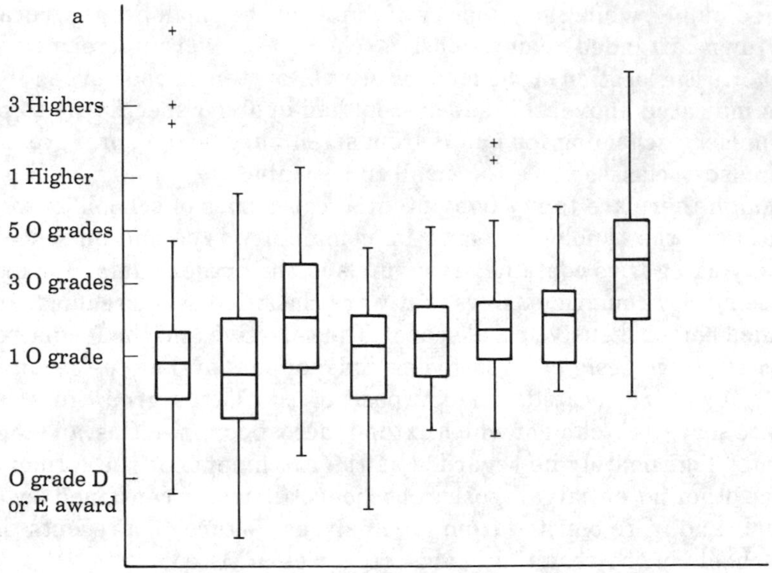
a
3 Highers
1 Higher
5 O grades
3 O grades
1 O grade
O grade D
or E award
1
2
3
4
5
6
7
8

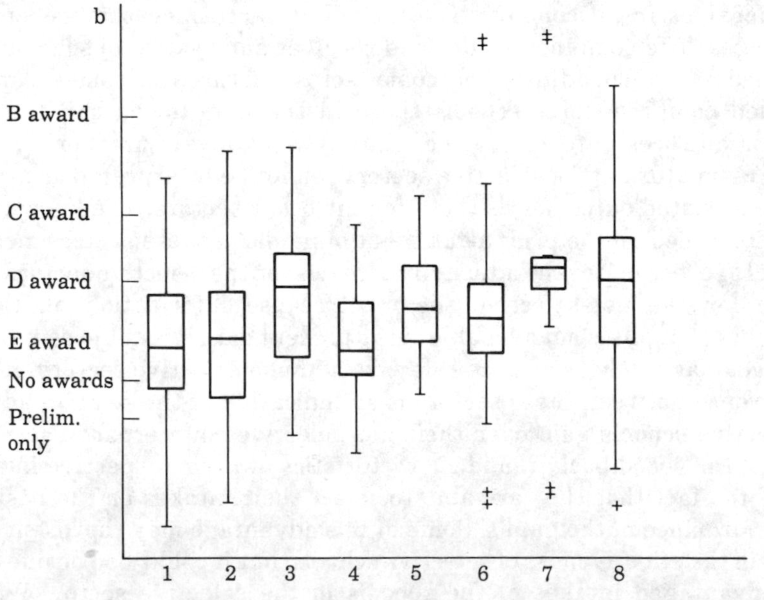
b
B award
C award
D award
E award
No awards
Prelim.
only
1
2
3
4
5
6
7
8

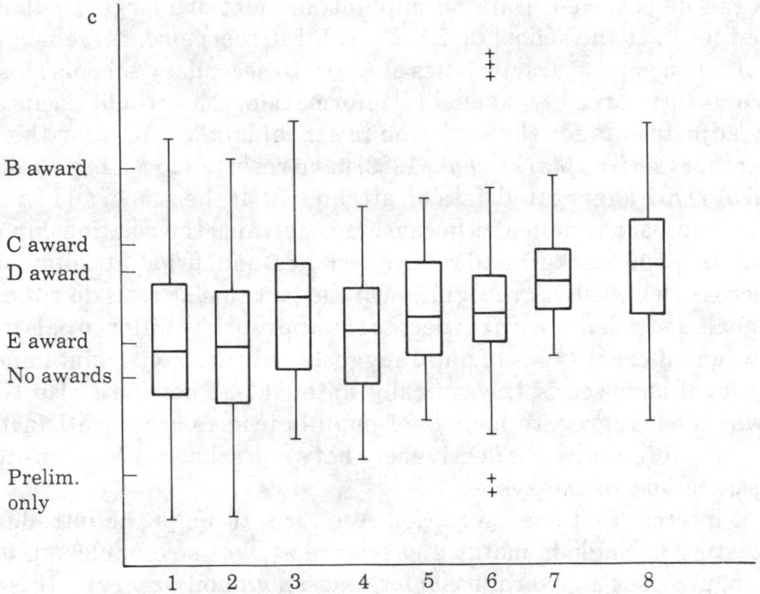

Figure 4.7 *Adjusted estimates of attainment for schools classified by selectivity and community type. a, Overall SCE attainment. b, English attainment. c, Arithmetic attainment*
Legend: 1, Feeder/receiver sub-systems (95 schools); 2, city creamed comprehensives (101 schools); 3, large burgh creamed comprehensives (26 schools); 4, rural uncreamed comprehensives (30 schools); 5, large burgh uncreamed comprehensives (31 schools); 6, small burgh uncreamed comprehensives (95 schools); 7, new town uncreamed comprehensives (9 schools); 8, selective education authority and independent schools (55 schools)

all potentially creamed of their more advantaged pupils, and the creamed large burgh sector are likely to be underestimated by the model.

DISCUSSION

The analyses presented above described three models that have been employed to assess the differences in outcomes among schools. The standards model is the implicit method that is employed when judging schools solely on the basis of their published examination results. Since the published results do not also include the necessary information to contextualize the raw unadjusted outcomes of schools, this model is not able to provide any insight into the relative progress that pupils make at different schools. Between 15 and 20 per cent, depending on outcome considered, of the unadjusted (raw) variation in pupil attainment lies between schools, and about half of this is attributable to differences in school intakes. Because school intakes account for such a large proportion of the unadjusted variation in pupil attainment, any informative assessment of the variation in the effectiveness of schools needs to adjust for the social background and prior attainment of pupils at their point of entry to schools.

Once differences in intakes have been taken into account, there is a further conceptual issue to be dealt with before appropriate estimates of the adjusted outcomes can be obtained. Data on pupil attainment are largely published in aggregated form, at the school or LEA level. Furthermore, there is a paucity of information on pupil characteristics at entry to secondary school. This means that there is little readily available information that would facilitate the necessary adjustments for the variation in school intakes. It is for this reason that researchers such as Marks *et al.* (1983) have resorted to a merging of census data on LEAs with aggregated data on attainment at the school and LEA level. But such an approach is deficient because it constrains the relationship of pupil attainment to pupil background characteristics and prior attainment to be uniform across all schools. A recognition of the fact that schools do not all share the same goals and policies with respect to the appropriate differentials in attainment between different types of pupil suggests that this constraint imposed by aggregate-level analyses is theoretically untenable. There are also technical reasons why such aggregate models of pupil outcomes are unsatisfactory for estimating the differences in effectiveness between schools, LEAs or other sectorial classifications of the system.[6]

It is of interest that the Education Act 1988, through the introduction of national testing in English, maths and science at ages seven, eleven, fourteen and sixteen, provides a general basis for assessing pupil *progress*. It is a great pity that this aspect of the assessment of standards is not applied to schools outside the public sector also. Evidence from the United States (Coleman *et al.*, 1983; Coleman and Hoffer, 1987) clearly indicates that there is much more variation within both the private and public sectors than there is between them. The most effective schools in the USA are spread across sectors. Thus, the major task in assessing the effectiveness of schools does not relate to whether they are in the public or private sector. There is no reason to believe that the situation will be different in the UK once a system of grant-aided schools is re-established, through the opting out provisions under the Act, over the next few years.

Although the schools that will obtain grant-aided status are likely to be drawn from those with high levels of pupil attainment, they will also be the schools with advantaged socioeconomic intakes. The progress that their pupils make may be no larger than that made by pupils in many other schools in the public sector. Indeed, there is evidence from the analyses presented above that some selective schools perform at levels below that of the twenty-fifth percentile school in any of the comprehensive sectors, despite the higher prior attainments of the pupils entering the former sector. If the prior attainments of pupils could have been taken into account in these analyses there would probably be many more selective schools with estimates of adjusted school outcomes that place them among the less effective schools in the system. Even without taking account of the overestimation of the adjusted outcomes for the selective sector, there are many schools in the comprehensive sector that have adjusted estimates that are higher than that for the median school in the former sector. This reinforces the importance of including all schools in the system in descriptions of the variation in effectiveness among schools, and therefore of the need to obtain assessment information for all schools that opt out of LEA control under the provisions of the new Act. In addition to these substantive arguments, it would be iniquitous to hold only one sector of the school system accountable for the public funds that it receives, while simultaneously failing to assess the effectiveness of the other sector that was also in receipt of public funds.

APPENDIX: NOTE ON READING BOXPLOTS

The grouped boxplot display is a means of comparing the main characteristics of several distributions in a single display.

1 The median (fiftieth percentile) of each plot is marked by a + sign, and/or a bar across the plot.
2 The lower and upper limits of the central box represent the twenty-fifth and seventy-fifth percentiles of the distribution (interquartile range), respectively. These points are referred to as the lower and upper hinges of the boxplot. The distance between the lower and upper hinges is thus the interquartile range for the data depicted by the boxplot.
3 The tails of a distribution are represented by the 'whiskers', and extreme points (outliers) are represented by a special symbol (one of the following: *, 0 (zero), 1), depending on the software employed to generate the graphics for the particular analysis. The length of the whiskers is determined by computing: hinge $\pm$ 1.5 $\times$ (interquartile range). Otherwise the whisker terminates at the largest/smallest value in the distribution. The more extreme points are denoted by special symbols, usually an asterisk. The various points in a boxplot will rarely be symmetric. In particular, the boxplots for skewed distributions usually have medians that are not at the centre of the interquartile range, and non-symmetric whiskers.
4 Where boxplots are based on samples from a population, it is more likely that the larger samples will contain outlier observations, the values of which may vary from sample to sample. Hence caution is required in comparing boxplots which are based on samples of varying size. However, where the boxplots are based on all observations in a fully enumerated population, rather than just a sample from that population, the population characteristics can be directly compared across plots.

ACKNOWLEDGEMENTS

This chapter reports research conducted with funding from the UK Economic and Social Research Council, and the Scottish Education Department, although the views expressed are not necessarily in agreement with those of either of these bodies.

NOTES

1 Cuttance (1980) provides references to the literature on this issue.

2 In general this argument applies to any of a wide range of variables that could be employed to control for variation in school intakes, such as social class, ethnicity, etc.

3 Additional references for the US studies are cited in Cuttance (1983).

4 This classification of schools was devised by Gray *et al.* (1983).

5 This usage of the terms 'established' and 'transitional' approximates that employed by Steedman (1983) in her study of English schools.

6 See Goldstein (1987) for a discussion of these issues.

REFERENCES

Aitken, M. and Longford, N. (1986) 'Statistical modelling issues in school effectiveness studies', *Journal of the Royal Statistical Society, Series A*, **149** (1), 1-43.

Burnhill, P. (1984) 'The 1981 Scottish School Leavers Survey', in Raffe, D. (ed.), *Fourteen to Eighteen: the Changing Pattern of Schooling in Scotland.* Aberdeen: Aberdeen University Press.

Burnhill, P., Lamb, J. and Weston, P. (1984) *Collaborative Research Dictionary and Questionnaires 1981.* Edinburgh: Centre for Educational Sociology, University of Edinburgh.

Coleman, J.S. and Hoffer, T. (1987) *Public and Private High Schools: the Impact of Communities.* New York: Basic Books.

Coleman, J.S., Hoffer, T. and Kilgore, S. (1983) *High School Achievement.* New York: Basic Books.

Cuttance, P.F. (1980) 'Do schools consistently influence the performance of their students?', *Educational Review*, **32**, 267-80.

Cuttance, P.F. (1983) 'Public and private schools, tax credits and tuition vouchers: a review of a comparison of the performance of public, Catholic, and private schools in America', *British Journal of Sociology of Education*, **4**, 363-73.

Cuttance, P.F. (1988a) 'Modelling variation in the effectiveness of schooling'. Unpublished manuscript, CES, Edinburgh.

Cuttance, P.F. (1988b) 'Intra-system variation in the effectiveness of schooling', *Research Papers in Education*, **3**, 183-219.

Cuttance, P.F. (1988c) 'The effectiveness of Catholic schooling in Scotland'. Unpublished manuscript, CES, Edinburgh.

Cuttance, P.F. (1988d) 'The effects of institutional differentiation in a school system: the legacy of Victorian and Edwardian educational developments'. Unpublished manuscript, CES, Edinburgh.

Goldstein, H. (1986) 'Multilevel mixed linear model analysis using iterative generalised least squares', *Biometrica*, **73** (1), 43-56.

Goldstein, H. (1987) *Multilevel Models in Educational and Social Research.* London: Griffin.

Goldstein, H. and Cuttance, P.F. (1988) 'National assessment and school comparisons', *Journal of Educational Policy*, **3**, 197-200.

Gray, J. and Hannon, V. (1986) 'HMI's interpretations of schools' examination results', *Journal of Educational Policy*, **1**, 23-33.

Gray, J. and Jesson, D. (1987) 'Exam results and local authority league tables', in *Education and Training, UK*, 33-41.

Gray, J., McPherson, A. and Raffe, D. (1983) *Reconstructions of Secondary Education: Theory, Myth and Practice since the War*. London: Routledge & Kegan Paul.

Gray, J., Jesson, D. and Jones, B. (1986) 'The search for a fairer way of comparing schools' examination results', *Research Papers in Education*, **1**, 91-119.

Hargreaves, D.H. (chairman) (1984) *Improving Secondary Schools. A Report of the Committee on the Curriculum and Organisation of Secondary Schools*. London: Inner London Educational Authority.

McPherson, A. and Willms, D. (1987) 'Equalisation and improvement: some effects of comprehensive organisation in Scotland', *Sociology*, **21**, 509-39.

Marks, J., Cox, C. and Pomian-Srzednicki, M. (1983) *Standards in English Schools*. London: National Council for Educational Standards.

Marks, J. and Pomian-Srzednicki, M. (1985) *Standards in English Schools Second Report: an analysis of the examination results of secondary schools in England for 1982 and comparisons with 1981*. London: National Council for Educational Standards.

Mortimore, P., Sammons, P., Stoll, L., Lewis, D. and Ecob, R. (1988) *School Matters: The Junior Years*. Wells: Open Books.

Raudenbush, S. and Bryk, A. (1986) 'A hierarchical model for studying school effects', *Sociology of Education*, **59**, 1-17.

Rutter, M., Maughan, B., Mortimore, P. and Ouston, J. (1979) *Fifteen Thousand Hours: Secondary Schools and Their Effects on Children*. Wells: Open Books.

SED (1947) *Secondary Education: A Report of the Advisory Council on Education in Scotland*. Edinburgh: HMSO.

Steedman, J. (1980) *Progress in Secondary Schools: Findings from the National Child Development Study*. London: National Children's Bureau.

Steedman, J. (1983) *Examination Results in Selective and Non-selective Schools*. London: National Children's Bureau.

Torrance, H. (1986) 'What can examinations contribute to school evaluation?', *Educational Review*, **38**, 31-43.

Willms, J.D. (1987) 'Differences between Scottish educational authorities in their examination attainment', *Oxford Review of Education*, **13**, 211-32.

Willms, J.D. and Cuttance, P. (1985) 'School effects in Scottish secondary schools', *British Journal of Sociology of Education*, **6**, 289-306.

Chapter 5

School Effects at A Level: Genesis of an Information System?

Carol T. Fitz-Gibbon

INTRODUCTION

In England and Wales, externally set and marked examinations ('public examinations') are taken at the age of sixteen by a majority of pupils and at eighteen by the 20 per cent or so who choose to stay on for advanced work. At age sixteen, pupils now sit General Certificate of Secondary Education (GCSE) examinations, but at the time the project described in this chapter was undertaken, there was a two-tier system involving Certificate of Secondary Education (CSE) and General Certificate of Education (GCE) O (Ordinary) level examinations. The examinations taken at age eighteen were and still are GCE A (Advanced) levels. The last two years of school (equivalent to the US eleventh and twelfth grades) are called the 'sixth form'. The academic sixth form, those studying for A levels, although representing a small percentage of the school population, is the pool from which most future professionals are drawn and, as such, it is of undoubted importance in the field of formal education. Grades received at A level are used to screen applicants for admission to universities and polytechnics, thus making them significant factors in many careers.

The effects that schools have on A-level results are difficult to assess in any one year because of the relatively small numbers of students in each school, but given their importance as a major academic hurdle for entry to the professions they are worthy of close scrutiny and detailed monitoring. In schools, sixth forms are highly valued for the chance they give staff to teach to a high academic level and to teach highly motivated pupils. The academic content is substantial, as illustrated by the fact that a pass at A level in a subject may give as much as two years' credit in the subject in US universities. Moreover, the schools receive more funds for A-level students than for students lower down the school.

This chapter describes a research project on school effects at A level, i.e. in sixth forms. The project has since developed into a performance monitoring system (Fitz-Gibbon, 1989) supported by seven local education authorities (LEAs) and covering the north of England from the Tees to the Scottish border. In 1983 a letter was sent to schools in two LEAs inviting them to collaborate with a university department of education in evaluating A-level work. Since the letter was sent 'cold' (the researcher had no previous contacts with the schools) and in view of the fact that responses to questionnaires are often as low as 20 per cent, it came as a surprise when about 50 per cent of the schools responded positively, attended a meeting and joined the project. Moreover, all these schools have since continued to participate each year. Given this successful collaboration over a long period it may be worth identifying some operational features of the project before considering the findings.

Originally schools were, of course, being offered a free data collection and analysis service - a free information system. Nevertheless, the comparisons of one school against another might have been seen as potentially damaging or embarrassing. Anxieties on this account were probably reduced by two procedures. Firstly, the LEA did not receive the results. Permission to approach the schools was originally sought from the two LEAs involved, but the understanding was that the results would go in confidence directly to the schools. Secondly, each school chose a code-name so that although it received all the data and could compare its 'effectiveness' with that of other schools, the identity of the schools was not generally known. Each school knew only its own code-name. This need for confidentiality had to be considered in preparing the reports each year. For example, the size of the sixth form had to be omitted from tables because this datum by itself could identify a school.

Another feature which may have helped to ensure initial and continuing collaboration was the stringent efforts made to keep demands on school personnel to a minimum. Since 1984, the researcher or specially employed data collectors have administered all the tests and questionnaires. Schools need only make students available for a 70-minute session. This arrangement has the added benefit of ensuring high-quality data. The conditions for the test and the atmosphere in which the attitude-questionnaire is administered can be well standardized from school to school. In addition to having the measures administered by the same person in all schools, standardization is further improved by having the explanations and instructions pre-recorded on an audio-tape. Every candidate hears exactly the same explanation and instructions, and timing is consistent from school to school. These strenuous efforts to standardize the data collection are considered necessary because any differences introduced by administration procedures would be confounded with schools, the unit of analysis. Thus 'school effects' might appear which were in fact due to differences in the data collection procedures.

The project was named the COMBSE project, standing for Confidential, Measurement-Based, Self-Evaluation. The confidentiality has been explained above. The following explanations of 'measurement-based' and 'self-evaluation' were provided in 1983:

> **Measurement-based:** The aim of research is to *discover* relationships. We do not start with faith in any particular model of how schools should teach for A levels or what their policies should be. Instead we are concerned to find what *measurable* aspects of pupils, schools and teaching strategies *actually* relate to examination results and to pupils' satisfaction.
>
> **Self-evaluation:** We hope to find measurements that will help to predict A-level results and indicate *how much* difference is possibly attributable to various factors. However, it is quite certain that there will be many variations in A-level results which will not be explicable in terms of the data we have collected.

> Schools will be the final interpreters of their own particular set of results, knowing, as they do, far more than we can measure. However, by extending the areas that are measured, self-evaluation can be more informed.

It is just as well that, from the start, there was an emphasis on self-evaluation. Researchers could not acquire the detailed knowledge of the situation in each school that would be needed to interpret the data. The project represented, rather, 'monitoring' and the provision of information to those who could not only interpret it in the light of their full understanding of conditions in their school, but also take action on the trends suggested by the data, if that were appropriate. Providing clear and fair feedback to schools on their performance may be a feasible way to improve schools - letting schools improve themselves. Indeed, a re-analysis of the Hawthorne experiments suggested that feedback on performance was the source of 'the Hawthorne effect' (Parsons, 1974).

Table 5.1 indicates some of the data collected each year of the project. After the first year (some findings from which were reported by Fitz-Gibbon (1985)) the major sources of data have been questionnaires and ability tests administered to students in the 'upper sixth', one term before the A-level examinations.

In addition to investigation of the effects schools appeared to have on examination results, attitudinal variables were also reported each year. Three summated scales will be considered here: attitude-to-the-subject (mathematics or English), attitude-to-the-school and self-reported level of effort. The items contributing to these scales are listed in the Appendix to this chapter, in which the reliabilities of the scales are reported. In short, the study has provided schools with 'fair performance indicators' for examination results, attitudes to the school, attitudes to the academic subjects and levels of effort.

SOME FINDINGS

This chapter uses data from 1157 pupils taking A levels in the years 1983 to 1986. It is now of historical interest as documentation of the kind of research which led into a major performance monitoring system. Furthermore, while this was a small-scale study, as school effects studies go, it was nevertheless on the kind of scale at which a small, single LEA might collect data on A levels, so it was worthwhile asking what kind of stability and what kind of significant differences could be found on such a scale. The data were also used to generate hypotheses which could later be checked on larger samples.

Examination Effectiveness Scores

In order to evaluate examination results 'in context', i.e. controlling for intake characteristics, pupil-level prediction equations were needed, predicting A-level grades from information about each pupil. The predictor variables available were prior achievement at O level, ability tests and socioeconomic status. Since like predicts like, it was expected that prior achievement at O level would provide the highest correlation with achievement at A level and this was indeed the case.

Table 5.1 *Measurement topics in the COMBSE project*

Data collection procedure	*Major variables measured*	*Year 1* *1983*	*Year 2* *1984*	*Year 3* *1985*	*Year 4* *1986*	*Year 5* *1987*
Report from school	A level grades per pupil	✓	✓	✓		✓
	Examination Boards used		✓	✓	✓	✓
	Teacher experience with A level	✓				✓
	Class size	✓	✓	✓	✓	✓
	School size	✓	✓	✓	✓	✓
Report from LEA	School EPA classification			✓		
	School history	✓				
Test given to pupils	Pupil ability on APM[a]			✓		✓
	Pupil ability on AH6[b]		✓			✓
Pupil questionnaire	Pupil background (SES) + AVOC[c]	✓	✓	✓	✓	✓
	Pupil's attitude to school	✓	✓	✓	✓	✓
	Pupil's attitude to subject	✓	✓	✓	✓	✓
	Pupil's study habits	✓	✓	✓	✓	✓
	Classroom processes				✓	✓
Teacher interview	Classroom processes	✓				
	Very able pupils	✓		✓	✓	
	Experience of examination boards	✓				
Teacher questionnaire	Teacher-predicted A level grades	✓				✓
	Very able pupils			✓	✓	✓
	Classroom ethos			✓	✓	✓
	Textbooks used				✓	✓

[a]APM: Advanced Progressive Matrices (Raven, 1962).
[b]AH6: An NFER-published test for high ability pupils, developed by Alice Heim.
[c]AVOC: Average O level and CSE grade (the ILEA scale).

There are several different ways in which O levels might be used for the prediction of A levels, such as the number of passes, the number of 'good' passes or a sum-of-points scale, reflecting both the numbers of O-level examination successes and the levels of grade awarded. In this study the average grade obtained on whatever O levels were taken was found to be the best predictor of A-level grades. This could have been because the number of subjects for which a candidate entered was a matter on which different schools had different policies and these policies would thus represent a confounding factor if allowed to affect the intake measure. The average O-level grade represents several hours of academic testing on topics taught by several different teachers. It is a good index of general academic ability.

The correlations between each pupil's average O-level grade and A-level grades were 0.56 in English and 0.59 in mathematics. The average O-level grade obtained by an individual pupil will be referred to as the pupil's O-level GPA (grade point average) to utilize a concept familiar to American readers and to avoid confusions with group averages. It had been the intention to use multiple predictors but once this O-level GPA was entered into the prediction equation socioeconomic status measures did not make any additional statistically significant contribution to the prediction. The effects of home background have probably had their major impact before students appear in the sixth form. (However, Smith (1987) reported a similar finding for younger pupils, fifth-formers: social class showed little effect after ability had been considered.)

There were, however, two major problems with the use of O levels as predictors. One was that the effects of schools may already have been apparent in these very grades so that A-level effects will have been affected to an unknown extent by 'school effects' at O level. Schools which had been particularly effective with O levels might look poor at A level simply because the good O-level grades made it appear they were working with pupils with high abilities. Nevertheless, the effects calculated with O level grades as the predictor could justifiably be regarded as measures of 'improvement', 'change' or 'value added' between O level and A level. The other problem with the use of O-level grades in prediction equations for A levels was that in upcoming years O-level results would no longer be available as O levels were set to give way to other examinations. Since the project was to continue it was important to have some measures which provided comparability from year to year. Although not a problem for the present analysis this situation needed consideration for the future.

It was in order to deal with both these problems that ability measures were collected in 1984 (the AH6: Heim *et al.*, 1983) and in 1985 (the Advanced Progressive Matrices: Raven, 1965). The strongest correlations between these measures and A levels were considerably weaker than those provided by O levels, as would be expected since it is almost always the case that achievement measures predict achievement better than ability measures predict achievement. The AH6 verbal score had a correlation of 0.37 with A-level English and the Advanced Progressive Matrices had a correlation of 0.31 with A-level mathematics (see Table 5.2). Although weak, these correlations were as strong as or stronger than correlations generally found with socioeconomic status, a measure which is often accepted as a satisfactory covariate.

Table 5.2 *Correlations between ability measures and A-level grades*

Ability measure	*n*	*English grade*	*n*	*Maths grade*
APM[a]	122	0.21	122	0.31
AH6[b]	129	0.34	154	0.28
verbal		0.37		0.21
numerical		0.16		0.30
diagrammatic		0.22		0.17

[a]APM: Advanced Progressive Matrices (Raven, 1965).
[b]AH6: Alice Heim 6 (Heim *et al.*, 1983).

Having located O-level GPA as a moderately good predictor and ability tests as weak predictors of A levels, we could develop 'examination effectiveness scores' for each school for each subject for each year, using either predictor. The regression lines used for reports to the schools each year were based on the data for that year. For this chapter, results have been pooled across the four years 1983 to 1986 and a single regression line used. (The small sample sizes for each of the ten schools precluded consideration of separate regression lines per school per year). For each school, the average of the pupils' residuals was designated the examination effectiveness score for the school.

Did the two predictors, prior achievement and ability, yield similar results? Yes, to a large extent. The correlations between the two types of residuals for individual pupils were 0.80 for both the AH6 and the APM with English candidates, and 0.85 and 0.75 respectively for mathematics candidates.

Levels of Analysis and Levels of Aggregation

As Plewis commented in a symposium on 'Statistical modelling issues in school effectiveness studies' (Aitken and Longford, 1986), 'it should not be forgotten that pupils are taught by teachers not by schools'. Many would argue that the major impact on the pupil is the particular teacher, so that it is at the teacher level that one should expect to find the maximum 'effects' of schooling.

In the COMBSE study the decision was made from the start to examine effects subject by subject, with English and mathematics chosen initially as subjects which represented the science/arts divide and which had relatively large enrolments. As shown in Table 5.3, this decision seems justified by the data. In an analysis of variance with mean O-level grade as a covariate, the effect of subject (English or mathematics) was highly significant *and* the interaction of subject with school was highly significant, indicating that different schools obtained good results in different subjects. This finding runs contrary to that of Willms and Cuttance (1985), in their study of Scottish leaving qualifications among fifteen schools. Willms and Cuttance found schools that were effective in English tended also to be effective in mathematics. Perhaps the younger age group accounts for the different finding. The implication of Table 5.3 is that, for A-level effects, to aggregate results across subjects would be misleading and would result in important variations being overlooked.

In short, it appeared to be the case that schools were not uniformly effective

Table 5.3 *The effects of subject (English or maths) and school attended on A-level grades achieved, with average O-level grade controlled*

Source of variation	*Sum of squares*	*DF*	*Mean square*	*F*	*Significance of F*
Average O-level grade	981.764	1	981.764	443.341	0.000
Subject	82.367	1	82.367	37.195	0.000
School	36.476	9	4.053	1.830	0.059
Subject school	57.717	9	6.413	2.896	0.002
Residual	2079.384	939	2.214		
Total	3232.474	959	3.371		

in getting A-level grades but might be effective in English and not effective in mathematics, or vice versa. If this kind of variation in effectiveness from department to department within a school is a general phenomenon then it casts doubt on the wisdom of parents or researchers trying to locate the best *school*. It might also be taken as an indication that efforts to improve education must be made *within schools*, department by department, rather than by setting schools in competition.

Since data in the COMBSE project were collected subject by subject, was the effectiveness of individual A-level teachers being investigated? No. Almost all the A-level classes were taught by a team of teachers so that the effects of a single teacher on A-level results could not be examined. The unit of aggregation in the COMBSE study is most properly thought of as the school *department*. Although individual teaching groups within schools (i.e. classes) were identifiable each year, changes in the composition of the teaching team from year to year meant that no information could be obtained on the stability of effects among classes. However, given the yearly feedback of effectiveness data, the schools themselves could make interpretations based on their intimate knowledge of conditions and personnel in the department each year. This was the 'self-evaluation' component of the COMBSE project. It bears repeating that an outsider collecting and analysing data will not have the detailed, qualitative knowledge of conditions that is available to personnel working in the schools. Furthermore, staff appraisal requires more complex information than that provided by objective data analyses.

The Magnitude of Differences in Effectiveness

The 'examination effectiveness score' employed in this study may be defensible but it fails to convey a sense of whether or not the differences between schools were sufficiently large to be of concern. Did it matter much whether a pupil attended a school with low or high examination effectiveness? Table 5.4 shows the actual distribution of the grades which were obtained by schools with the lowest and schools with the highest effectiveness scores.

For both English and mathematics the probability of getting an 'A' or a 'B' was approximately twice as high in the most effective schools as in the least effective. In the most effective schools the chance of a 'Fail' or the derisory

Table 5.4 *Percentage of pupils who obtained various grades at the least and most effective schools*

Schools	*n*	*A-level grade*						
		Fail	*O*	*E*	*D*	*C*	*B*	*A*
English								
Three least effective	75	33	20	24	5	8	7	3
Two most effective	90	3	24	21	13	12	15	11
Mathematics								
Two least effective	154	8	31	15	20	12	9	5
Three most effective	157	10	17	18	17	13	12	13

n: Number of pupils.

O-level pass was half that in the least effective schools in English and about 70 per cent as great in mathematics.

Causal Attributions for 'Effectiveness'

Although the teaching-team approach to A levels provided a comfortable reason to stay clear of issues of teacher effectiveness, it left open the question of how effectiveness might be explained or understood. What causes a school department to be effective? One seeks more than simply the statement that there are effects of various magnitudes. Explanations of why there are effects are needed.

There are many ways forward on this question, most of which will require, initially, the collection of qualitative information about teaching practices and the management of the school department. This information should be collected on site *by someone who is unaware of the effectiveness data.* Meanwhile, from a distance, a start can be made on collecting some evidence of associations between classroom processes and effectiveness scores. Since 1986 the project has collected process data about what happens in classrooms, using questions some of which matched those in Gray *et al.* (1983). By regarding pupils as 'raters' and using the class as the unit of analysis, some scales which have reasonably high degrees of inter-rater consistency and which differentiate between classrooms have been developed. A scale assessing the amount of pupil talk was constructed by asking about the frequency of such activities as 'discussion in groups', 'working in pairs', 'presenting your work to the class' and 'listening to another student present work to the class'. A visit to several schools by someone unaware of the data on the pupil-talk scale produced a glowing report of the amount of pupil participation in lessons in exactly the English department which had the highest score on the pupil-talk scale, thus providing some reassurance of validity for the scale as a measure of classroom events. This process variable did not, however, correlate significantly with examination effectiveness scores. Given the small sizes of samples for each year it is important to collect several years' data before drawing conclusions. Work of this kind, relating statistical descriptors and ethnographic descriptions, is urgently needed.

Another scale, 'examination emphasis', was moderately reliable for English but for mathematics there was more variation between pupil reports within classrooms than between classroom averages, making an unsatisfactory scale. Again the importance of dealing with different academic subjects differently is emphasized.

This search for processes that relate to effectiveness scores is important for two major reasons. One is that if effective processes can be located, it may be possible for these to be adopted elsewhere with good results. The search for effective processes is the search for 'alterable variables' (Bloom, 1979) or 'tractable variables' (Willms and Cuttance, 1985). In contrast, locating effective teachers would still leave open the question of how they were effective and whether or not they could be copied. A question on which there is still very little evidence is the amount of variance in effectiveness accounted for by non-imitatable teacher variables, such as personality or charisma, and the amount which is accounted for by processes which could be adopted by most teachers. Only experiments will even begin to resolve this issue.

Another reason for the importance of the search for process variables which have some predictive validity is that they might be our only chance of explaining the unstable outcomes from year to year, from school to school - for the outcomes *were* unstable, as will be discussed below. Faced with instability in the data, one has to ask if effectiveness was 'really' varying from year to year or whether the instability was almost entirely due to poor models and/or variables with low reliability and validity. Finding process variables which 'explain' some of the variations in effectiveness is thus an important test of the models used in school effectiveness research.

Stability of Effectiveness Scores from Year to Year

Table 5.5 indicates that there were no trends in examination effectiveness from year to year (no significant main effects for year) but there were highly significant interactions between year and school, indicating different schools were effective from year to year. (Again this emphasizes what seems to be the futility of a search for effective *schools*: the results would depend upon which year's data were examined.)

One way to index the stability from year to year for several variables, including examination effectiveness, was to compute KR-20 as a measure of the reliability of the school means from year to year (McKennell, 1970). Results of this analysis are shown in Table 5.6. This index of reliability is perhaps better called an index of relative stability. If the schools in the sample maintained roughly the same rank order from year to year and if the variation within schools was small compared to the variation between schools, then KR-20 would be large.

There was considerable relative stability among schools in the ability of pupils staying on into the sixth form (0.75 for English and 0.87 for mathematics). In other words, their intakes were stable, a finding consistent with the stable population patterns associated with north-east England. In the sixth form, however, many aspects changed from year to year so that instability might be expected and was indeed evident, with low relative stability on mean raw A-level scores and on examination effectiveness scores (mean residual gains) with the

Table 5.5 *ANOVA: the effects of cohort (data year) and school on A-level grades adjusted for O-level GPA*

Source of variation	*Sum of squares*	*DF*	*Mean square*	*F*	*Significance of F*
English					
Covariate (O-level GPA)	450.947	1	450.947	218.829	0.000
Data year (1983, '84, '85 or '86)	3.742	3	1.247	0.605	0.612
School	30.130	9	3.348	1.625	0.106
Data year by school	114.533	24	4.772	2.316	0.001
Residual	799.561	388	2.061		
Total	1398.913	425	3.292		
Mathematics					
Covariate (O-level GPA)	618.995	1	618.995	295.026	<0.001
Data year (1983, '84, '85 or '86)	2.799	3	0.933	0.445	0.721
School	76.230	9	8.470	4.037	0.000
Data year by school	96.397	25	3.856	1.838	0.008
Residual	1038.561	495	2.098		
Total	1832.981	533	3.439		

Table 5.6 *KR-20 for school mean values from years 1984, 1985 and 1986*

Variable	*English*	*Maths*
O-level GPA	0.75	0.87
Raw A-grade	0.26	0.35
Exam. effectiveness score	0.20	0.61
Attitude-to-the-subject[a]	[b]	0.47
Attitude-to-the-school[a]	0.19	0.20
Reported effort[a]	0.50	[b]

[a]Summated scales described in the Appendix.
[b]Essentially zero. More variation within than between.

exception of mathematics effectiveness. Among the changes which might explain this variation in the data were changes in teachers and, in a few cases, in examination boards or syllabuses.

The Pulling Power of Some Mathematics Departments

Another variable which came close to the O-level GPA in being stable from year to year was the ratio of the number of candidates choosing mathematics to the number of those choosing English. Nationally this ratio was about 1.4; that is, about 40 per cent more candidates entered for mathematics than entered for English. The schools in the COMBSE study showed a considerable range, from 0.6 to 4.5 in 1986, for example. Some mathematics departments were attracting many more entrants than English departments. This was dubbed the 'pulling power' of the mathematics department. The pulling power scores showed a KR-20 value of 0.82, indicating that mathematics departments were fairly consistently popular or unpopular.

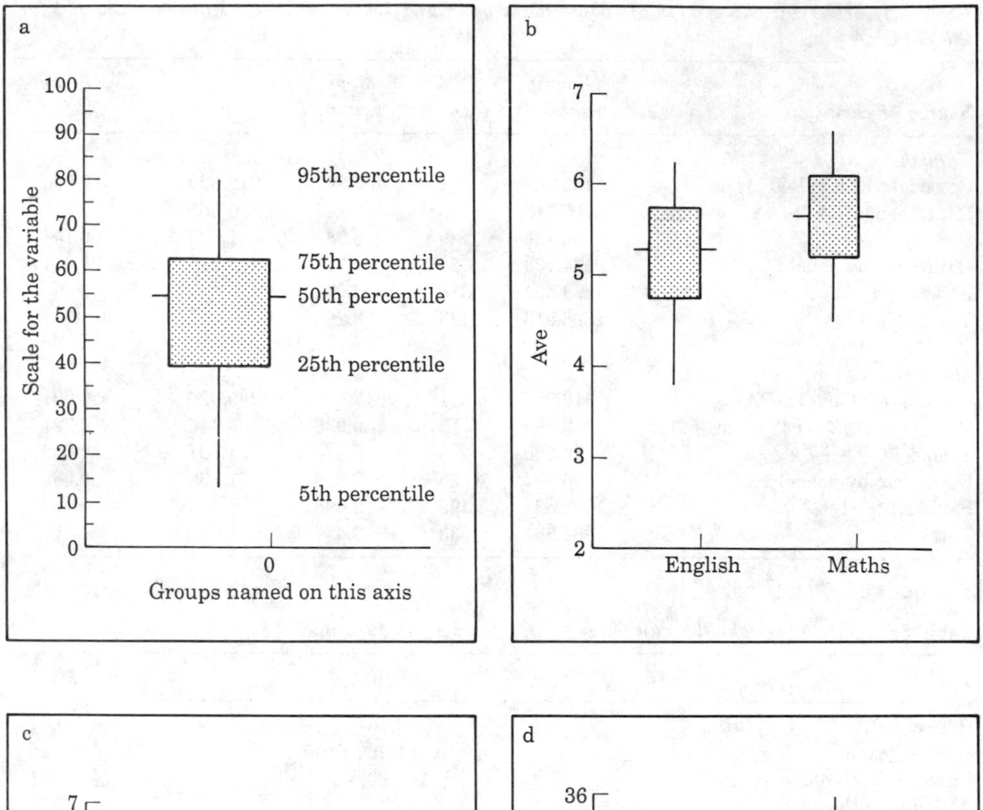

Figure 5.1 ***Attainments of candidates for A-level English and mathematics on prior achievement and ability measures, a, Key. b, Mean O-level grades of all candidates. c, Mean O-level grades of successful candidates. d, Advanced matrices, e, AH6 verbal. f, AH6 numerical. g, AH6 diagrammatic***

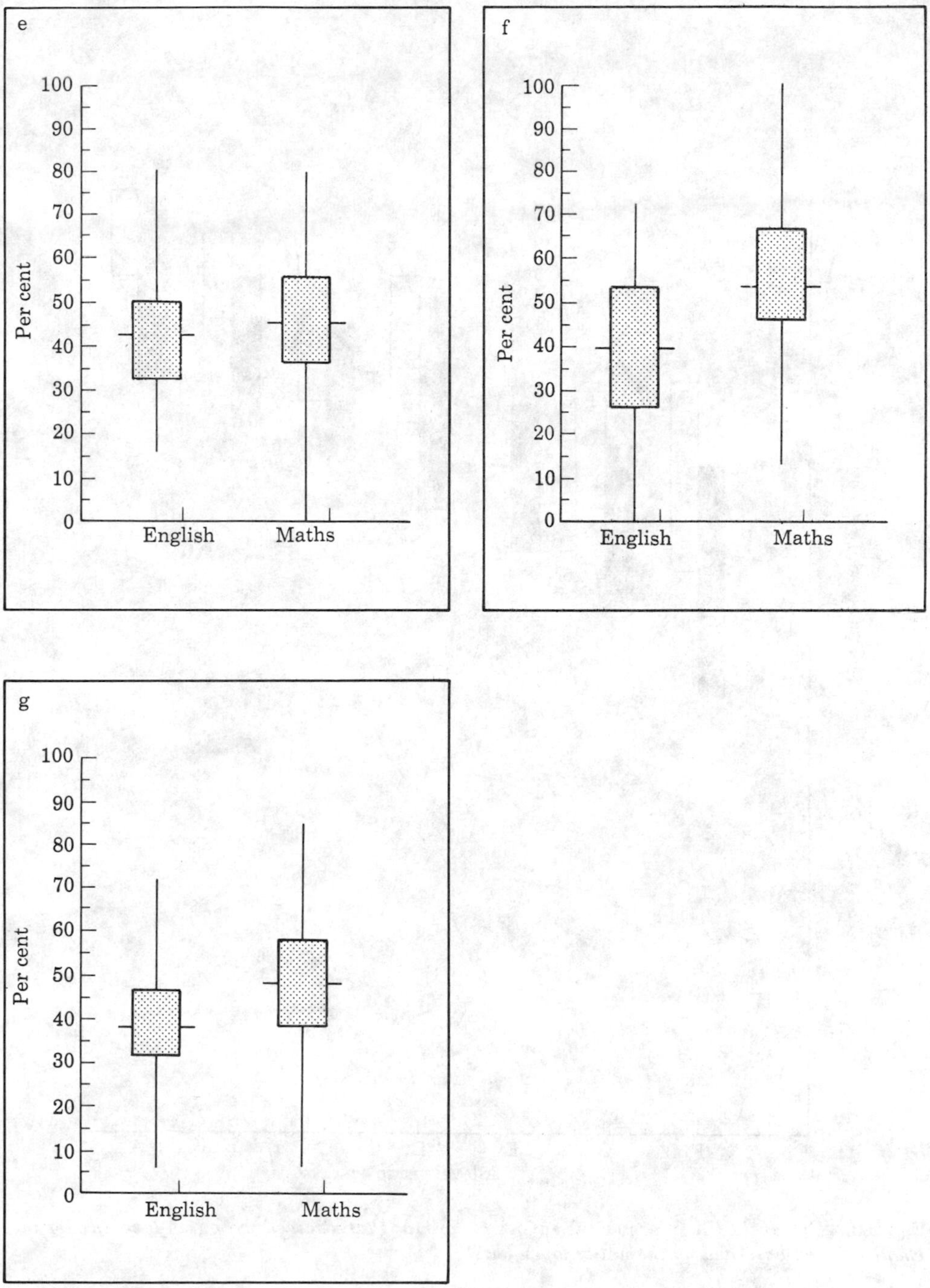
e
f
g
Per cent
100
90
80
70
60
50
40
30
20
10
0
English
Maths

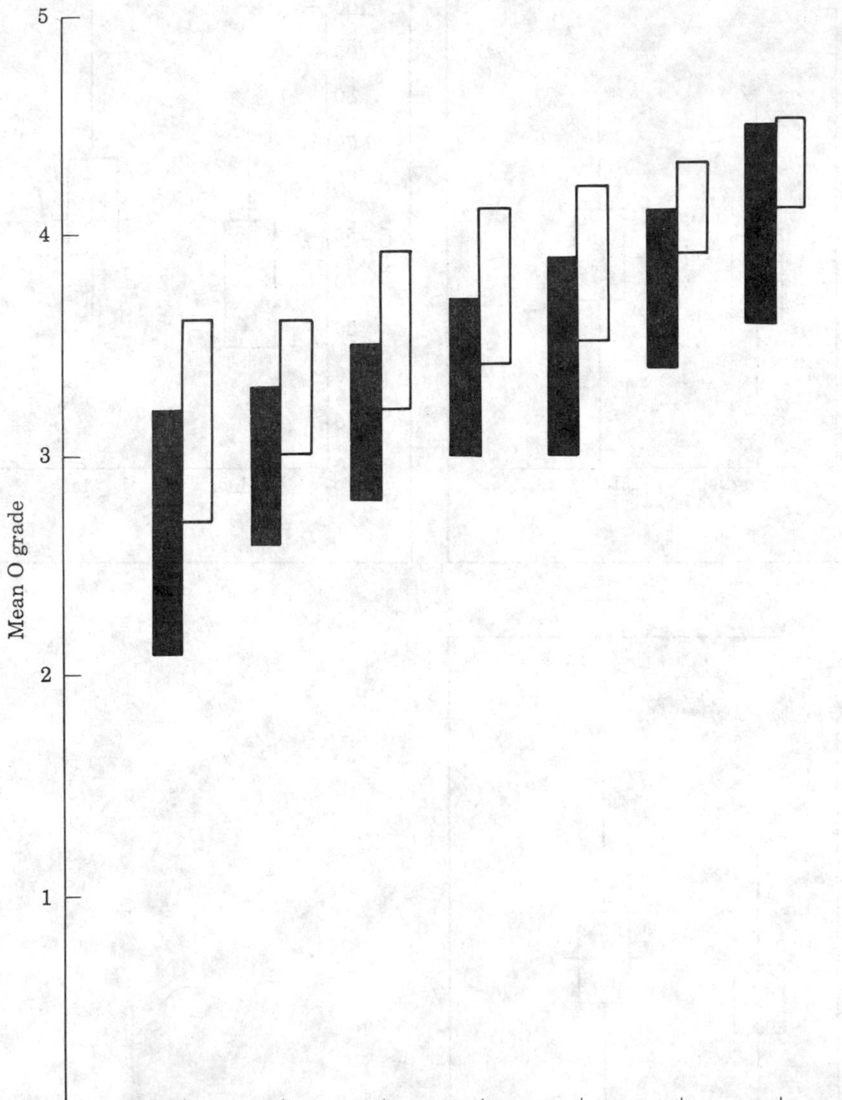

Figure 5.2 *O-level GPA interquartile ranges for groups that attained various A-level grades in English (filled bars) and mathematics (open bars)*

The Higher Ability of Mathematics Candidates

It was clear that mathematics generally attracted more able pupils. The ability tests reported above served to confirm a pattern which was clear from examination of O-level GPAs: on average mathematics candidates were substantially more able than English candidates. Graphs for O-level GPAs, the Advanced Progressive Matrices and the AH6 subscales are presented in Figure 5.1.

Other studies have arrived at the same conclusion (Smithers *et al.*, 1984; Smithers and Robinson, 1987). Whether one looks at O-level GPA, ability as measured by the various subscales of the AH6 or the scores (of another cohort) on the APM, the result replicates again and again: mathematics candidates were substantially more academically able. On mean O-level grades the lower quartile score for successful mathematics candidates was about the same as the median score for successful English candidates. The 'effect size' or standardized mean difference was 0.67, implying a difference of about two-thirds of a standard deviation. On the APM the effect size was even larger: 1.02. On the AH6 the effect size was 0.62 on the full scale.

Was a 'D' in mathematics worth a 'B' in English? Mathematics candidates were more able than English candidates but a similar proportion failed. This implied that the mathematics examination at A level was more difficult than the English examination at A level. Under such an examining system, making efforts to attract the hesitant, borderline pupil into mathematics A level might have been dangerous. Schools had to warn their students that they were more likely to fail mathematics than English, other things being equal. The bars in Figure 5.2 represent the range from the lower to the upper quartile on the distribution of O-level GPA for pupils who attained the indicated grade at A level. In other words, each bar represents the spread of average O-level grades for the middle half of the group of pupils. It can be seen that the range of abilities of the middle 50 per cent of candidates who obtained a 'D' in A-level mathematics was almost exactly the same as the range for those who obtained a 'B' in A-level English.

This difference in examination difficulty at A level is not a law of nature; it is a policy decision and one which needs reconsideration. Should mathematics be left as so much more difficult than English? Do we need to push people out of mathematics so early? Should we then be surprised that many otherwise well educated people feel mathematically illiterate, that there is a shortage of people with mathematical competencies in so many professions and, in particular, a shortage of mathematics teachers?

SENSITIVITY TO SCHOOL EFFECTS

Table 5.6 presented indices of stability of means from year to year and it was notable that there was considerably more stability in effectiveness in mathematics than in English (0.61 as opposed to 0.20). A slightly different question to ask of the data relates to the proportion of variance explained by the variable 'school' (or school department in the present study). This 'proportion-of-variance-accounted-for' measure can be thought of as indicating the effects which schools can have relative to the large amount of variation in the data owing to differences among pupils.

Discussions of the proportion-of-variance-accounted-for by schools have generally set the figure quite low. For a sample of comprehensive schools Aitkin and Longford (1986, p. 15) reported a figure of 7 per cent for effects on O-level achievements as indexed by a sum-of-points scale. Willms (1987), employing the Scottish School Leavers Surveys of 1977, 1981 and 1985, reported a figure of about 10 per cent.

In addition to examining the proportions of variance in examination effectiveness, one could also ask to what extent schools had effects on the three scales mentioned earlier: attitude-to-the-subject, attitude-to-the-school and effort. Except for attitude-to-mathematics, these attitude scales were not significantly correlated with prior achievement or ability measures. Consequently, if there were to be any control for differences in school intakes it would have to be by means of socioeconomic status (SES). The somewhat surprising finding here was that more positive attitudes were associated not with higher SES but with lower SES of pupils. *Post hoc* explanations spring to mind. It could be that higher SES students in the sixth form were more inclined to be critical and students from lower SES backgrounds were more inclined to be appreciative. Again these hypotheses need exploration by qualitative methods. For our purposes here, SES was used as a covariate to control for some intake differences when examining attitudes.

Susceptible Outcomes

There may be some outcomes that can be little affected by anything schools can do, whereas schools may have a large impact on other outcomes. Which outcomes are, or are not, sensitive to school effects? *A priori*, one might hypothesize that mathematics would be more sensitive to schooling than English. Poor instruction in mathematics may have worse effects than poor instruction in English and likewise particularly good instruction in mathematics might make more of an impact than particularly good instruction in English, particularly on achievement. Another way of putting this hypothesis is that pupils are more dependent on schooling for learning mathematics than for learning English literature.

The proportion-of-variance-accounted-for was computed from one-way ANOVAs treating schools as a random factor. The results are presented in Table 5.7. In Figure 5.3 this proportion-of-variance-accounted-for by schools has been graphed for each of the four outcomes, with separate bars for English and mathematics.

In the present data the proportion-of-variance-accounted-for by schools was about 6 per cent in mathematics as compared to only 1 per cent in English. It appeared that among mathematics candidates achievement and attitude-to-the-subject were far more susceptible to school effects than they were among English candidates, as hypothesized above. One could say that in this sample the proportion of variance accounted for was about six times larger for mathematics than for English. When we examine the outcome most closely related to the school, however, namely the pupil's attitude to the school, the proportion of variance was very large in English (over 15 per cent) although very small in

Table 5.7 *Susceptibility to school effects among four dependent variables*

DF (N – 1)	*English or Maths*	*Dependent variable*	*Controlling for*	*Proportion of variance accounted for (random model)*	*F*	*p*
A-level grades with no control variables						
425	English	A-grade		0.384	6.11	<0.001
533	Maths	A-grade		0.102	2.54	0.01
Four dependent variables as plotted in Figure 5.2						
425	English	A-grade	GPA	0.010	1.41	0.18
533	Maths	A-grade	GPA	0.057	4.04	<0.001
207	English	Att. to sub.	SES	0.004	1.08	0.38
251	Maths	Att. to sub.	SES	0.111	3.99	<0.001
289	English	Att. to sch.	SES	0.155	5.83	<0.001
346	Maths	Att. to sch.	SES	0.092	4.28	<0.001
280	English	Effort	SES	0.016	1.43	0.17
341	Maths	Effort	SES	0.000	0.90	0.52

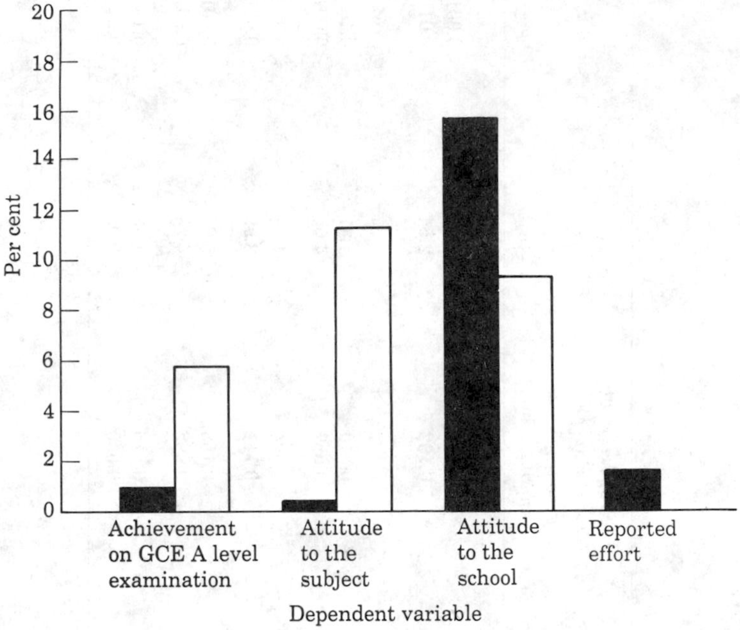

Figure 5.3 *School effects: percentage of variance on the random effects model for English (filled bars) and mathematics (open bars)*

mathematics. Are English candidates more aware of, or more responsive to, school 'atmosphere' than mathematics candidates?

Turning to the question of school effects on behaviours, examination of the self-reports of effort showed exceedingly small effects. Yet teachers try hard to influence the effort that pupils expend. These findings suggest another hypothesis: if effort is little affected but achievement (in mathematics) is, perhaps good results depend upon the quality of the work done, not the quantity of time expended on the work. The more effective teachers do not set more work than the less effective teachers, but set better work or teach better. But this is only a hypothesis, going beyond the data available.

Carroll, in his seminal 'Model of school learning' article, commented that we often think that motivation (effort or perseverance) is a behaviour that can be influenced while academic achievement is determined by fixed abilities. The facts might be otherwise.

> 'Aptitude' is regarded as relatively resistant to change, whereas it is the hope of the psychologist that he can readily intervene to modify 'perseverance'.... To some extent, this feeling is justified not only by logic but also by research findings - by the research on the apparent constancy of the IQ.... On the other hand, if aptitude is largely a matter of prior learnings, it may be more

> modifiable than we think. Whereas, conversely, some kinds of clinical findings suggest that motivational characteristics of the individual may be much harder to change than one might think.
> (Carroll, 1963, p. 731)

From the current data this would seem to be the case for mathematics: the variance attributable to the effects of schools was approximately 0 per cent for effort as opposed to 5.7 per cent for achievement. In English both effects were small (1.6 per cent for effort and 1 per cent for achievement).

Susceptible Sub-groups of Pupils

In addition to examining the extent to which various outcomes are susceptible to schooling, one might ask whether schools have different amounts of impact on different groups of pupils (cf. Reynolds and Reid, 1985).

Do school effects differ with respect to the ability level or socioeconomic status of pupils? We might hypothesize that pupils who are either more able or from more affluent backgrounds are in a better position to compensate for a poor instructional programme - they have more resources either within themselves or at home on which they can draw if they are not learning at school. Indeed there were several schools in the COMBSE sample in which pupils reported the use of private tutors. Given these personal or financial resources, were high ability or high SES pupils less susceptible to school effects than less able or lower SES pupils? Were low ability and low SES pupils more susceptible to school effects because they were more dependent on schools, having fewer alternative resources?

Table 5.8 presents the proportions of variance accounted for when sub-groups of high and low SES, and high and low ability, were examined. The hypothesis that pupils of low ability or low SES would be the more 'vulnerable' did *not* appear to be supported by the data. At A level, the schools appeared to have had more effect on more able pupils. This conclusion applied to achievement, attitude-to-the-school and attitude-to-the-subject but not to effort.

Post-hoc, what are the possible explanations? One consideration is the nature of the A-level scale. A levels show little differentiation at the lower end of the ability continuum: nationally 50 per cent received an E or failed. There was more differentiation at the upper range, in the D, C, B and A grades. It is in this range that the effects were detectable. One might also suggest that schools have the greatest effects on pupils for whom the curriculum is best suited. The A-level curriculum was best matched to the abilities of the more able pupils. However, while not supported by the present dataset, the 'disadvantaged are more dependent on schools' hypothesis does receive support from data presented by Cuttance in this volume. This serves as a warning not to assume that effects at one level of the educational system have the same patterns as effects at another level.

While the findings on the sub-groups of pupils will need more replication, being based on small numbers and yielding some surprising results, the illustration that mathematics is more sensitive to schooling than English is so much in

Table 5.8 *Susceptibility to school effects among sub-groups*

DF (N – 1)	*Sub-group*	*Dependent variable*[a]	*Proportion of variance accounted for (random model)*	*F*	*p*
English sample broken down by SES and ability					
130	Low SES	A-grade	– 0.064	0.26	0.98
159	High SES	A-grade	0.027	1.39	0.20
279	Low ability	A-grade	0.009	1.24	0.26
145	High ability	A-grade	0.015	1.17	0.31
68	Low SES	Att. to sub.	0.016	1.11	0.37
138	High SES	Att. to sub.	0.019	1.26	0.27
128	Low ability	Att. to sub.	– 0.010	0.87	0.55
78	High ability	Att. to sub.	0.135	2.05	0.05
128	Low SES	Att. to sch.	0.024	6.00	< 0.001
160	High SES	Att. to sch.	0.310	7.34	< 0.001
182	Low ability	Att. to sch.	0.167	4.48	< 0.001
106	High ability	Att. to sch.	0.178	2.84	0.005
124	Low SES	Effort	0.079	2.00	0.04
155	High SES	Effort	– 0.028	0.63	0.77
270	Low ability	Effort	0.039	2.07	0.03
143	High ability	Effort	– 0.022	0.76	0.65

Maths sample broken down by SES and ability					
155	Low SES	A-grade	– 0.025	0.63	0.77
187	High SES	A-grade	0.061	2.26	0.02
231	Low ability	A-grade	0.049	2.14	0.03
301	High ability	A-grade	0.067	2.98	0.002
81	Low SES	Att. to sub.	0.013	1.10	0.37
169	High SES	Att. to sub.	0.154	3.77	0.002
110	Low ability	Att. to sub.	0.171	3.17	0.002
140	High ability	Att. to sub.	0.138	3.03	0.002
154	Low SES	Att. to sch.	0.023	1.34	0.22
191	High SES	Att. to sch.	0.174	4.27	< 0.001
144	Low ability	Att. to sch.	0.054	1.78	0.08
201	High ability	Att. to sch.	0.129	3.69	< 0.001
150	Low SES	Effort	0.023	1.34	0.22
190	High SES	Effort	0.019	1.33	0.22
229	Low ability	Effort	– 0.012	0.73	0.68
304	High ability	Effort	– 0.002	0.95	0.48

Negative variance proportions imply that the model did not hold. They are usually set to zero.
[a]The same variables were controlled for as in Table 5.7.

conformity with expectations and intuitions that it seems likely to become a robust finding. It has implications that may not be uniformly welcomed: efforts to improve achievement may be more likely to result in measurable improvements if they are concentrated on mathematics rather than on English teaching, at least in the sixth form. On the other hand, since there is national concern over levels of mathematical competencies, findings that schools do affect mathematics achievement must be welcome.

CONCLUSIONS

Two kinds of conclusion arise from research: those which can be fairly said to have arisen directly from the data and those at which the researcher has arrived as a result of conducting the research project. The latter, based it might be said on 'experiential' rather than formal learning, must be regarded as closer to opinions than to findings, but they are often important.

Conclusions Arising from the Data

From the data collected over four years from ten comprehensive schools, it would seem to be the case that:

1 Schools varied significantly and substantially in the level of A-level grades their students attained, even after taking account of prior achievement or ability.

2 Schools that appeared to be effective in getting good grades in English were not necessarily the same ones that were effective at getting good grades in mathematics.

3 There was considerable variation from year to year in the effectiveness of English and mathematics A-level work. Since it is known that there were changes in the schools in such areas as teachers, examination boards and syllabuses, this year-by-year fluctuation would be expected. More data would be needed to explain some of the year-by-year fluctuation, including qualitative data and classroom process data.

4 Socioeconomic status was very weakly correlated with achievement in A-level work. An ability measure or a prior achievement measure is therefore a necessity for use as a co-variate in data at this level of the educational system.

5 In this sixth-form sample, socioeconomic status correlated negatively with attitude-to-the-school: pupils from homes with parents in professional jobs were less satisfied than students whose parents were in lower-status jobs. This finding is contrary to the pattern generally expected in younger pupils.

6 Mathematics appeared to be more sensitive to school effects than English. The variance in examination results which could be attributed to schools was about six times larger among mathematics students than among English students.

7 School effects on expressed attitudes were stronger than their effects on achievement, in terms of variance accounted for.
8 School effects on the level of effort reported by pupils were surprisingly small and not statistically significant. This finding contrasts with the feeling teachers have that they affect the effort students make.
9 Candidates for A-level English were considerably less able, as a group, than candidates for A-level mathematics. A D in mathematics A-level tended to be awarded to candidates with the same range of ability as those obtaining a B in English.

Conclusions Arising from the Experience of the Research

The following conclusions cannot be said to arise directly from the data but rather from reflection upon the data and upon the experience of collecting and analysing the data and feeding them back to schools.

1 The school department is the desirable unit on which to focus as a first level of aggregation in school effects studies. Because there are significant differences between the effectivenesses of departments within the same school, aggregation to the level of school will mask important effects. Furthermore, the school department is a unit which is *managed*. Information on effectiveness can actually be used by a school department. It is less clear how to go about improving a whole school.
2 School personnel need assistance in interpreting and using school effectiveness data. It is not enough simply to send out the reports each year.
3 As the quantity of data becomes larger, more sophisticated analysis strategies will become possible and desirable, utilizing computer programs written especially to handle hierarchical, nested data (Aitkin and Longford, 1986; Goldstein, 1985; Raudenbush and Bryk, 1986).

Finally, the most important conclusion drawn was:

4 The logical outcome of school effectiveness research is the creation of monitoring systems to supply schools with regular measures of effectiveness. The monitoring systems must provide fair indicators of performance, not only on cognitive goals but also on other outcomes of concern. This information must be collected in collaboration with school departments and reported back to school departments. They are close enough to the events to interpret the data and take action where necessary. If this monitoring is to be fair it must develop from the base of information and experience which is being slowly built up by research into school effectiveness.

APPENDIX: THE SCALES USED

The A-level Scale

This was a modification of the scale used by UCCA. It is extended at the lower end to distinguish between an O-level pass (coded 0) and an outright Fail (coded −1). (These grades became roughly 'N' and 'U' in 1987).

5 points for an A
4 points for a B
3 points for a C
2 points for a D
1 point for an E
0 points for an O
−1 point for an F

Attitude to the Subject Scale

Six items were summed to yield the attitude-to-English scale or the attitude-to-mathematics scale. These were all five-point Likert-type items on the questionnaire. Stated positively, these items were:

17 Not finding it hard to get down to work in the subject.
18 Looking forward to lessons in the subject.
19 Liking examinations in the subject.
20 Thinking about the subject outside class.
21 Not regretting having chosen the subject.
22 Preferring the subject to others being studied.

In the 1986 data the reliabilities of this attitude-to-the-subject scale were:

0.72 in English ($n = 175$)
0.76 in mathematics ($n = 245$)

Attitude-to-the-school Scale

Six items were summed to yield the attitude-to-the-school scale, all from Likert-type items on the questionnaire. Stated positively, these items were:

1 Liking school.
2 Liking lessons.
3 Liking the teachers.
4 Feeling one was being treated like an adult.
5 Thinking the atmosphere in the school was good for sixth formers.
6 Reporting one would recommend the school to others.

Previous work has shown that sixth formers place considerable importance on being treated in an adult fashion. The reliabilities of this scale were:

0.83 in English ($n = 182$)
0.77 in mathematics ($n = 247$)

Effort Scales

'Effort' was assessed by summing the responses to the following items on the questionnaire:

1 Time spent per week on homework, categorized on a six-point scale.
2 Time spent per evening on homework for all subjects.
3 Not doing homework while watching TV.
4 Getting work in on time.
5 Doing more than just the required amount of work.
6 Working hard.
7 Being one of the hardest workers in the class.

A person obtained a high score on the effort scale, therefore, to the extent that he or she reported spending time on the subject and on homework in general, not watching TV while doing homework, getting work in on time, doing more than only what was required, working hard and being one of the hardest workers in the class. The reliabilities of the two scales were as shown below:

0.65 in English ($n = 166$)
0.65 in mathematics ($n = 225$)

Socioeconomic Status Scale

Socioeconomic status was assessed in the following way:

I Professional: accountant, doctor, lawyer, clergyman, etc. coded 6
II Intermediate: Member of Parliament, nurse, manager, etc. coded 5
III Skilled non-manual: clerical worker, sales representative, etc. coded 4
III Skilled manual: bus driver, butcher, bricklayer, etc. coded 3
IV Partly skilled: barman, fisherman, postman, etc. coded 2
V Unskilled: kitchen hand, labourer, office cleaner, etc. coded 1

The reliability of the SES index was:

0.55 in English ($n = 122$)
0.57 in mathematics ($n = 148$)

ACKNOWLEDGEMENTS

The author wishes to thank the Department of Education and Science for a small grant, Peter Clarke for collecting the 1987 data so effectively, Patrick Eavis for 'blind' visits to English departments and most useful descriptions thereof, Tony Edwards and Peter Cuttance for helpful comments on a draft and, especially, all the participating schools and colleges.

REFERENCES

Aitken, M. and Longford, N. (1986) 'Statistical modelling issues in school effectiveness studies', *Journal of the Royal Statistical Society, Series A*, **149** (1), 1-43.

Bloom, B.S. (1979) *Alterable Variables: The New Direction in Educational Research*. Edinburgh: Scottish Council for Research in Education.

Carroll, J.B. (1963) 'A model of school learning', *Teachers College Record*, **64**, 723-33.

Fitz-Gibbon, C.T. (1985) 'A-level results in comprehensive schools: the COMBSE project, year 1', *Oxford Review of Education*, **11** (1), 43-58.

Fitz-Gibbon, C.T. (1989) 'Using performance indicators: educational considerations', in Levacic, R. (ed.) *Financial Management in Education*. Milton Keynes: Open University Press.

Goldstein, H. (1985) 'Multi-level mixed linear model analysis using iterative generalised least squares', *Biometrika*, **73** (1), 43-56.

Gray, J., McPherson, A.F. and Raffe, D. (1983) *Reconstructions of Secondary Education: Theory, Myth and Practice since the War*. London: Routledge & Kegan Paul.

Heim, A.H., Watts, K.P. and Simmonds, V. (1983) *Manual for the AH6 Group Tests of High-level Intelligence*. Windsor: NFER.

McKennell, A.C. (1970) 'Attitude Scale construction', in O'Muircheartaigh, D. and Payne, G. (eds) *The Analysis of Survey Data*. Vol. 1: *Exploring Data Structures*. Chichester: John Wiley.

Parsons, H.M. (1974) 'What happened at Hawthorne?' *Science*, **183**, 922-32.

Raudenbush, S. and Bryk, A.S. (1986) 'A hierarchical model for studying school effects', *Sociology of Education*, **59**, 1-17.

Raven, J.C. (1965) *Advanced Progressive Matrices. Sets I and II*. London: H.K. Lewis.

Reynolds, D. and Reid, K. (1985) 'The second stage: towards a reconceptualization of theory and methodology in school effectiveness research', in Reynolds, D. (ed.) *Studying School Effectiveness*. Lewes: Falmer Press.

Smith, I. (1987) 'Educational and vocational opportunities at 16+', *ESRC Newsletter*, **61**, 19-20.

Smithers, A.G. and Robinson, P. (1987) 'Mixing A levels: hard choice or soft option?', Paper presented to the Thirteenth Annual Conference of the British Educational Research Association, Manchester, 2-5 September.

Smithers, A.G., Collings, J.A. and McCreesh, F.J. (1984) 'The growth of mixed A level courses', *Research in Education*, **32**, 1-16.

Willms, J.D. (1987) 'Differences between Scottish educational authorities in their examination attainment', *Oxford Review of Education*, **13** (2), 211-32.

Willms, J.D. and Cuttance, P. (1985) 'School effects in Scottish secondary schools', *British Journal of Sociology of Education*, **6** (3), 289-306.

Chapter 6

Differences between Comprehensive Schools: Some Preliminary Findings

Louise S. Blakey and Anthony F. Heath

This chapter gives some preliminary findings from the Oxford University School Effectiveness Project. The main aims of the project are:

1 To discover what differences, if any, exist between comprehensive schools in their educational and social outcomes.
2 To determine how far such 'outcome' differences can be accounted for by differences in school intake.
3 To identify which schools perform significantly better or worse than expected, given their intakes.
4 To discover whether these discrepancies between observed and expected outcomes can be attributed to particular school characteristics and policies.

The project has two main components: firstly, a quantitative study of a sample of over 2000 fifth-year pupils in fifteen comprehensive schools; secondly, a qualitative investigation of those schools found to be exceptional in their performance. The quantitative part of the study is concerned primarily with *establishing* the differences between schools in their intakes and outcomes. It is, however, unlikely that statistical analysis will be able to *explain* satisfactorily any such differences in effectiveness. The qualitative study of particular schools will therefore be used to explore the social processes which generate the differences in effectiveness.

The major theoretical perspective which informs our work is broadly a Weberian one. That is to say, we assume that a school brings together a variety of actors - teachers, parents and the pupils themselves - with their own distinctive orientations and objectives. We reject a unitary conception of the school or of the concept of effectiveness. Schools are not cohesive, unidimensional institutions with members united on all fronts. The sociology of teacher and pupil subcultures has shown clearly that this is not the case. The different actors involved may have quite different goals. A school which is effective in helping the academically ambitious achieve their goals of university entrance may not be so effective in helping the children whose aspirations are to win apprenticeships. We must not simply ask *whether* a school is effective but *who* it is effective for.

The fifteen participating schools vary substantially in their intake, history, organization and popularity with parents. Information has been collected not only on the pupils' cognitive ability and social class background but also on ethnicity, parental interest, household composition, family size, pupil health and receipt of free school meals. While the LEA in which they lie may be thought of as a relatively affluent and advantaged county (although by no means exceptionally so), it is clear that there are sociologically interesting differences between schools in the county. For the fifteen schools in this study the average ability score (measured on the AH2 Group Test of General Ability) ranges from 51 to 67. Differences in outcome, not surprisingly, are present too. We have collected detailed information on examination performance, attendance and truancy, career expectations and destinations (although in this paper we shall limit ourselves to the examination measures). Again, the differences between schools are considerable. In 1985 one of the thirty-nine schools in the county had only 36 per cent of its pupils gaining one or more higher grades in GCE O level or CSE while another had 70 per cent. For the fifteen schools participating in the study the range was almost as great: 36 to 64 per cent.

Our primary concern was to explore what outcome differences remain after we have controlled for intake. We were particularly concerned with the robustness of the differences. Even the measurement of examination performance, let alone measurements of truancy or occupational destinations, is fraught with problems. For example, differing measures of examination performance can be used: thus we can measure the average number of O level passes per pupil, or the percentage of pupils obtaining 'passes' in main subjects such as English and mathematics, or we can use a composite scale which takes into account lower-level grades as well. It is not self-evident that a school will do equally well on all three criteria. Indeed, to some extent they may be in conflict. A school that places its priority on O level 'passes' in main subjects may therefore have fewer teaching resources to devote to 'less able' pupils attempting CSE. Different measures may thus tap different school priorities. There will be no single 'correct' measure of an effective school, even if we equate effectiveness with examination performance. The choice of measure is not a technical matter but a normative one reflecting the researcher's values and priorities.

SCHOOL OUTCOMES

We recognize that there are many possible measures of school outcomes and that in limiting ourselves in the present chapter to examination outcomes we are taking a narrow view of education. We shall try to rectify this in future publications.

We recognize, too, that different measures of examination outcomes are possible. Here, we shall report two distinct measures: firstly, the percentage of pupils obtaining five O-level passes (grades A, B and C at O level or grade 1 at CSE) in the 'main' academic subjects of English and French, history and geography, maths, physics, chemistry and biology; and secondly the average number of 'scalepoints' in all subjects and at both CSE and GCE. (In making these calculations we have included 'early entries' but excluded 'double entries' in the same subject at both CSE and GCE. Parental entries have also been included.)

Five O-level passes in 'main' subjects can be thought of as a traditional measure, reflecting the pre-war concept of matriculation (where pupils had to obtain passes at School Certificate in a specified range of subjects). Matriculation was the requirement for pupils wishing to go on to university, and it is probably still the case that pupils obtaining five O-level passes in these main subjects can hope to win a place at university or polytechnic. The implicit assumption behind this traditional measure, then, is that the purpose of schooling is the preparation of pupils for higher education. It might therefore be thought an appropriate measure for evaluating grammar schools, but of questionable value when assessing comprehensive schools which are expected to provide educational targets for the whole ability range. In assessing comprehensive schools, therefore, 'scalepoints' have become the standard measure.

Scalepoints are assigned as follows:

CSE grade			1	2	3	4	5	U
GCE grade	A	B	C	D	E			U
Scalepoints	7	6	5	4	3	2	1	0

Clearly scalepoints take account of the whole range of performance in the main public examinations, but it should be pointed out that the equal intervals between each grade are only an assumption of the researchers who created the scale. It could plausibly be argued, and indeed tested empirically, that the gap between grades 1 and 2 at CSE in terms of their economic value in the labour market was much greater than that between grades 4 and 5. Alternatively if one used a criterion such as intellectual difficulty rather than marketability, one might be able to make a case for 'stretching' the scale elsewhere. None of the measures is value-free.

Table 6.1 shows how the fifteen schools (all of which have of course been given pseudonyms) fared on these two measures. The range of outcomes between the schools is substantial. As might be expected, there is some bunching in the middle of the distribution with a few schools standing out at either extreme. Thus Meadowpark and Greenford stand out, taking the top two places on both measures of examination outcome, while at the other end Royston, Shackleton and Stanford lag behind, taking the bottom three places on both measures.

Initially, then, it would seem that both measures of outcome yield the same general picture of examination effectiveness. That there should be some correlation between the measures is hardly surprising, given that five O-level passes will make a substantial contribution of scalepoints to the school average, and given that the pupils' social background might be expected to affect both measures equally. It must be said, however, that the correlation between the two measures is in fact remarkably high.

For the academic trying to assess the factors that are *in general* associated with school effectiveness, then, it will make very little difference which measure is taken. If, however, we are concerned as parents with the performance of *individual* schools, the different measures may yield somewhat different answers. The clearest example concerns Croxley and Oakwood, which as it happens are neighbouring schools between which parents might very well wish to choose. On the traditional measure of five O levels in main subjects there is

Table 6.1 *Examination results at the fifteen schools*

	Percentage of pupils obtaining 5 GCE passes in main subjects	*Average Scalepoints per pupil*	*n*
Meadowpark	19	29	134
Greenford	17	30	203
Weston	13	24	210
Croxley	11	27	204
Preston	10	24	155
Craighill	10	22	237
Oakwood	10	21	198
Venables	9	18	161
Ormond	7	25	121
Scott	7	21	196
Enfield	7	23	199
Bellamy	6	21	199
Shackleton	5	16	125
Stanford	3	11	116
Royston	1	15	301

no real difference between the two schools. But on the average scalepoints criterion a clear gap opens up, as Oakwood falls in the rankings while Croxley moves up one place and, more importantly, almost equals the performance of the two leading schools - Greenford and Meadowpark. The implication is that Croxley and Oakwood may be equally effective for pupils who have their sights on university but differentially effective for those who plan to leave school at sixteen and try their luck in the labour market.

CONTROLLING FOR INTAKE

Table 6.1 presents a 'league table' of school outcomes and, as is well known, such league tables cannot be regarded as measures of school effectiveness. The school performances which they depict will be in part the product of exogenous factors such as the character of the school's intake rather than of endogenous factors such as the quality of teaching.

Strictly speaking, we do not have measures of intake in the present study (although as a shorthand we shall continue to refer to them as controls for intake). Instead we have various estimates of the pupils' characteristics as measured at age fifteen. Specifically, the AH2 test (short time limits) was administered and the pupils completed a short questionnaire which asked them, *inter alia*, for their parents' occupations and whether or not parents visited school on open days and the like. In our analysis we distinguish between four parental classes - professional and managerial, clerical, skilled manual, and semi- and unskilled manual (based on the head of household's occupation) - and we distinguish between parents who were reported 'always', 'sometimes' and 'never' to visit school (based on whichever parent visited most frequently).

One point to note here is that none of these measures can be regarded as truly exogenous. The social class intake, the level of parental visiting and even measured ability may all be influenced by the school. Thus there may be some element of parental choice as to which school a child attends, given the presence of a large number of private schools in the area, and the social class intake of a state school may therefore be in part a function of the school's reputation and its ability to attract affluent parents away from the private sector. Parental interest may also be a function of the school's efforts to involve parents in its work. And unless one believes that the AH2 test is a pure measure of 'native ability' (whatever that is), it is likely that the pupils' educational experiences within the schools will have had some effect on their test scores by the time they have reached the age of fifteen. On the other hand, there are inevitably some exogenous 'out of school' factors which we have failed to measure adequately. We have no measure of parental education, for example, and according to theories of cultural capital these may be important determinants of the child's ability to appreciate what the school has to offer.

We are, then, faced with the inevitable problem that our statistical models will be mis-specified to some unknown extent; on the one hand there are unmeasured exogenous variables of unknown importance, and on the other the measured exogenous variables will to some unknown extent be influenced by the endogenous variables. If we are lucky, these unknowns will cancel out, but we should assume that we will be unlucky and that there will be errors of unknown magnitude in our results. However, on Christopher Jencks's principle that the magnitude of these errors is almost certainly less than if we had simply consulted our prejudices, which seems to be the usual alternative, we shall now proceed to our statistical analysis.

Our first step is to regress the pupils' scalepoint scores in the public examinations on their scores for the three 'exogenous' variables (AH2 scores, parental visiting and parental social class) and on the 'endogenous' variable of the school attended. Both scalepoint and AH2 scores are treated as continuous variables, but the other measures are all entered in the equation as dummy variables. In entering a set of dummies, one of them is suppressed (for statistical reasons) and the suppressed variable in effect becomes the yardstick by which the others are compared. Thus, in the case of the schools, Enfield was chosen to be suppressed (as it appeared to be an average performer) and the regression coefficients for the other schools tell us how much better or worse they performed than Enfield, controlling for the other variables in the equation. To remind us of this procedure, Enfield has been included in the following tables but with zero coefficients. In the case of the parental class set of variables, the professional and managerial category is the one suppressed, and in the case of parental visiting, the category 'sometimes visit' is suppressed.

In Table 6.2 we report: the unstandardized regression coefficients for each of the variables (the *B* coefficients); the statistic *T*, which is the ratio of the *B* coefficient to its standard error; and the significance of *T*. The significance of *T* tells us whether the regression coefficient in question is statistically significantly different from zero. Thus in the case of the school variables, it tells us whether pupils at the school in question performed significantly differently, controlling for the exogenous variables, from pupils at Enfield (which by fiat has been assigned a zero coefficient).

Table 6.2 *Scalepoints regressed on measured ability, home background and school*

	B	*T*	*Significance of T*
AH2	0.6	31.2	0.000
Clerical	– 2.9	– 2.9	0.01
Skilled	– 3.5	– 5.3	0.000
Semi-skilled	– 4.5	– 5.2	0.000
Always visit	4.6	7.0	0.000
Never visit	– 4.0	– 4.5	0.000
Croxley	5.4	4.1	0.000
Greenford	4.5	3.5	0.000
Meadowpark	3.2	2.3	0.05
Weston	2.6	2.0	0.05
Ormond	2.1	1.4	n.s.
Enfield	0	0	0
Preston	– 0.2	– 0.1	n.s.
Craighill	– 0.6	– 0.4	n.s.
Bellamy	– 1.4	– 0.8	n.s.
Venables	– 1.6	– 1.1	n.s.
Oakwood	– 1.6	– 1.1	n.s.
Scott	– 2.2	– 1.4	n.s.
Royston	– 2.6	– 1.9	n.s.
Stanford	– 3.7	– 2.2	0.05
Shackleton	– 6.5	– 4.0	0.000

The overall equation explains 53 per cent of the variation in pupils' examination scores, which is rather satisfactory by the usual social science standards. As might be expected, measured ability is the single most powerful predictor of examination score, while social class background and parental interest are also highly significant predictors.

Even after controlling for these exogenous variables, however, significant differences between schools persist, albeit somewhat reduced from those of Table 6.1. For example, Table 6.1 showed that pupils at Meadowpark obtained on average 6 more scalepoints than those at Enfield. Table 6.2 now shows that this difference, after controlling for intake, is reduced to 3.2 points, still a statistically significant difference. Similarly, Table 6.1 showed that pupils at Stanford obtained on average 12 fewer scalepoints than those at Enfield; Table 6.2 shows that this difference is reduced to 3.7 points once we control for the pupils' ability, social class and parental visiting. In other words, some of the differences between schools are reduced, although by no means eliminated. The overall range between top and bottom school, for example, has been reduced from 19 points to 11.9 points, still a substantial difference. It suggests (assuming that our statistical models are not too badly mis-specified) that a pupil of average ability and home background who had the good fortune to attend Croxley would end up with nearly 12 more scalepoints (equivalent to an extra two O-level passes) than a similar pupil who attended Shackleton.

More generally, however, although the differences are smaller, Table 6.2 shows a very similar pattern to Table 6.1. There is a large group of schools in the middle which are not significantly different from each other. There is a 'tail' of high-performing schools which are virtually identical to the top group of Table 6.1: Croxley, Greenford, Meadowpark and Weston. And there is a 'tail' of low-performing schools which is again almost identical to the bottom group of Table 6.1: Royston, Stanford and Shackleton. There are, however, some changes of interest between the two tables. Most notably, Croxley has moved up from third to first and the gap between Croxley and Enfield, for example, has actually widened from 4 points to 5.4 after controlling for ability and home background. At the other end, Stanford has moved off the bottom: whereas in Table 6.1 it was 5 points behind Shackleton, in Table 6.2 it is 2.8 points ahead.

One reason for the similarity of Tables 6.1 and 6.2 is that we have not taken into account 'contextual effects'. The statistical model from which Table 6.2 is derived controls for the *individual* pupil's characteristics but takes no account of contextual effects such as the characteristics of his or her peers at school. As every parent knows, a child will be influenced by the attitudes of peers. These peer-group influences will in turn be related to the nature of a school's catchment area. Thus it is no accident that the schools at the top of Tables 6.1 and 6.2 include some of the socially most advantaged in the study, while those at the bottom include some of the most disadvantaged.

In explaining a pupil's performance, then, we need to take account *both* of his or her own social class background *and* of the background of the other children in the school. That is to say, we need both individual-level and school-level measures of social background. Unfortunately, with a sample of only fifteen schools it is difficult to make much statistical progress with school-level variables, and we shall not pursue the matter in detail here. Table 6.3, however, gives an overview of two main contextual variables: the proportion of pupils from professional and managerial background, and the proportion of 'high ability' children attending each school (those whose scores on the AH2 test were 0.5 standard deviations above the overall mean for the fifteen schools).

Table 6.3 *School composition*

	Percentage of pupils from professional and managerial homes	*Percentage of pupils with 'high' AH2 scores*
Meadowpark	58	34
Oakwood	54	44
Weston	48	24
Greenford	46	34
Croxley	42	35
Enfield	39	39
Craighill	37	49
Ormond	36	22
Bellamy	35	28
Preston	33	34
Shackleton	31	36
Venables	29	26
Stanford	29	14
Royston	23	24
Scott	20	34

It is apparent that, for these fifteen schools at least, social class mix is more closely associated with the school's academic success than is its ability mix. This provides an interesting contrast with the individual-level analysis which showed that the individual pupil's examination score is more closely associated with his or her ability than with social background. These two findings are not in any way contradictory: there is no logical reason for school-level contextual variables to operate in the same way as individual-level ones. On theoretical grounds, indeed, we might well have expected that pupil sub-cultures would be moulded more by social class than by ability, and, as we have already suggested, pupil sub-cultures are likely to be one of the prime sources of contextual effects.

It is also important to note that contextual effects do not fall neatly into the categories of 'exogenous' and 'endogenous' variables. From the teacher's point of view, the social composition of the school is largely given and outside his or her control. It is one of the facts of school life with which a teacher must cope as best he or she can in trying to obtain good, examination results. We should clearly control, therefore, for these contextual effects if we are to assess the schools' teaching. In contrast, from the parent's point of view, in choosing between schools, the social composition of the school will be highly relevant. For the parent the differences shown in Table 6.2 *before* controlling for the school's social composition would seem to be the relevant ones to consider.

In choosing between schools, however, a parent does not necessarily want to know how *on average* children are expected to fare at the schools in question, which is all that Table 6.2 can tell us. An above-average school performance can in theory be made up in many different ways. An elitist school, for example, might achieve an above-average performance by concentrating attention on its more able pupils and ensuring that they obtain large numbers of O-level passes. An egalitarian school may concentrate attention on the less able pupils and ensure that they all obtain some CSE passes. As we said earlier, it is worth asking not only whether a school is effective but who it is effective for.

To explore this question we divided pupils into those of low, middle and high measured ability. (Average ability pupils were defined as those whose AH2 scores fell within 0.5 standard deviations of the overall mean). We then calculated the mean number of scalepoints that these three categories of pupil obtained at each of the fifteen schools. The results are shown in Table 6.4. This shows several different school profiles, but we should be cautious in our interpretations since in many cases the numbers of pupils involved will be small. Schools like Oakwood, for example, have few low-ability children while Stanford has few high-ability children. Many of the variations in Table 6.4 could be attributed to chance and measurement error.

Some patterns are discernible, nevertheless. There are just two schools where examination results are consistently above average for all three ability groups - Meadowpark and Greenford. And there are five schools - Shackleton, Scott, Venables, Royston and Stanford - which are consistently below average. These two lists of schools are by now rather familiar, representing as they do the socially advantaged and the socially disadvantaged schools respectively. This suggests that contextual effects operate 'across the board': even less able pupils in a socially advantaged school will tend to have better-than-expected

Table 6.4 *Average scalepoints by school and ability*

	Ability group		
	Low	*Middle*	*High*
Greenford	15	27	45
Weston	12	28	45
Meadowpark	14	26	43
Croxley	12	29	41
Ormond	17	30	37
Enfield	14	21	37
Oakwood	10	22	36
Bellamy	13	21	34
Preston	18	24	35
Venables	9	22	35
Craighill	16	24	33
Scott	12	22	33
Royston	8	21	31
Stanford	8	15	30
Shackleton	10	15	29
Overall	12	24	37

performance while more able pupils in a socially disadvantaged school will tend to have worse-than-expected performance.

These results, incidentally, refute the view that was sometimes expressed in the days of the selective system that it was better to be one of the ablest pupils in a secondary modern than a struggling pupil at the bottom of a grammar school. The ablest pupils in the quasi-secondary modern Stanford, for example, are pulled down towards the Stanford average, while the least able in the quasi-grammar Greenford are pulled up.

We have, then, some schools which perform consistently above average while there are others performing consistently below simple average (such as Enfield). More interestingly, however, we can look for what might be termed egalitarian and elitist patterns. Let us define an egalitarian school as one which does better-than-average for the less able pupils but worse-than-average for the more able pupils. An elitist school can be defined as the converse. Interestingly, two clear examples of egalitarian schools can be found in this sample of fifteen schools (Craighill and Preston) but none can be found of elitist schools.

Whether these results would be replicated in a larger sample of schools is a moot point. But they do confirm our original suspicion that schools might not be equally good or bad for all types of pupil.

SCHOOL POLICIES: CONSTRAINT OR CHOICE?

As we stated at the beginning of this chapter, it is implausible that statistical analysis of fifteen schools' results could satisfactorily explain the schools' relative levels of success with the different groups of pupil. There are, however, some negative points which we can make. First, schools are not wholly constrained by their intakes, their past histories or their institutional arrangements. Conventional wisdom might have suggested that a former grammar school with a large nucleus of able pupils would have been most successful while a former secondary modern with no sixth form of its own would have been least successful. In practice, matters are not so simple. One of the schools that consistently appears at the top of our tables is a former secondary modern with no sixth form, while there is a former grammar school with a socially advantaged intake that consistently appears in the middle. (Interestingly, the one single-sex girls' school in our sample is another of the schools that consistently appears at the top.)

The social composition of a school, that is, the contextual effect, would appear to be much more constraining. As we have seen, the schools at the top of Table 6.2 all have socially advantaged intakes; the schools at the bottom all have socially disadvantaged intakes. But even so, the schools are not wholly constrained. Shackleton and Venables, for example, have very similar (disadvantaged) social composition, but Venables manages to move up into the group of schools with middling performance while Shackleton does not. Similarly, Oakwood and Greenford have similar (advantaged) intakes but Oakwood falls down into the middling group. To be sure, no socially disadvantaged school manages to transcend the contextual effects and climb into the top third of Table 6.2, and no advantaged school manages to fall to the bottom. The social constraints, then, are very real. There would seem to be clear limits to what can be expected of the staff of the schools. Our guess is that even a school with poor staff morale may be protected from poor results by a favourable mix of pupils, while even the best morale and teaching may not suffice to overcome an unfavourable peer-group culture among the pupils. We should not expect teachers to compensate for the class structure and its associated sub-cultures.

The qualitative part of the research will be used to shed some light on these hypotheses. In the present chapter, however, we shall pursue some of the choices that are available to schools, specifically the neglected topic of examination entry policy.

The schools differed widely in their entry policies, with respect to both the number of subjects for which pupils were entered and the balance between CSE and GCE. Some of the differences will of course be related to the pupils' measured ability but, as Table 6.5 shows, it is also notable that a pupil's social class background and whether or not his or her parents visit school regularly are significantly related to the number of subjects for which he or she is entered.

Table 6.5 is analogous in format to Table 6.2, except that we report the standardized (beta) regression coefficients rather than the unstandardized. We do this because, in order to approximate better to the assumption of normality, we have cubed the dependent variable. This makes the unstandardized coefficients harder to interpret, whereas the standardized ones can be interpreted as measures of the relative importance of the various independent variables. Table 6.5, then, shows that, even after controlling for the exogenous variables, pupils at some schools are entered for many fewer subjects than those at other schools. Pupils of similar test score and social background are entered for many fewer subjects at Bellamy than at Ormond, for example. We also found that the balance between GCE and CSE entries varied markedly between schools. Stanford, for example, favoured CSE to a far greater degree than did Oakwood.

Table 6.5 *Number of subjects taken (cubed) regressed on measured ability, home background and school*

	Beta	*T*	*Significance*
AH2	0.50	22.9	0.000
Clerical	– 0.02	– 1.1	n.s.
Skilled	– 0.06	– 2.5	0.02
Semi-skilled	– 0.08	– 3.5	0.001
Always visit	0.14	5.9	0.000
Never visit	– 0.05	– 2.3	0.02
Ormond	0.09	3.6	0.001
Croxley	0.09	3.0	0.005
Royston	0.07	2.4	0.02
Weston	0.07	2.5	0.02
Meadowpark	0.06	2.3	0.05
Greenford	0.01	0.3	n.s.
Enfield	0	0	0
Venables	– 0.02	– 0.6	n.s.
Craighill	– 0.02	– 0.9	n.s.
Shackleton	– 0.04	– 1.7	n.s.
Scott	– 0.05	– 2.0	0.05
Preston	– 0.07	– 2.8	0.01
Stanford	– 0.07	– 2.8	0.005
Oakwood	– 0.09	– 3.3	0.001
Bellamy	– 0.13	– 5.2	0.000

These differences in school entry practice do seem to be genuinely endogenous rather than exogenous. In other words they are the results of school policy - of choices made by the staff - rather than the consequences of social constraints. Thus a school like Royston, which has a very disadvantaged social composition, is one of the most generous in its entry practices while Oakwood has a very restrictive policy despite its advantaged composition. Schools are not wholly the prisoners of their social environments.

Do these differences in policy and practice make any difference to the pupils' eventual examination scores? It could be argued that, if pupils take fewer subjects, they will obtain better marks in each subject and thus end up with the same overall score. As the Black Paper writers used to argue, although in a different context, more may mean worse. We can test this hypothesis easily enough by repeating the regression analysis of Table 6.2 but with the inclusion of number of entries as an additional independent variable. Table 6.6 gives the results.

There are several notable features of this analysis. First, we manage to increase very substantially the variance explained. R increases from the 0.53 of Table 6.2 to 0.71 in Table 6.6 when number of subjects entered is added as an independent variable. We must emphasize, however, that this represents an improvement in the explanation of *individual* differences in scalepoints, not necessarily in *school* differences.

Before moving to school differences we should note that number of subjects entered appears to have taken over as the single best predictor of scalepoints, but we should remember that Table 6.6 shows only the *direct* effects of the listed variables. AH2 scores will also have *indirect* effects mediated by number of

Table 6.6 *Scalepoints regressed on AH2 score, parental class and parental visiting, number of subjects entered and school*

	B	*T*	*Significance of T*
Number of entries	3.5	25.9	0.000
AH2 score	0.4	20.6	0.000
Clerical	– 2.7	– 3.3	0.001
Skilled	– 3.1	– 5.7	0.000
Semi-skilled	– 3.3	– 4.6	0.000
Always visit	3.0	5.5	0.000
Never visit	– 2.2	– 3.1	0.01
Greenford	4.4	4.2	0.000
Croxley	4.2	3.8	0.001
Weston	3.3	3.0	0.01
Bellamy	2.5	1.9	n.s.
Meadowpark	1.7	1.5	n.s.
Preston	1.5	1.3	n.s.
Oakwood	0.9	0.7	n.s
Scott	0.1	0.1	n.s.
Enfield	0	0	0
Stanford	– 0.2	– 0.1	n.s.
Craighill	– 0.3	– 0.2	n.s.
Ormond	– 0.5	– 0.4	n.s.
Venables	– 0.5	– 0.5	n.s.
Royston	– 2.6	– 2.4	0.02
Shackleton	– 3.6	– 2.7	0.01

entries, and the overall effect of AH2 score will still be larger than that of number of entries. More generally, we should note that the other background variables, and indeed school attended as well, will also have both direct and indirect effects.

Turning now to the school differences, we can note from Table 6.6 that school entry policy does indeed account in part for the school differences of Table 6.2, but it does so only in part. Thus, on the one hand the school regression coefficients of Table 6.2 are generally reduced in size in Table 6.6. But on the other hand, statistically significant school differences still persist in Table 6.6 even after controlling for number of subjects entered.

Let us consider some specific examples. In Table 6.2 the regression coefficient for Croxley was 5.4, showing that, controlling for individual social background and AH2 score, pupils at Croxley obtained 5.4 scalepoints more than those at Enfield (the reference point for the school dummy variables). This difference has fallen to 4.2 scalepoints in Table 6.6. Some of the original difference, then, can be attributed to Croxley's more generous entry policy, but pupils of similar AH2 score and home background who enter for the same number of subjects still get better results at Croxley than at Enfield. Similarly, we find that the regression coefficient for Stanford has fallen from 3.7 in Table 6.2 to 0.2 in Table 6.6. In other words, pupils of similar AH2 score and home background at Enfield and Stanford get similar results in the subjects they take, although pupils at Stanford are entered for decidedly fewer subjects.

Regression analysis does not enable us to answer in any definitive way the hypothetical question of whether pupils at, say, Stanford would have obtained better overall results if their school had operated a more generous entry policy. For that we need 'action research' in which we monitor the consequences of actual changes in school policy. It is perhaps worth noting, however, that the schools with the most restrictive entry policies - Bellamy, Stanford, Oakwood and Preston - all tend to 'underachieve' on the evidence of Table 6.2 (although not in all cases at a statistically significant level). Equally, with one exception, the schools with a generous entry policy - Ormond, Croxley, Royston, Weston and Meadowpark - tended to 'overachieve' on the evidence of Table 6.2. The exception is of course Royston, but we should remember that Royston is one of the schools with the most disadvantageous contextual constraints.

Schools, then, do appear to have some choices open to them, but the constraints of the contextual factors are quite restrictive. Some schools do a better job than others, but even the best cannot compensate for society.

ACKNOWLEDGEMENTS

We would like to thank the ESRC for their support of this study and the LEA and schools involved for their co-operation. All maintained secondary schools within one LEA were asked if they would consider participating in the project. Twenty-six expressed an interest and after further consultation fifteen of these decided to go ahead. Further work into the explanation of the school differences is in progress.

Chapter 7

Changing a Disruptive School

Bill Badger

THE BACKGROUND TO THE STUDY

The intractable problem of disruptive behaviour has traditionally been dealt with in the sphere of the school pastoral and disciplinary system, the educational psychologist and, if all else has failed, the exclusion and suspension procedure. Until very recently the major emphasis has been on the 'treatment' of the disruptive *pupil*.

The concentration on the *school* as a focus for examination and change, rather than on the individual pupil, is a phenomenon of the 1980s, and as yet only partially developed. It has, however, a number of highly pragmatic antecedents:

1 A generally growing unease and dissatisfaction with the efficacy of the child-centred approaches to tackling disruptive behaviour in schools. This unease has been expressed not only from the chalkface but from within the ranks of educational psychologists. Gillham's *Restructuring Educational Psychology* (1978) would exemplify the clearly self-critical movement here.

2 Current economic climates which render referral to special education outside the normal school barely feasible, and which anyway will continue to assure a significant shortfall in educational psychological provision for answering the calls to deal with disruptive behaviour.

3 The Warnock Report and 1981 Education Act, in which the major emphasis for dealing with *all* special educational needs is placed within the normal school.

4 Tangentially (some may argue more centrally) the increasing unacceptability of corporal punishment as a means of dealing with disruptive behaviour.

5 In a generalized way, the feeling increasingly expressed both within and outside the education system that as society itself changes, so many of the tacitly accepted rules of school will have to change as well. Passive obedience of, and respect for, the teacher is by no means so easily come by these days, some would argue. Schools *have* to change if they are to survive, it is thought.

A one-year fellowship to the Centre for Educational Research and Development at Lancaster University formed the basis for the study of the incidence of disruptive behaviour in a Cumbrian comprehensive school. The underpinning of the research came from three sources:

- The school differences/school effects work of Reynolds *et al.* (1976), Reynolds (1982), Rutter *et al.* (1979), Rutter (1983), Galloway *et al.* (1982) and many others.
- The school change work with specific reference to disruptive behaviour of Lawrence *et al.* (1983).
- The 'teacher as researcher' concept, promoted by Laurence Stenhouse and developed at University College, Cardiff by Davie (1981) and Lewis (1981).

Each of the three strands will be looked at separately and their inter-relatedness will be traced.

School Differences/School Effects

The relevance of this work to the current study is considerable. If, as the work of Coleman *et al.* (1966), Jencks *et al.* (1972) and perhaps Plowden (Department of Education and Science, 1967) appeared to suggest, there is a minimal effect that schools can have on their pupils, then trying to change pupils is a fairly vacuous exercise. However, almost all the work done in the 1960s and 1970s, which portended to show the minimality of effects of schools on pupils, looked at pupil *abilities* and *attainment* of various sorts. The current study's focus is on *behaviour* within schools and there is a limited degree of cross-reference possible between these earlier studies and the current one.

Power *et al.* (1967, 1972), Reynolds *et al.* (1976) and Gath *et al.* (1977) are among the earlier workers who claimed to find behavioural/delinquency rate differences between schools which could not be accounted for by factors outside the school. These were very much 'black box' researches but fitted well enough with feelings within schools in the 1970s that things could be done to make schools more congenial and relevant.

Fifteen Thousand Hours (Rutter *et al.*, 1979) marks a watershed for school effectiveness studies. The huge literature generated by the report would fill a book on its own, and the arguments as to whether Rutter *et al.* did indeed show how schools affect pupils on the basis of the statistics used continue until now. Certainly the conclusions tie in well enough with the work of Reynolds *et al.* (1976) in South Wales secondary schools, in which, putting it simply, data on pupils' abilities and personalities on intake did not seem able to explain the variation of outcomes between the schools. Galloway *et al.* (1982), looking specifically at exclusion and suspension rates among Sheffield secondary schools, found differences between the schools that could not, by any means they chose, be explained by catchment area or intake variations.

Rutter (1980) concludes in a discussion of his data that eight important within-school influences on school outcomes could be identified. These can be summarized as: academic balance, reward and punishment systems, environment, pupil responsibilities, homework, teacher modelling, classroom management and leadership characteristics. Reynolds (1982) concludes that: 'the key to successful modification of school practice is likely to be in the phenomenological world of schooling - in the perceptions and relationships that govern teacher and pupil actions.'

All told, there appears to be convincing evidence that school differences exist, and that these differences are connected with effects on behaviour and attainments of pupils. It is not suggested that the differences and effects have as much influence on pupils as do home background and environment. Nevertheless, Reynolds and Reid (1985) are happy to conclude that the work reviewed so far, 'has begun to indicate that there are substantial differences in the effectiveness of different schools'. Rutter, however, is concerned about causality. Do the differences *cause* the effects? He finds 'strong circumstantial evidence' (Rutter, 1983) that they do, but adds a comment which forms the *raison d'être* of the present study: 'Firm and unambiguous evidence on causation can only come from experimental studies in which school practices are deliberately changed. If the effect is truly causal, the change should be followed by the predicted alterations in school outcomes.' Both Rutter and Reynolds point out that such studies would be difficult, and in any case have, as yet, barely been attempted.

The Work of Lawrence, Steed and Young on Disruptive Behaviour

The work of Lawrence *et al.* since 1977 has focused on disruption in schools, and crucially stems from two studies of secondary schools (1977, 1981) in which levels of disruptive behaviour were recorded by non-observational methods. It is this pioneering work which has appeared most closely, to date, to answer the appeal by Rutter and Reynolds for work on *changing* school systems. In the two studies, techniques were devised to obtain data on levels and patterns of disruption over varying periods of time. This recording was used in both cases to form the basis of a report to the schools. Subsequent meetings with staff were held to look at implications for school organization and management, the object being to orchestrate change to minimize the occurrence of disruptive behaviour.

Neither study was able to proceed beyond this point, and neither study was followed up by more school-based research. However, the framework in these two studies was established for an analysis of disruption in an entire school, and guidelines set out for development of the work into a full-scale school-change operation. In this work, which has now been widely reported (Lawrence *et al.*, 1978, 1983), the academic 'school differences' background is acknowledged and, with specific targeting on disruptive behaviour, school processes can be analysed with a view to determining causal relationships. The Lawrence approach has been used, in the current study, as a basic tool to fashion a framework on which to hang a complex analysis of organizational and interpersonal factors within a school which appear likely to bear on patterns and levels of disruptive behaviour.

The Teacher-Researcher Concept

Analysis of disruptive behaviour, in terms of school processes rather than as produced by characteristics of individual pupils, is a fascinating area of study, the complexities of which need the closest consideration (Badger, 1985a). It is not possible to obtain useful data without the closest knowledge of the workings of the individual school under scrutiny.

The current study began by relying heavily on the active co-operation of staff at the school. While it is truc that it remained the researcher's responsibility alone to produce a report, much of the data gathering and contextual analysis was only possible because about twenty members of staff gave a great deal of time to the project. As the project proceeded, the work of Davie (1981) and Lewis (1981) became more obviously relevant. In Cardiff, a part-time MEd course has existed since 1979, in which the underlying propositions have been that schools can change *only* if the problems are initially adequately analysed and if school staff (in particular headteachers) are willing to change. To this end, staff are seconded with the specific blessing of their headteachers to work as teacher-researchers within their own schools on a part-time attendance basis at Cardiff. As Davie (1981) points out, once the 'right' question is asked, with the experience and resources at their disposal teachers 'need no expert outside to help them'.

I am concerned here with the teacher-researcher movement. Stenhouse (1975) strongly advocated the concept but it takes considerable practice to validate it. Current experience, however, indicates that Reynolds and Reid (1985) are right when they argue that using teachers and researchers could make available 'a large data base on processes and outputs ... particularly since teachers may well be highly sensitive observers of within-school practices'. The failure of traditional INSET courses to acknowledge how primary schools work as organizations is discussed by Mountford (1984). The solution, as he sees it, is to be found within the teacher-researcher concept, looking at institutional effectiveness rather than at the problems of individual teachers.

School differences, in both cognitive and behavioural terms, not accountable for by external factors, have been found in a number of studies. For such results to be translated into school practice, it is clearly essential for attempts to be made to change schools within pre-determined parameters, and for ensuing results to be measured. In behavioural terms, such attempts to date have been almost wholly neglected. The work of Lawrence *et al.* provides an introduction into this intensely difficult area and for a practical application of the research method, the teacher-as-researcher concept became an essential element of the current project.

THE CURRENT STUDY

Much of the above theoretical and experimental background came to be seen as cohesive only as a result of the attempts to formulate the approach of this particular study of disruptive behaviour. As indicated above, the specific non-observational method developed by Lawrence *et al.* formed the basic tool of analysis, which was agreed upon with the school at an early stage. However, complications became evident almost from the beginning, and many new avenues became apparent, into which a few tentative steps were taken as the research progressed. As perhaps is often the case, more questions were raised than answers produced.

The school eventually chosen was a purpose-built (1967) comprehensive school in the west of the county of Cumbria, of some 1200 pupils serving a mixed rural/urban population and taking in children of the disadvantaged and unemployed as well as those of endoctored scientists. Initial visits were productive and welcoming, and while some of the wholly urban west coast schools clearly produced more problematic school behaviour, this school's willingness to help and genuine interest in the research made it the final choice.

Initial visits took place in October 1983, a pilot study (see below) was run during November of that year, and a full scale survey was carried out during February and March 1984. The report on both these periods of research was presented to the school in May 1984. Unfortunately (from the point of view of the research), teachers' industrial action continued for the remainder of the summer term of 1984 and no planned staff discussion was able to take place on the report. From September 1984 a sequence of meetings took place, and these meetings continued. The school staff have maintained a gratifying level of interest, particularly the headteacher, and as indicated earlier the whole process of discussion and decision-making on the basis of the report has developed into a study in its own right.

Given a free hand, and the unique privilege that went with it, of working with the utmost co-operation within a large comprehensive school as researcher over an extended period of time, it was decided to make at least an initial analysis of every significant-looking process or pattern that emerged. In all, fourteen approaches were explored. Only *one* of these comprises the original Lawrence non-observational method; many of them sprang directly from staff suggestions and initiative. There was a deeply held feeling that if disruptive behaviour was really going to be looked at, then no process, relationship or nuance thereof should be ignored. The result is still an incomplete analysis of the complexity of in-school factors involved, but at least some parameters have been made clearer and bones assembled in an identifiable skeleton.

The report itself, though of intrinsic value, can be seen as only one of a series of stages in this attempt at school change. The stages can be described as follows:

1 Extended discussion and familiarization with the subject school; laying down of agreed ground rules and objectives; mutual building of confidence and credibility; formulation of some form of contract. This stage extended over a number of visits, with attendance at staff meetings, and discussions with staff at all levels, though predominantly with the senior management team. It extended into stage 2, which followed in the autumn term of 1983.

2 Using the basic, if modified, Lawrence *et al.* tool of non-observational monitoring, a two-week period of research was undertaken over a third of the school. Because of the defined

'house' structure, two houses, their staff and pupils, were the population involved. This stage produced interesting information on disruptive patterns within this segment of the school, with apparent trends in years and sex of pupils involved, day of the week and period of the day, subject from which referred, class and house of pupil. Staff at this stage discussed these initial results at a series of formal and informal meetings, and a unanimous view was that the apparent findings were of such interest that a larger exercise was needed to throw more light on them, and that the implications involved were of such complexity that only by a larger and more wide-ranging study could any practical meaning be put on them.

Consequently, with the full backing of the head, a third stage was planned to delve further into the variations in behaviour found in the pilot study. This was then conducted over a four-week period in the spring term of 1984, and involved the entire school.

3 The full study. Since it was agreed that much more information was needed if there was to be a realistic look at change, an *ad hoc* committee of eleven staff formed itself around the project to act as both instigator and facilitator of the requirements of the study. As a result, working from the basic approach of non-observational recording of disruptive incidents, a further thirteen approaches were outlined and acted upon. In each case the aim was clarification - the provision of additional perspectives and viewpoints and the inclusion of as much information on the workings of this complex institution as was possible in the time.

While the difficulty of obtaining *any* behaviour data which do not have an element of subjective 'tainting' is recognized (Badger, 1985a), the following approaches are grouped with reference to the degree of subjectivity apparently inherent in them. Group 1 data were gathered without reference to staff in any direct way. Group 2 data were gathered by and through staff, but in a mainly quantitative way. Group 3 data were gathered from staff, pupils and others at a mainly individual and reflective level, with little reference to quantitative methods. All three levels appear to be essential in a whole-school analysis of this kind.

Group 1 Quantitative data collected by the principal researcher

(a) Analysis of referrals to the school 'quiet room' over a two-year period (this is a process by which teacher-pupil conflict situations are defused by an immediate referral of pupils to a 'quiet room' staffed at all times by senior staff). All referrals are documented, and referral records extend back for seven years.

(b) Analysis of the school detention book over two years.

(c) Analysis of the physical/environmental attributes of all classrooms. This was devised on the instigation of staff to look for possible links between disruptive levels and classroom attributes.

(d) Meteorological data, again from staff. An attempt to correlate weather patterns over the course of a complete academic year with referrals to the quiet room.

Group 2 Quantitative data collected by staff

(e) Monitoring of 'high level' disruptive incidents over four weeks, the original underpinning of the survey.

(f) Monitoring of 'low level' disruptive incidents (a development of (e) following pressure from staff for ways of recording more trivial incidents).

(g) A class matrix - a replication of work done by Lawrence *et al.* (1981) to look at whole classes and the behavioural dynamics within them, mainly undertaken by one member of staff.

(h) Profiles of twenty difficult pupils - a further Lawrence-type replication, but including attainment and ability data.

(i) Behavioural links between feeder primary schools and the subject school - in response to primary staff requests (Badger, 1985b).

Group 3 Qualitative data

(j) Interviews on pupils who had been involved in 'high level' incidents.

(k) A sixth form questionnaire, instigated and largely co-ordinated by staff, to ascertain the views of recent clients of the system.

(l) Pupil essays, as employed by Lawrence *et al.*, involving pupils from each year writing essays on behaviour from the view-point of a 'fly on the wall'.

(m) Staff interviews with fifty teaching staff plus caretaking and kitchen staff, giving tape-recorded semi-structured interviews of twenty to thirty minutes on their perceptions of the problems and causes of disruptive behaviour in the school.

(n) Recording of many informal discussions and communications with different members of the school community over an eight-week period.

The report on the survey as outlined covers ninety-six pages and is difficult to summarize. It was produced as a document internal to the education authority and even within the authority was not circulated outside the school, apart from within a small number of officers with a particular interest in the project.

This report was presented to the school as a basis for discussion and implementation of school change. It was by no means complete as a summary of all the implications derivable from the data collected. Much interpretative material was drawn from the data separately, but was deliberately not included in the report to the school. The intention was to allow the data (albeit in summary form) to be worked on by the staff themselves. The extent to which this was indeed possible, and the processes by which the school imposed its own priorities on examination of the data, will be summarized at a later point.

The results from the survey, both as contained in the report to the school and as shown in a later analysis (Badger, 1985b), can be summarized under a number of headings.

Findings across the Approaches

Recurring themes are clear enough, emerging from varying perceptions and analyses in the different approaches used. These are most readily identified from the numerical data obtained, but also emerge from the interview personal report material. They can be summarized as follows.

Sex of pupils involved in disruptive incidents The ratio averaged out at 2.75: 1 male to female, which was derivable from quiet room analysis, detention book analysis, high level disruption figures and pupil profiles.

The day of the week most prone to disruption This was Monday, and was derived from quiet room analysis, high level disruption figures and low level disruption figures (see Figure 7.1).

The period of the day most prone to disruption This was period 5 (i.e. the last period in the afternoon), and was derived from quiet room analysis, high level disruption figures and low level disruption figures.

The higher rate of experience of disruption for individual members of staff rather than individual pupils This was derivable from quiet room figures, high level disruption figures and low level disruption figures. During 1983, five pupils accounted for 11 per cent of the referrals to the quiet room but five staff accounted for 30 per cent of the referrals to the quiet room.

Data from the Interview and Personal-Report Approaches

The sixth form questionnaire material The number of completed questionnaires returned on a voluntary basis was thirty-six, which represents 52 per cent of the entire sixth form. It appears from this material that disruptive behaviour, as defined, was seen by sixth-form students as an important influence on their previous five years of school experience.

Thus 90 per cent of responses refer specifically to classroom disruptive activity, and 86 per cent of students consider that it had prevented them from working properly. Sixty-nine per cent had experienced ‘quite a lot’ or ‘a lot’ of

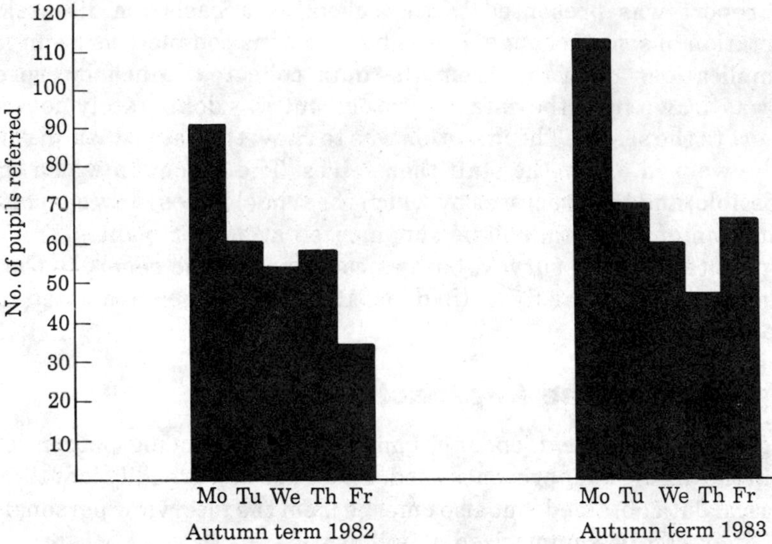

Mondays for autumn 1982 were 40 per cent higher than the next highest day (Tuesday).
Mondays for autumn 1983 were 61 per cent higher than the next highest day (Tuesday).

Figure 7.1 *Referrals to the school quiet room by day of the week*

it; 27 per cent thought it had caused them to obtain lower exam results than might otherwise have been the case. The specific behaviour referred to included:

deliberate teacher provocation	61%
general talking	53%
ignoring and defiance of teacher	36%

In terms of causes, the pupils argue for:

peer group pressures	50%
boredom, non-interest	44%
resentment of school itself	25%

The interviews of pupils involved in 'high-level' disruptive incidents

Here we are looking for causes of particular episodes of highly disruptive behaviour, as perceived by the pupils involved in the incidents. They can be summarized as follows:

Teacher pre-determinants:
- teacher too soft
- teacher too loud
- teacher not willing to listen
- teacher simply 'a new one'
- teacher not even-handed.

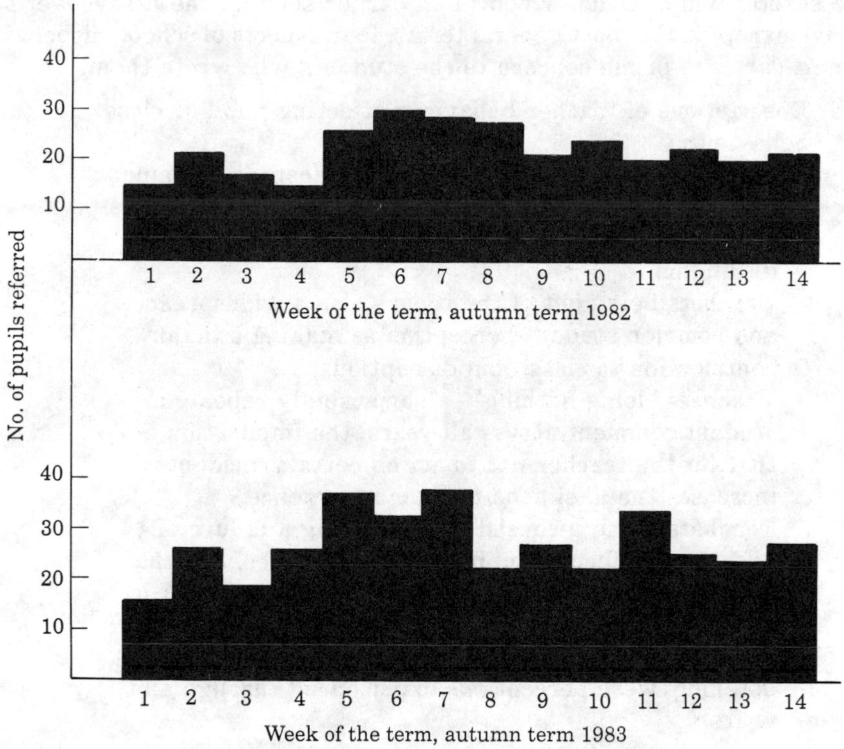

Figure 7.2 *Referrals to the school quiet room by week of the term*

Lesson pre-determinants:

lesson boring
lesson theoretical not practical.

Pupil pre-determinants:

pupil 'in a mood'
pupil unable to do the work
pupil 'led on' by others
pupil affected by last lesson
pupil 'labelled'
pupil 'didn't realize'
pupil doing it 'for a laugh'.

Teacher characteristics or approaches which lessen the likelihood of such behaviour include when the teacher 'takes time over a pupil' and when the teacher 'has a sense of humour'.

A summary of the material produced in pupil essays Two hundred and fifty essays were analysed using a pair of classes for each of the first five years in the school. While, as described in an earlier section, the essays were non-directive except in the most general terms, four aspects of school misbehaviour became clear as of prime concern to the students who wrote them.

1 Descriptions of teacher behaviour affecting pupil or class behaviour:

   Teachers being late to lessons - a widespread comment from all years and all classes, seen in numerical terms as the commonest contributory factor to classroom disruption.

   Teachers being out of the room - also a widespread and common student perception as making a major contribution to classroom disruption.

   Teachers 'doing nothing' - a surprisingly repeated student comment across all years, the implication being that for the teacher not to act on certain incidents increases the likelihood of their recurrence.

   Teachers being inconsistent - implying a failure of different teachers to uphold the same rules, and that individual teachers did not remain consistent over a period of time.

   Teachers being 'too soft', 'shouting too much' and 'not listening' were perceptions experienced through all years.

2 Descriptions of pupil behaviour itself. Here widespread differences in perceived disruption levels were found between the years. Differences between classes in the same years were also marked. Many pupils expressed extreme perceptions of the levels of disruption in their classes. Allowing for junior Hawthorne effects, these perceptions have major implications for the school. Teachers 'crying' or 'breaking up' were observations scattered throughout the essays. A mutual antipathy between academically oriented pupils ('boffs') and others was a common observation throughout the fifth year.

3 Descriptions of out-of-lesson activity. Areas of concern to students, listed in decreasing order of frequency, are as follows: smoking, graffiti, theft, littering, solvent abuse, 'bunking off'. The commonness of smoking, and the perceived failure of the school to influence it, was referred to throughout all years and classes. The failure of teachers to 'know' about widespread theft was referred to in all years.

4 A description of movement around the school. The time between lessons was described commonly as both a great source of relief and a potential source of disruption. Dinnertime was seen by pupils in all years as a time of frustration. The science block stairs were viewed by all years as a source of particular difficulty of movement, younger pupils clearly

suffering significantly in the process. Bus queues and bus loading were areas of unhappiness for many younger pupils. Overall, this approach indicated quite specific areas of concern both inside and outside classrooms, which could well be followed up on a 'whole-school' basis.

The staff interviews Fifty staff were interviewed, as indicated, representing a 63 per cent sample. A large amount of material was obtained and categorized. A summary is very difficult, as it seems likely that sheer frequency of a particular comment or observation is not an adequate measure of its necessary relevance or significance. Allowance for this has been made as far as practicable.

Although no clear consensus emerged on the perceived increase or decrease of disruption in the school, staff were in broad agreement that it was low-level disruptive behaviour which caused the bulk of the problem. The effect on staff of this, in terms of strain and tiredness, was commonly experienced. Many staff referred to a 'lack of respect' and generally low standard of 'pupil to teacher' behaviour. This problem of the minor disruptions, the 'low attaining ethos' was referred to in the fifty interviews.

Commenting on causes, staff echo many of the feelings of the pupils:

teacher lateness
movement around the school
anonymous teacher - pupil relationships
staff inconsistency
lack of time
failure in communications
delay in dealing with problems
lack of pupil guidelines
lack of adequate staff support
inadequate curricula
the physical openness of the school
personality clashes (teacher-pupil, teacher-class)
class 'chemistry'.

There was a unanimous agreement that the major school sanction - detention - was little better than useless, but that no alternative appeared practicable. Suggested approaches to tackling the perceived disruption problem can be listed. All staff mentioned one or more of the following. They are presented in descending order of frequency:

find more time
develop an improved staff support system
improve teacher-pupil relationships in the classroom
discuss the problem widely
improve parental relationships
find a way to improve the detention system.

The Effects of the Measured and Perceived Levels of Disruption

Evidence here can come very largely only from the recorded perceptions of people within the school, given that we are not undertaking a comparative school effectiveness study. There are no exam results to compare with other schools, no delinquency figures. Even if there were, we would still be unable to tease out the *effects* of behaviour measured. The question here is how people *feel* affected. A lesson which is 'disrupted' within the terms we have used is by definition adversely affected - we are here looking at what the participants see as the effects on themselves.

Students in the sixth form in 86 per cent of the sample saw the disruption as in some way preventing them from working properly when they were lower down in the school. They 'lost concentration' and 'lost out on quite a bit of work', or 'treated it as a laugh, but now regret it'. Fifty-eight per cent felt that it gets the school 'a bad name' and 27 per cent felt that it had directly affected their exam results. Thirty-five per cent felt it was quite serious or very serious as a problem.

Pupils in the lower part of the school gave a far less objective account of the matter but individuals registered strong reactions. 'It's disgusting when the teacher goes out of the room'. 'It's terrible . . .'. Overall, younger pupils did not use value judgements on classroom behaviour, but a number of comments express sympathy with the experiences of some of the teachers: 'some teachers are a little scared of the pupils, they send the teacher out in tears', or 'the teacher comes in and tries to get order, but the kids keep on talking'. Perceptions across the years vary, with some alarm and sympathy in the first year, and general acceptance in the fifth year. As one 'disrupter' explained, 'When I first came I was a goody goody, but I saw other kids talking back to teachers - I never thought of that, now I can't stop.'

Many staff, as has already been shown, are affected by levels of disruptive behaviour, whether or not they see the problem as increasing. The effect on the rest of the school of the handful of 'hard cases' has already been discussed. Additionally, the low-level disruption is seen as denying productive working atmospheres in many cases. It clearly takes a toll at a personal level as well. The following are representative of large numbers of teacher comments: 'I feel my emotional energy draining away.' 'It takes too much energy to solve - my willingness to fight is eroded.' 'I've had a couple of incidents which left me unfit to teach.' Perhaps less dramatically, but overall more insidiously: 'It affects my attitude, if they disrupt I get less interested myself.'

In summary, what are the school-based factors that appear to be linked to levels and patterns of disruption?

Pupil factors

1 Thirty-eight pupils, comprising 3 per cent of the population, are perceived to cause a disproportionately large amount of disruption in the school.

2 Of these, 82 per cent are perceived by the school to be of below average attainment levels.

3 A smaller fraction still - perhaps five pupils (0.4 per cent) - are perceived by staff as causing such severe problems as to be beyond the control of normal school measures and in need of removal from the main school.

4 Throughout the different approaches, a ratio of 2.75: 1, male to female, appears to reflect the likelihood of pupils of one sex being involved in disruptive incidents.

5 While the fifth year clearly poses significant behavioural problems, the third year looks to be the time when disruption is increasingly likely to be felt by staff.

Teacher factors

6 Teacher characteristics most commonly perceived by pupils as linked with pupil misbehaviour are: 'being too loud', 'being too soft', 'not listening', 'not doing anything about . . .' and 'being inconsistent'.

7 Teacher lateness to lessons was perceived in all student-based approaches and throughout teacher interviews as a primary factor linked with classroom disruption.

8 There appears little doubt that a small number of teachers experience extreme and chronic difficulty in maintaining behavioural standards in their lessons.

Classroom factors

9 The concept of the 'difficult class' persisting through its school life is recognized by both staff and pupils.

10 Both classes and pupils appear to behave in some lessons in ways which are directly linked with their experiences in their previous lesson.

11 Teacher-pupil relationships in general are seen by both staff and students as being less than conducive to adequate classroom behaviour in many cases. This is in spite of what should be seen as a generally relaxed and caring atmosphere engendered throughout the school.

12 Boredom with the subject in hand, and an impatience with the theoretical at the expense of the practical, are seen by a number of pupils as reasons for their disruptive behaviour.

13 All the above may combine to lead to a generally unconstructive level of classroom discipline in which some pupils either actively provoke or deliberately ignore the wishes of the teacher to promote an atmosphere of non-work.

14 In mixed-ability classes, some pupils report on the unhelpful relationship between the higher attaining pupils and the lower attaining ones. The atmosphere produced is perceived by some as destructive of optimum attainment levels.

Timetable and temporal factors

15 Of the five days in the school week, there is strong evidence from all the numerical data obtained that Mondays are particularly prone to disruptive behaviour. The reasons for this are unexplained to date. They could be seen as linked with mere timetable factors, e.g. the most disruptive classes or pupils working with the least effective teachers, in subjects more prone to disruption, etc., all on Mondays. This appears less than likely as the phenomenon holds true over two distinct academic years, but other aspects of Monday school functioning may still be linked. The other view might be that pupils and staff are affected by the fact that it *is* Monday, that weekend factors or start-of-the-week factors are involved.

16 Afternoon periods, over two academic years and as measured from a number of approaches, are much more prone to disruption than morning ones. The last period of the day is up to 60 per cent more likely to produce disruptive behaviour than the first three morning periods. Again, further investigation is required but directions to look at here would appear to involve school-based factors more obviously than in the 'day-of-the-week' figures.

17 There is some indication, over a two-year period, that disruptive behaviour increases as the half-term approaches, with peak figures apparent in the weeks before either full-term or half-term holidays.

Whole-school organizational factors

Clearly a number of the factors already described have connection with 'whole-school' processes and organization, but others can only be described at this level.

18 There are fewer teachers able to use single classrooms as their bases than many would like. This links with teacher lateness, decorative order of room, and more subtle teacher-control factors, quite apart from enhanced job satisfaction.

19 Movement around the school appears to be connected with certain types of disruptive behaviour. Particular areas of the school cause particular problems, which in turn are likely to be reflected in behaviour in succeeding lessons. Both teacher and pupil lateness to lessons will be affected. The stairs in the science block are singled out as uniquely problematical in this area, but a number of other locations are difficult. Movement generally between lessons is cited by staff, pupils and ancillary staff as productive of conflict in both direct and indirect ways.

20 The lack of behavioural guidelines for pupils to follow is

perceived by many staff as directly linked with disruptive behaviour. The 'federal' approach to both instigation and implementation of rules appears to be a disjointing influence on pupil behaviour, with a consequent overemphasis on personal control by individual staff both in and out of lessons.

21 There is some failure of school rule enforcement in areas such as smoking, littering, 'bus' behaviour and 'bunking off' which, combined with the above, appears to be linked with levels of disruption throughout the school.

22 Current sanctions, mainly detentions, are not seen by either pupils or staff as being at all effective in curbing disruptive behaviour.

23 Some failure in communications between staff is felt by many to be of significance in allowing levels of disruptive behaviour to be inadequately checked. Pupils perceive that action may well not be taken against them when this involves staff in communication with each other. This perceived lack of communication also involves failure in pursuit of common goals of behaviour across the school, and in contact between senior management and staff. These communication difficulties are clearly linked with both staff and pupil criticisms of inconsistencies and failure of rule enforcement.

24 While the majority of staff interviewed see the level of staff support as higher than in other schools, many still regard it as inadequate. The isolated teacher in a classroom under pressure from a difficult class or pupil still feels vulnerable and less able to contend with the difficulties than he or she would if supported more firmly and closely than is the case.

25 Both staff and pupils indicated that lack of time was a major factor linked with behavioural problems. From a pupil point of view a teacher who had time was a 'good one' and by implication less liable to experience disruption. If that time was used to listen to a pupil then so much the better. From a staff point of view time became the most crucial commodity of all. Time to listen, to communicate, to meet, to discuss, to support, to move from lesson to lesson, to prepare lessons, to counsel, to meet parents, to work effectively. Lack of time, above all, is perceived as an all-embracing contributor to behavioural problems throughout the school.

As has been described earlier, a number of other potentially linked factors, such as class size, sex of teachers, subject under study, condition of rooms and time of the lesson, were examined in the same light as the above, and found in the current study to have little or no clear link with behavioural levels. No doubt many other factors which perhaps would have clear links were not examined at all. On the whole, curricular links were not subjected to close examination, though it should be said that very little evidence of such a link in this particular school was indicated in either the numerical or perception-based data gathered, an exception being the reference by some pupils to 'boredom' following an excess of 'theory' type lessons.

FROM RESEARCH TO ACTION

Here is the situation as it stood at the beginning of the term following the research described above:

1 A school indicated willingness to co-operate in a project aimed at making a survey of levels and patterns of disruptive behaviour with the specific intention of unearthing possible processes and relationships which might bear on the problem.
2 After a series of discussions a project was planned involving active staff co-operation. At this stage the school, through its senior management, agreed that it would try to implement any change that might be indicated as a result of the research.
3 The project was undertaken. A considerable amount of data was generated and links between disruptive behaviour and existing school processes were implied in the report on the survey. Some of these putative links were confirmed in extensive structured interviews with members of the school community. What is to be done next?

In this case the headteacher decided to formalize a series of meetings. Copies of the report were made available to all staff and it was made clear that, using three remaining weeks of the summer term and the ensuing holidays, staff should familiarize themselves with it. There therefore followed: a senior management meeting; six house meetings; seven department meetings; and one full staff meeting. Following the final staff meeting a working group was formed from eleven members of staff who had been closely involved with the survey, to be chaired by the senior researcher. All the senior management, house and departmental meetings asked to produce reports on their deliberations, outlining which aspects of the report were considered and giving an indication of the tone of discussion on each one. The committee collated all the meeting reports, and members produced syntheses of specific topics gleaned from numbers of different meeting reports.

As already emphasized, the analysis and report were seen as valuable only to the extent that the school felt able to act thereon. The areas picked out by staff from the report as worthy of further consideration and, if possible, action were:

movement around the school
time to deal with and discuss both pupils and problems
consistency between staff, and on rules
rearrangement of teaching groups
staff support

length of lessons
communications
positive sanctions
quiet room procedures
below-average groups
attractive environments
the need for teacher bases
primary school practice
lateness to lessons
curriculum
timetabling - day of the week and time of day
pupil-teacher relationships
the sixth-form block
male-female disruptive patterns.

It will be noted that this list of staff priorities by no means corresponds fully to the list of twenty-five factors derived by the author from the survey data as showing evidence of relationships with disruptive behaviour. These two lists perhaps serve to illustrate a distinction between school-based empirical research mediated externally, and school-focused research with teachers acting as researchers in their own schools. In this case the school's own list has been the one from which further work has followed.

Many difficulties have arisen. All have been coped with to date. The decision-making procedure has become a major issue in its own right. How *does* a school change, even given that its members can agree on specific directions to work in? What power can the headteacher delegate in this? To what extent are less-senior members of staff prepared to act in a co-ordinating or even decision-making role? How do you actually go about changing things?

The results of the current study give an indication of a number of areas of school functioning which appear to be linked to levels of disruptive behaviour, but at the stage reached so far it is quite clear that school change directed towards whole-school behavioural problems is an immensely complex area of study. A number of examples will illustrate this.

1 From the data available for this particular school, afternoon periods show much higher levels of disruptive behaviour than morning ones on all measures applied. Similarly, Mondays as analysed retrospectively over a two-year period show on average over twice as many serious disruptive incidents as Fridays. One is left, on this evidence, not with a policy for school change, but with a far-reaching analytical exercise to answer questions on timetabling patterns, pupil concentration spans, diurnal rhythms, teacher fatigue, and above all on the patterns within other schools. Is one dealing here with a school-specific problem, or some common phenomenon of schooling?
2 Within this specific dataset there is evidence that teacher

lateness to lessons is a significant factor in pupils' disruptive behaviour. Again, there is no evidence on *what* to change. Clearly one needs to look at the need for more teacher bases, less pupil movement and the timetabling of teachers in a way that minimizes lengthy movement between lessons. One also needs to look at *why* teachers who have no obvious reasons for being so are late, and here the vicious cycle of difficult classes and teacher trepidation comes into play.

3 The most commonly reported area of dissatisfaction from both teacher and pupil viewpoints relating to the incidence of disruption was the lack of *time* for staff to deal with it. Here perhaps it is more clear what change is required - more time - but the problem of how to provide it, at the right time, in the right place, with the right teacher-pupil match, is in practice a highly troublesome one.

The behavioural committee, meeting sixteen times over a twelve-month period, has taken single issues from the initial report and subsequent staff meetings, and attempted to tease out the school-specific implications. It has made proposals to senior management for school change strategies to tackle the issues in question. Three detailed papers were prepared:

- on movement around the school;
- on the provision of time
  - for meetings about problem pupils
  - to deal with problem pupils;
- on an integrated procedure for follow-up of pupils referred to the quiet room.

A further paper on the development of a full staff support programme is in preparation. The senior management group introduced a major revision of the school detention system on the basis of the original report to the school. The school is attempting to change itself. What happens is a different story.

REFERENCES

Badger, B. (1985a) 'Behavioural problems - some cautionary notes', *Maladjustment and Therapeutic Education*, **3** (2), 4-11.

Badger, B. (1985b) 'Behavioural problems - the primary/secondary link', *School Organisation*, 5 (2), 185-93.

Coleman, J.S. *et al.* (1966) *Equality of Educational Opportunity*. Washington, DC: US Government Printing Office.

Davie, R. (1981) 'Behaviour problems in schools and school based in service training', in Upton, G. and Gobell, A. (eds) *Behaviour Problems in the Comprehensive School*. Cardiff: University College Cardiff.

Department of Education and Science (1967) *Children and Their Primary Schools*. London: HMSO. (The Plowden Report)

Galloway, D., Ball, C., Blomfield, D. and Seyd, R. (1982) *Schools and Disruptive Pupils*. Harlow: Longman.

Gath, D. *et al.* (1977) *Child Guidance and Delinquency in a London Borough*. Oxford : Oxford University Press.

Gillham, B. (1978) *Restructuring Educational Psychology*. Harlow: Longman.

Jencks, C. *et al.* (1972) *Inequality*. New York: Basic Books.

Lawrence, J., Steed, D.M. and Young, P. (1977) *Disruptive Behaviour in a Secondary School*. London: Goldsmiths' College. (Educational Studies Monograph 1.)

Lawrence, J. *et al.* (1978) 'Non-observational monitoring of disruptive behaviour in school', *Research International*, **4**, 38.

Lawrence, J. *et al.* (1981) *Dialogue on Disruptive Behaviour*. London: PJD Press.

Lawrence, J. *et al.* (1983) 'Coping with disruptive behaviour', *Special Education*, **10** (1), 9-12.

Lewis, J. (1981) 'Leadership in educational change', in Upton, G. and Gobell, A. (eds) *Behaviour Problems in the Comprehensive School*. Cardiff: University College Cardiff.

Mountford, B. (1984) 'Developing staff resources', *School Organisation*, **4** (3), 229-35.

Power, M.J. *et al.* (1967) 'Delinquent schools', *New Society*, 19 October, 542-3.

Power, M.J., Benn, R.T. and Morris, J.N. (1972) 'Neighbourhood, schools and juveniles before the courts', *British Journal of Criminology*, **12**, 111-32.

Reynolds, D. (1982) 'The search for effective schools', *School Organisation*, **2** (3), 215-37.

Reynolds, D. and Reid, K. (1985) 'Towards a reconceptualisation of theory and methodology in school effectiveness studies', in Reynolds, D. (ed.), *Studying School Effectiveness*. Lewes: Falmer Press.

Reynolds, D. *et al.* (1976) 'Schools do make a difference', *New Society*, 29 July, 223-5.

Rutter, M. (1980) 'Educational criteria of success - a reply to Acton', *Educational Research*, **22** (3), 170-4.

Rutter, M. (1983) 'School effects on pupil progress - research findings and policy implications', *Child Development*, **54**, 1-29.

Rutter, M., Maughan, B., Mortimore, P. and Ouston, J. (1979) *Fifteen Thousand Hours: Secondary Schools and Their Effects on Children*. Wells: Open Books.

Stenhouse, L. (1975) *An Introduction to Curriculum Research and Development*. London: Heinemann.

Chapter 8

Issues in School Effectiveness

Peter Mortimore

INTRODUCTION

Writing about *issues* in any field is daunting: doing so in the field of school effectiveness and school improvement is particularly so because of the relative youth of the subject matter. It is, after all, only twenty years since Weber published his seminal work and, by doing so, invited us to ask the simple question of whether some schools were more effective than others (Weber, 1971). It is, of course, only in the past thirty or so years that educational research itself has come to prominence as a subject in its own right, rather than as a subsidiary subject of psychology or sociology.

Despite the daunting nature of the task, however, it is important that researchers in any field - and perhaps more especially in a youthful area of study - pause periodically in their investigations and reflect on the worth of all this endeavour. As part of this process it is highly appropriate to attempt to identify the key issues of that field. In a field in which - despite its youth - one of the most striking characteristics is its international nature (with committed researchers coming from the United States and Canada, Australia, the United Kingdom and an increasing number of other European countries led by the Netherlands), it may well be right to call these universal issues, despite the somewhat grandiose nature of the term.

My intention, in this chapter, is to select nine issues and to identify at least some of the debates that surround them. In this context the number nine has no significance other than its manageability: it could have been twenty or thirty. Similarly, other researchers may well have compiled a quite different list. These issues are merely those that seem to me - at this stage of the development of our chosen field - to be important. In some cases the issues I have chosen are to do with methodological problems and are amenable to solutions. In others, they concern the context in which we work, and are related to societal problems which simple solutions are unlikely to solve.

In some ways, it is an idiosyncratic list: four issues are concerned with research matters and deal with technical questions of investigation; one is what I have termed a pivotal issue and deals with the interface between research on school effectiveness and school improvement projects; two are about improvement programmes; one deals with the question of international co-operation; and the final issue, naturally, is focused on future developments. (I have tried to structure this collection into a model but with little success. The first four research issues could be defined as basic building blocks and the three issues concerned with school improvement could be described (in the Fullan *et al.*, 1990, idiom) as 'cogs', but there remain one pivot and two antennae, pointing vaguely at the international community and the future!)

SAMPLING

Sampling is a very obvious issue to begin with. It is discussed at the start of most academic courses devoted to research methods. Its importance should never be underestimated. If, as a community of researchers, we aim to produce work which deserves to be taken seriously by policy-makers - in the United States, the work of Congressman Gus Hawkins is a prime example of such attention (House of Representatives, 1986) - the sample used in our research must be large enough and suitable enough to permit reasonable generalization.

Drawing on some of the work with which I have been associated, the sample of secondary schools chosen for *Fifteen Thousand Hours* (Rutter *et al.*, 1979) was small because it had been determined by earlier work. It served its purpose well but was far from ideal and, in the Harvard University Press edition of the book, an appendix has been added to explain its use. In the later *School Matters* study (Mortimore *et al.*, 1988), the sample of primary schools was both random and, when checked, representative: fifty junior schools drawn from a population of over 650.

Size of sample, however, is not the only criterion and Reynolds (1990) has drawn attention to the fact that many of the major studies of school effectiveness have used samples from populations of disadvantaged schools. We also need to investigate the mechanisms of effective schooling in *advantaged* areas, just as, I suggest, we need to do so in schools that serve a wholly minority community. To obtain similar findings in groups of schools with such different student bodies would add considerable weight to the strength of our arguments; to obtain different findings would be an interesting challenge to those arguments. Between the various research studies, we surely need to cover the range of possible samples, not only so that we can indulge in meta-analysis techniques (which in the field of school effectiveness present difficulties) but so that our school improvement follow-up work can be built on the most secure foundations.

MEANS OF MEASURING OUTCOMES

School outcomes studied in many of the school effectiveness investigations have been restricted to pencil and paper tests of cognitive skills. In American work, this has meant an almost exclusive focus on English and maths tests. In the United Kingdom, the focus has been broader and, in fact, some of the pioneering work was devoted to the study of measures of delinquency (see Mortimore, 1991, for a discussion of the methods and findings of British research). The details of the British work, however, are not well known in the United States and claims are sometimes made that the non-cognitive and the affective outcomes have been neglected in studies of school effectiveness.

Fifteen Thousand Hours used four outcomes of which only one - public examination results across the range of the curriculum - was cognitive. The other three - attendance, behaviour and delinquency - focused on the non-cognitive development of students. In *School Matters* the list of outcomes is even longer: reading, maths (written), maths (practical), writing, speaking, attendance, behaviour, self-image and a range of attitudes to school. Such a list enabled us to chart the progress and development of students with a reasonable degree of confidence that we were tapping their all-round capabilities. Even so, we were not monitoring the full range of the school curriculum. We were unable to measure the humanities, social studies, aesthetic subjects and physical and religious education (the latter included by law in the United Kingdom). In these areas we found the variation between schools to be so great that there was little basis for valid comparison. Interestingly, the introduction, from 1989, of an English and Welsh National Curriculum will enable future studies to make up this deficiency.

In my view, the adoption of a broad range of outcome measures is essential if studies are to address, adequately, the all-round development of students, and if they are to be used to judge the effectiveness of schools. In *School Matters*, for example, we found considerable variation in effectiveness, with some schools appearing particularly effective on cognitive outcomes, others seemingly effective on non-cognitive outcomes, and a group of fourteen schools straddling both areas. A replication of this approach with a sample of secondary schools might generate some interesting data.

METHODS OF ANALYSIS

Over the past ten years developments in statistical techniques and in computer programs to handle large data sets have been impressive. In England, for example, the work of Murray Aitkin (Aitkin *et al.*, 1981) and Harvey Goldstein (1984, 1987) has expanded considerably the range of available techniques. In particular, the development of multi-level analysis and of programs to handle it enables the data to be treated in an appropriate manner, rather than being reduced to a single level. Thus differences between classes, year groups and schools can be recognized rather than aggregated together arbitrarily.

These developments are welcome. They represent a considerable improvement from standard multiple regression techniques (Preece, 1989) and go some way towards solving the difficulties identified by Purkey and Smith (1983) and Gray (1989). But, as all researchers should be aware, sophisticated techniques of analysis cannot compensate for inadequate measures and the best analysis depends on a matching of appropriate techniques with correctly specified high quality data.

THE RELATIONSHIP OF OUTCOME TO PROCESS TECHNIQUES

My final 'research' issue poses as a problem something that often passes as unproblematic: the way different sorts of measures are linked, both conceptually and in terms of data relationships.

Conceptually, the division of variables into inputs, processes and outcomes, although subject to criticism on grounds of an over-mechanistic approach, has proved helpful in enabling a clarification of the question of how to study schools. Using this model, student outcomes (measured, as I have noted, in various ways and on a number of dimensions) can be adjusted to take account of the level of the student on arrival at the school (intake measures). These adjusted outcomes, by a process of 'backward-mapping' (Murphy, 1990), can be related to a series of process measures, provided they have been collected contemporaneously and so are related to the conditions that the target students would have experienced.

The statistical techniques used for backward mapping have usually been based on some form of correlation. While few techniques are more easily used to clarify relationships, the difficulty with correlations - as is widely recognized - is determining the direction of influence. Thus, distinguishing whether higher achievement is influenced by higher expectations or vice versa is impossible unless other information is available. Occasionally, it is possible to use a cross-lagged technique to investigate such a question. This was the case in *School Matters* when my colleagues and I were able to investigate the relationship between reading problems and behaviour difficulties. Interestingly, our use of this technique illustrated that *each could be an antecedent condition for the other*. For some students, reading difficulties preceded any signs of behaviour difficulties, while for others early behaviour difficulties were followed by the identification of reading problems. In my judgement, the linkage between the outcome and the process variables in empirical work is often weak. In view of the use that is made of the findings of research, it is obviously of the utmost importance that techniques of backward mapping be improved and the experience of such techniques be increased, perhaps through the further development and extension of multi-level methods.

These are the four issues that I have selected concerning research on school effectiveness. As I noted in my introduction, however, there are a number of others that could equally well have been addressed. I turn now to my 'pivotal' issue, which stands between the research on school effectiveness and the developmental work on school improvement.

MODELS FOR SCHOOL IMPROVEMENT

The issue here is simple: are the processes identified by the various research studies in this area necessarily the best models for school improvement work?

Factors such as sensitive headship, the careful management of students and teachers, the care of students, the quality of the environment and the positive climate of the school have been identified as being important in a number of different studies (Mortimore, 1991). These factors have been shown to be associated with greater student progress; they have emerged from studies of good practice. There is a question, however, as to whether they are necessarily appropriate for schools which do not *yet* have good student outcomes. Furthermore, do such factors rest on other conditions that have had to be secured previously?

This possibility of necessary *antecedent variables* is difficult to explore since, by their nature, such variables are likely to be unobtrusive or, in some cases, to be transient conditions. A concrete example may clarify the issue. *A new headteacher is appointed to a run-down school where students' outcomes are very poor and teachers are demoralized. Parents are extremely vocal in their criticisms and the community is hostile to students and staff.* Is this a situation in which sensitive leadership and careful management are needed or, before these can be employed, are more dramatic gestures necessary? The answer to this question will depend on different philosophies of management and it seems likely that a variety of strategies could be adopted, *provided these were suited to the style and skills of the new headteacher.* My personal view, however, is that the factors that have been identified in the effective schools research can be adopted, rather than the new headteacher adopting a quite different style and expecting to alter his or her actions at a later date. This *is* a personal view; others may argue for a much more authoritarian style to suit the crisis conditions of the school.

This example illustrates the complexity of the issue. Satisfactory resolution may emerge from a study of the burgeoning literature on school change.

This issue, which I have termed pivotal, leads away from studies of school effectiveness to the area of *school improvement*. The next two issues to be considered arise from attempts to improve schools.

THE IMPETUS FOR CHANGE

In the section above an example of a run-down school was cited. The unsatisfactory state of such a school provided an impetus for change. Unfortunately, most countries will have some schools in similar states because of a variety of circumstances to do with the history of the management of the school or its environment, funding or political circumstances. There are, however, other sources from which the impetus for change may spring. Governments in a number of countries - most notably in the United States, New Zealand and the United Kingdom - are currently seeking reforms of different aspects of schooling. This pressure for change does not stem directly from particular examples of schools that are failing - although it may be strengthened by public discussion of such schools - but rather from a general criticism that *all schools are inadequate for the needs of our changing societies*.

While different governments will put different glosses on this argument, it is clear that this attitude is not restricted to particular countries or to governments of particular political hues. While I - as someone who has worked in the education service for over twenty-five years - feel a defensive loyalty to schools as they are now, I also acknowledge that as the needs of societies change, schools, which tend to be highly conservative institutions, need also to be modified. Where I dissent from the actions of some governments is that I do not accept that the most effective way to secure change is to heap blame on schools and opprobrium on teachers, often for outcomes beyond their control. I also believe that change cannot be introduced overnight by hostile legislation, but rather that these things can be best achieved co-operatively over a suitable time period.

The reality for many teachers in many parts of the world, however, is that governments, ably assisted by a teacher-unfriendly media, are endeavouring to force change on schools. In the phrase adopted from George Bernard Shaw by Michael Fullan, they are attempting to change schools by 'brute sanity' (Fullan, 1982). In the United Kingdom, for example, schools are being expected to:

- introduce a National Curriculum with an associated programme of individual student assessment;
- operate a local management of schools system of site-management on the basis of formula-funding;
- compete with each other for students under an open enrolment scheme.

In the United States and in some Canadian provinces, programmes of school restructuring are being introduced for similar reasons to the British reforms. Australia and New Zealand, too, are involved in programmes of school reform.

The impetus for system-wide change has also been strengthened by the demands of higher education. In the United States, for instance, Bloom (1987) and Burton Clark (1985) - both university professors - have criticized the quality of current applicants for higher education (and, in the case of Bloom, the quality of higher education itself) and have predicted dire consequences at societal level. Such arguments have lent considerable weight to the pressure for reform.

What must not be overlooked in any consideration of system-wide concerns, however, is the initiative of individual schools and their supporting bodies (local education authorities in the United Kingdom; school boards in North America) to welcome and embrace change in the search for greater effectiveness. Many schools have grasped the school effectiveness literature and used this to assist and support their own development. For a variety of reasons, there has been more activity of this sort of North America than in the United Kingdom (Mortimore, 1991) but in places as far apart as San Diego in southern California (Chrispeels and Pollack, 1989) and Halton County in Greater Toronto (Stoll and Fink, 1989) school improvement work is flourishing.

Where a support team - funded by a school board or state department - can work sensitively to support an individual school's request for greater effectiveness, the conditions are positive for change. Having provided a reasonable legislative framework, governments - in my opinion - would do well to encourage this type of co-operative endeavour rather than the bullying and deriding tactics that are more commonly employed.

In summary, then, the impetus for change can stem from a number of different sources. System-wide change emanates from governments; individual school change can be stimulated by the local education authority (school board) or by the school itself, either because a crisis has developed or because it is searching for greater effectiveness.

THE LIMITS OF CHANGE

In many ways this is the most difficult issue that I have chosen to discuss. This is because, while in so much writing about schools it is tacitly assumed that all schools have an equal chance of improvement, the reality is that schools in all countries vary enormously in their conditions and in the nature of their student intakes. The acceptance of this reality is not to condone a defeatist attitude by teachers of disadvantaged students but merely to note that judgements of school effectiveness have to be carried out in sensitive ways, using sophisticated methodology.

Such judgements of schools frequently involve comparisons of one school with another. To ensure that like is compared with like, however, is difficult. In terms of cognitive development, any examinations or tests that are norm-based and that have high failure rates (or criteria-based assessments that are pitched too high) will demonstrate that - in general - schools serving disadvantaged populations are likely to achieve less than their more advantaged peers. Of course, some individual students will 'buck the system': some of the disadvantaged will be academically successful just as some of the advantaged will fail to achieve. The odds of academic success, however, remain firmly in favour of the advantaged.

In the United Kingdom, where for historical reasons standards in public examinations have been pitched high (five higher-level grades in the General Certificate of Secondary Education for entry into advanced study or more prestigious occupations), this is a particular problem. Average students, having achieved at an average level, drop out of school at age sixteen feeling that their schooling has been a failure. From the point of view of the functioning of society this assessment system performs the task of sorting individuals into particular sets of aspirations and expectations about future life styles. It is efficient in that, on the whole, young people believe this judgement and accept their role in society but, in my view, is totally unacceptable on the grounds of equity or of the national interest. Although it might have served the country well in earlier times, the waste of the potential 'cooled out' by the system is surely far too serious to be tolerated by a modern country competing for trade and industry and needing highly trained and motivated workers.

For schools, which have to operate this system of role-selection, the price is considerable alienation for many students. Since there is a strong relationship between academic success and social advantage, it is clear that for schools serving disadvantaged populations, the proportion of alienated students is likely to be much higher (Mortimore and Blackstone, 1982). Yet such schools are powerless to alter this as they have to operate within the examination framework of the system. The limits of change, therefore, for such schools are clearly defined: they can maximize the opportunities for individual talented students, but the odds against acknowledged success will remain stacked against them, no matter how efficient the school might be in enabling disadvantaged students to make progress.

In the United States, with a history of lower drop-out at the end of the statutory school years and greater opportunity for higher education, the situation is less clear cut. From the point of view of school improvement studies, it is still possible to follow the advice of the late Ron Edmonds that 'if you want to change a school you need to start at the bottom with the least successful students; the rest will automatically improve' (Edmonds, 1982).

The capacity of the advantaged (whether students or adults) to get more out of any situation, however, poses a serious problem to school improvement. If a school's overall achievement is improved, yet there remains a large differential between advantaged and disadvantaged students within the school, has much been gained? In my judgement the answer is some, but with reservations. *School Matters* found that *disadvantaged* students in the most effective schools could perform better than advantaged students in the least effective ones. My reservations exist because of the failure to maximize the chances of *all* students. There is no obvious solution to this problem. Restricting coaching classes to the disadvantaged, though logical, would be likely to generate enormous resentment among groups of students. While it is possible to discriminate positively with resources between schools (Sammons *et al.*, 1983), doing so between students is likely to be divisive.

INTERNATIONAL CO-OPERATION

The issues arising from school effectiveness and school improvement are often common to a number of countries but, all too frequently, both researchers and policy-makers are relatively ignorant of other situations. My own knowledge, for example, of developments in the Netherlands has increased considerably since the inception of the International Congress of Effective Schools and its journal *School Effectiveness and School Improvement*. I am still disappointed, however, when I discover that American scholars are unaware of much British and Canadian work.

This prompts me to pose the question of whether an international study would be an appropriate way of bringing together teachers from different countries. Clearly such a study would need a great deal of planning so that a number of alternative strategies would be open to the planning team and the maximum value could be extracted from it. My own view is that such a study would be worthwhile and, if it took the form of a series of replications, could add considerably to our understanding of many practical concerns, as well as to the theoretical underpinnings of the work.

I am uncertain, however, as to whether such an international study would best be directed towards a further investigation of school effectiveness, or whether it would be more useful to focus on school improvement. As always there are costs and benefits to either choice. A large-scale study of, say, secondary schools drawing on established research instruments and analytical techniques would strengthen the repertoire of studies and, undoubtedly, would strengthen our understanding of the characteristics of effective schools. Yet it would take time and would not necessarily further our knowledge of how to *change* schools. On the other hand, a study of school improvement could address more immediately questions concerning change, but it would have to be built upon a foundation of various *national* rather than *international* studies.

On balance, I think my own preference is for a study of school improvement, on the grounds that governments are already engaged in school reform and the time scale for work which could inform (and in some cases rescue) these government initiatives is short. Such a study would, hopefully, avoid the successive bureaucracy and government interference that so often characterizes international projects. It is likely, in my view, that a number of researchers in different countries would welcome the opportunity to participate in such a study if funding could be procured. Who the appropriate body to co-ordinate the work would be is, however, an open question. Perhaps this chapter, reflecting the mood of the Special Interest Group on School Effectiveness, will act as a stimulus to funding bodies. At a time of such world change, few investments in the future could be more worthwhile than the improvement of schools.

THE FUTURE

The final issue to be presented in this chapter raises the danger that both researchers and policy makers may be restricted to an outmoded model of schooling. Such a model has a number of features:

- large groups of children and adolescents are controlled by adults;
- a considerable proportion of time is spent in passive roles;
- knowledge, and the day, are separated by bells or sirens;
- assessment is mainly carried out using expensive, formal techniques of testing.

My own position is that while schools have to work to this model, I want to help them to be as effective as possible, but that I also believe other - perhaps more appropriate - models should be developed. Who is better equipped to share in this task than those who have studied school effectiveness? Such people, whether researchers or practitioners, should be aware of the difficulties of change and of the need for cogs that fit rather than grate (Fullan *et al.*, 1990). A new model of schooling dedicated to producing effective learners, who are also caring and responsible people, is surely a worthwhile ambition?

These are my nine, somewhat idiosyncratic, issues. I am well aware that I may have neglected important areas - such as the different amounts of resources that similar schools have access to - but I have endeavoured to focus on issues that have arisen directly from my experiences of empirical research on school effectiveness. I hope the international network of those interested in these ideas will respond to my suggestions and that funding agencies, including governments, will be far-sighted enough to support this vital work.

ACKNOWLEDGEMENTS

I wish to acknowledge the debt I owe to the research teams of which I have been a member and to Jo Mortimore for her helpful comments on an earlier draft of this chapter.

REFERENCES

Aitken, M., Anderson, D. and Hinde, J. (1981) 'Statistical modelling of data on teaching styles', *Journal of the Royal Statistical Society*, **144** (4), 419-61.

Bloom, A. (1987) *The Closing of the American Mind*. New York: Simon & Schuster.

Chrispeels, J. and Pollack, S. (1989) 'Equity schools and equity districts', in Creemers, B., Peters, T. and Reynolds, D. (eds) *School Effectiveness and School Improvement: Proceedings of the Second International Congress*. Lisse: Swets & Zeitlinger.

Clark, Burton R. (1985) *The School and the University*. Berkeley: University of California Press.

Edmonds, R. (1982) Personal communication, Arizona, April.

Fullan, M. (1982) *The Meaning of Educational Change*. New York: Teachers College Press.

Fullan, M., Bennett, B. and Rolheiser-Bennett, C. (1990) 'Linking classroom and school improvement', *Educational Leadership*, May, 13-19.

Goldstein, H. (1984) 'The methodology of school comparisons', *Oxford Review of Education*, **10** (1), 69-74.

Goldstein, H. (1987) *Multilevel Models in Educational and Social Research*. London: Charles Griffin.

Gray, J. (1989) 'Multilevel models: issues and problems emerging from their recent application in British studies of school effectiveness', in Bock, R.D. (ed.) *Multilevel Analysis of Educational Data*. New York: Academic Press.

House of Representatives (1986) Proceedings and Debates of the 99th Congress, Second Session. *Congressional Record*, Washington, DC.

Mortimore, J. and Blackstone, T. (1982) *Disadvantage and Education*. London: Heinemann Educational Books.

Mortimore, P., Sammons, P., Stoll, L., Lewis, D. and Ecob, R. (1988). *School Matters: The Junior Years*. Wells: Open Books.

Mortimore, P. (1991) 'Effective schools from a British perspective: research and practice', in Bliss, J. and Firestone, W. (eds) *Creating Effective Schools*. London: Prentice-Hall.

Murphy, J. (1990) Paper presented at the International Conference on the Study of School Effectiveness and the Practice of School Improvement, Boston, MA, 16 April. In this volume (Chapter 9).

Preece, P. (1989) 'Pitfalls in research on school and teacher effectiveness', *Research Papers in Education*, **4** (3), 48-69.

Purkey, S. and Smith, M. (1983) 'Effective schools: a review', *Elementary School Journal*, **83** (4), 427-52.

Reynolds, D. (1990) Paper given at the Conference of the International Congress for School Effectiveness and School Improvement, Van Leer Institute, Jerusalem. In this volume (Chapter 10).

Rutter, M., Maughan, B., Mortimore, P. and Ouston, J. (1979) *Fifteen Thousand Hours*. Wells: Open Books.

Sammons, P., Kysel, F. and Mortimore, P. (1983) 'Educational priority indices: a new perspective', *British Educational Research Journal*, **9**, 1.

Stoll, L. and Fink, D. (1989) 'An effective schools project - the Halton approach', in Reynolds, D., Creemers, B. and Peters, T. (eds) *School Effectiveness and Improvement: Proceedings of the First International Congress*. Groningen: RION; Cardiff: University of Cardiff.

Weber, G. (1971) *Inner-city Children Can Be Taught to Read*. Washington, DC: Council for Basic Education.

Chapter 9

Effective Schools: Legacy and Future Directions

Joseph Murphy

INTRODUCTION

Over the past year, I have been asked twice to reflect on the health of the effective schools movement. As Chair of the School Effectiveness and School Improvement special interest group (SIG) of the American Educational Research Association (AERA) I was invited to prepare a column for the SIG newsletter on any topic I wished to write about. I was also afforded the privilege of delivering the summary remarks at the International Conference on the Study of School Effectiveness and the Practice of School Improvement that preceded the 1990 annual AERA meeting in Boston. The honour notwithstanding, both assignments caused me a good deal of uneasiness. In the first case, I didn't have the slightest idea of what to write about or where to begin. In the second the situation was even worse. That is, it was evident early on that anything that I was likely to say would be said more thoroughly and eloquently by the three conference presenters (Creemers, 1990; Levine, 1990; Reynolds, 1990). Not surprisingly, after I read the finished papers, this turned out to be the case.

The more I reflected on these opportunities that refused to go away - despite regular attempts to relegate them to the outer recesses of my mind - the more obvious it became that tried and true response avenues - a review of the literature, a discussion of the usefulness of the research, a tracing of the history of effective schools - were not the paths to be followed. Rather, what seemed to be needed was an epilogue to the rich body of work undertaken by researchers and practitioners in the effective schools movement. It was also clear that the report should not be linear in design; should not be the close of our play. Rather, it should be a prologue to the future, or more precisely one person's conception of the future of effective schools.

From the safe harbour of my academic office, I began my labours as many of my colleagues would, with a (scholarly!) analysis of the problems and difficulties endemic to effective schools work. Although an advocate for the effective schools movement, I had subjected the corpus of the research to such extensive critiques in the past (see Murphy *et al.*, 1983, 1985; Murphy, 1988) that revisiting the issue was not a particularly arduous task. As I continued my work in this fashion, however, it became increasingly - and, because I was quite far along in this activity before I came to this realization, painfully - obvious that this approach was not likely to provide the new perspectives and deeper insights that I had hoped to uncover. What began to take shape was a belief that micro-level critiques of effective schools research and applications overlook the fundamental contributions that the effective schools movement has brought to education. This is not to deny the importance, for example, of research on the applicability of effectiveness correlates in varied contexts. Nor does my conclusion gainsay discussions about the most appropriate outcome measures to employ in assessing effectiveness. What is true, however, is that these critical analyses almost invariably ignore the real legacy of the effective schools movement - the core principles that comprise its infrastructure. It also became apparent that the directions for future work indicated by the critical analyses of research done to date provide too limited a vision of the future for effective schools. A broader perspective seemed to be needed.

Given these reflections, the choice of paths I selected will not be surprising. For the international conference, I tried to capture what I believed was the legacy of effective schools. I asked the following question: as we head off into the next generation of effective schools work, what should we take with us from our past? I left room for only four items in the satchel. This was the epilogue. For my colleagues in the School Effectiveness SIG, I attempted to sketch out a story of what we needed to be about in the future. This was the prologue. This chapter captures both sets of thoughts.

THE LEGACY OF EFFECTIVE SCHOOLS

As I culled the pages containing the knowledge base and values of the effective schools movement, I sought out those things that were truly indispensable - principles and findings that could not be ignored without producing disastrous consequences for tomorrow's youth. I was astonished to discover how quickly items could be discarded. Perhaps most surprising, especially to those among us who maintain a content orientation about effective schools - who see this field of research as a body of knowledge to be transported from school to school - was the fact that the correlates themselves were not among these essential items. It became clear that the correlates were simply a means to an end - student learning. What were important were the principles that supported the correlates. I was forced to acknowledge that the correlates themselves might look quite different in the future. Factors that helped produce high and equitable levels of student performance under the current system of schooling might not be those that would work in a different world (Murphy and Evertson, 1990). Those that were appropriate in one context, the United States for example, might not travel well to others, such as the Netherlands (see Creemers, 1990). More importantly, I concluded that as the knowledge base of education - the educational production function, if you prefer - evolves, the correlates are likely to undergo significant alterations. For example, we know now that a focus on basic skills can be counter-productive, especially for so-called 'at risk' youth. Students learn best when basic and higher order skills are taught simultaneously (Hawley, 1989).

This discovery concerning the non-essential nature of the correlates in no way negates their historical importance. It simply means that, as currently defined, they may no longer be needed, whereas other items are clearly essential. A close reading of the early effective schools researchers reveals that they understood this (S. Stringfield, personal communication). In addition, leading figures in the effective schools movement, such as Larry Lezotte, are already engaged in efforts to see how correlates such as leadership and monitoring will change as the organizational and governance structures of schools are altered and as our knowledge of the teaching-learning process evolves.

What, then, should we focus upon in our plans for effective schools in the future? I would suggest that we concentrate upon the following four aspects - three principles and one finding - of the effective schools movement.

The Educability of Learners

Underlying the effective schools movement is a fundamentally different conception of student learning, one that is captured eloquently in the dominant aphorism of effective schools advocates: all students can learn. Schools historically have been organized to produce results consistent with the normal curve, to sort youth into the various strata needed to fuel the economy. There is a deeply ingrained belief that the function of schooling is to sort students into two groups: those who will work with their heads and those who will toil with their hands (Goodlad, 1984). David Seeley captures this operating principle nicely when he reports that

> up to now, the actual operating goal of American society [and other nations as well] - whatever the ideal of rhetoric, or the commitment of individual schools or teachers - has been to provide educational services for all children, but to expect a 'bell curve' distribution of success, with large numbers of children falling in the 'mediocre' or 'failure' range.
>
> (Seeley, 1988, p. 34)

The effective schools movement represents a significant departure from this way of thinking. A psychologically based model of learning is displaced by a sociological perspective that underscores not what students bring to the school, but the conditions of learning available once they get there (see Miller and Brookover, 1986). The fundamental belief is that, given appropriate conditions, all students can learn. This is the most important principle of effective schools that we need to take with us into the future.

A Focus on Outcomes

For a variety of reasons (see Meyer and Rowan, 1975), educators - at least those in the United States - have avoided serious inspection of the educational process. Even less attention has been devoted to examining educational outcomes. The quality of education has historically been defined in terms of two interrelated inputs - wealth (and the extra resources wealth allows schools to secure, such as better facilities, more equipment, additional staff, and so forth) and the socioeconomic status (SES) of students. Given the chance, parents move into high-income, high-SES school districts and out of low-income, low-SES ones. The inescapable conclusion, even to the most casual observer, is that the good schools are to be found in the former group and the bad schools in the latter one.

The effective schools movement was the first collective effort to challenge this prevailing view of assessing quality. In Finn's (1990, p. 586) terms, effective schools proponents realized that the input and output ends of the oar 'were not firmly joined at all. Indeed they were more like two separate oars, capable of moving independently. To pull the one labeled "inputs," however energetically, did not necessarily have an effect on the one labeled "outcomes".' They also saw quite clearly the pernicious effects of the operant definition of effectiveness on large groups of students. Effective schools advocates argued persuasively that rigorous assessments of schooling were needed and that one could judge the quality of education only by examining student outcomes, especially indices of learning. Equally importantly, they defined success not in absolute terms but as the value added to what students brought to the educational process. Finally, and most radically divergent from prevailing practice, they insisted that effectiveness depended on an equitable distribution of learning outcomes across the entire population of the school. This focus on the equitable distribution of the important outcomes of schooling needs to guide us as we travel into the future.

Taking Responsibility for Students

When quality education is defined primarily in terms of resources and student SES, when failure is an inherent characteristic of the learning model employed, and when the function of schooling is to sort children into 'heads' and 'hands', it is not difficult to discern responsibility for what happens to students - accountability lies elsewhere than with school personnel. Indeed, the prevailing explanations for student failures before the effective schools movement were focused on deficiencies in the students themselves and in the home/community environments in which they were nurtured: 'in short, since the beginning of public education, poor academic performance and deviant behavior have been defined as problems of individual children or their families' (Cuban, 1989, p. 781).

Effective schools researchers and practitioners were the first group to reject this philosophy. As Cuban (1989, p. 784) correctly notes, 'the effective schools movement shifted the focus of efforts to deal with poor academic performance among low income minorities from the child to the school'. Thus, the third major contribution of the effective schools movement is its attack on the practice of blaming the victim for the shortcomings of the school itself, its insistence upon requiring the school community to take a fair share of the responsibility for what happens to the youth in its care.

Attention to Consistency throughout the School Community

One pundit has described a school as a collection of individual entrepreneurs (teachers) surrounded by a common parking lot. Another says a school is a group of classrooms held together by a common heating and cooling system. While I acknowledge the hyperbole in these definitions, I also realize that it is the accuracy of the statements that brings a smile to our faces when we hear them for the first time. The picture they convey captures an essential condition of schools (at least of those in the United States): they are very loosely linked organizations. What unfolds in one classroom may be quite different from what happens in another. Activity in the headteacher's office is likely to have little impact on either classroom. A unified sense of mission is generally conspicuous by its absence. Curriculum is not well integrated across grade levels or among various programme areas. We claim to teach one thing (objectives), while we generally teach something quite different (textbooks), and almost invariably test students using assessment instruments (norm-referenced achievement tests) based on neither.

Perhaps the most powerful and enduring lesson from all the research on effective schools is that the better schools are more tightly linked - structurally, symbolically and culturally - than the less effective ones. They operate more as an organic whole and less as a loose collection of disparate sub-systems. There is a great deal of consistency within and across the major components of the organization, especially those of the production function - the teaching-learning process. Staff, parents and students share a sense of direction. Components of the curriculum - objectives, materials, assessment strategies - are tightly aligned. Staff share a common instructional language. Expectations for performance are similar throughout the school community and rewards and punishments are consistently distributed to students. This overarching sense of consistency and co-ordination is a key element that cuts across the effectiveness correlates and permeates better schools. We need to ensure that it is a defining characteristic of the schools of tomorrow, however they are specifically organized and governed.

THE FUTURE: EXPANDING THE BASE

Early in the last decade of the twentieth century, we find the effective schools movement flourishing and in a reasonable state of health, despite the fact that the overall well-being of the movement has been adversely affected in a modest way by regular attacks on its findings by members of the academic community. Somewhat more damage has been inflicted by zealots within the effective schools camp itself - those folks who have passed beyond the boundaries of advocacy and have lost their ability to see where our work can be improved.

Overly adverse critics and misguided friends do not pose the most serious problem for the effective school movement, however. The real challenge, from my perspective, is staunchly to adhere to the principles of the movement at the same time that we allow it to grow, by incorporating what we continue to learn about effective education for all children and young adults. What areas require additional scrutiny? What is on the horizon that we should analyse and possibly incorporate into the effective schools model?

Firstly, we need to continue to address the issue of how to help schools become effective. As noted earlier, effective schools research provides us primarily with a content knowledge base - identification of the correlates. Process issues - school improvement matters - require considerable attention as well. Progress has been made here. The change of name of the AERA SIG to School Effectiveness *and School Improvement* is a symbol of that progress.

Continued work on intertwining content and process to reach the objectives inherent to the effective schools model is needed.

Secondly, much more attention should be devoted directly to curriculum and instruction - especially to knowledge that has evolved over the past ten years in these areas. A number of practitioners and academics have argued the need for a more efficacious blending of research on the teaching-learning process with findings from effective schools. Although the latter line of work focuses on the importance of mastery of basic skills and systematic monitoring of student progress, the effective schools spotlight has been directed too infrequently upon activities unfolding in individual classrooms. This needs to change. Our knowledge about the teaching-learning function has grown tremendously since the completion of the most influential effective schools investigations. As noted earlier, lessons from cognitive psychology about the importance of teaching higher order and basic skills *concomitantly* need to find a home in our framework. Likewise, significant findings about instructional models such as co-operative learning - models that not only facilitate the production of desired outcomes but are consistent with the underlying fabric of the movement discussed above - should be worked into the school effectiveness framework.

Thirdly, we need to rejoice in - rather than engage in turf battles with - the work of more recent investigators that is centred on the equity issues that are so integral to our mission. There are others who are uncovering important information about helping all students succeed and developing reasoned proposals in this area that we should be aware of and use. In the United States, the work of Henry Levin at Stanford and the studies conducted by Robert Slavin and his colleagues at Johns Hopkins appear to be particularly worthy of our attention.

Fourthly, we need to examine what the restructured schools movement offers for school effectiveness and school improvement. School effectiveness studies have been largely silent on two issues that are central to discussions of restructured schools - changing authority and governance structures and work redesign - while paving the way on the third - accountability defined in terms of outcomes. Serious investigations of what these radical changes to the educational system hold for us in terms of reconfiguring the model and redefining the correlates themselves are required (see Reynolds, 1990).

The challenge for the future is to incorporate lessons from a broad array of investigatory lines of work that are relevant to and consistent with the basic principles of effective schools outlined above. The four areas reviewed are representative of areas to be examined.

REFERENCES

Creemers, B.P.M. (1990) 'Effectiveness and improvement: the case of the Netherlands', Paper presented at the International Conference on the Study of School Effectiveness and the Practice of School Improvement, Boston. (Chapter 3 in this volume)

Cuban, L. (1989) 'The "at-risk" label and the problem of urban school reform', *Phi Delta Kappan*, **70** (10), 780-4, 799-801.

Finn, C.E. (1990) 'The biggest reform of all', *Phi Delta Kappan*, **71** (8), 584-92.

Goodlad, J.I. (1984) *A Place Called School: Prospects for the Future*. New York: McGraw-Hill.

Hawley, W.D. (1989) 'Looking backward at educational reform', *Education Week*, **9** (9), 32-5.

Levine, D. (1990) 'Unusually effective schools', Paper presented at the International Conference on the Study of School Effectiveness and the Practice of School Improvement, Boston. (Chapter 2 in this volume)

Meyer, J.W. and Rowan, B. (1975) 'Notes on the structure of educational organizations: revised version', Paper presented at the annual meeting of the American Sociological Association, San Francisco.

Miller, S.K. and Brookover, W.B. (1986) 'School effectiveness versus individual differences: paradigmatic perspectives on the legitimation of economic and educational inequalities', Paper presented at the annual meeting of the American Educational Research Association, San Francisco.

Murphy, J. (1988) 'Methodological, measurement, and conceptual problems in the study of administrator instructional leadership', *Educational Evaluation and Policy Analysis*, **10** (2), 117-39.

Murphy, J. and Evertson, C. (1990) *Restructured Schools: Looking at the Teaching-Learning Process*. Nashville, TN: Peabody College of Vanderbilt University, The National Center for Educational Leadership.

Murphy, J., Hallinger, P. and Mitman, A. (1983) 'Problems with research on educational leadership: issues to be addressed', *Educational Evaluational and Policy Analysis*, **5** (3), 297-305.

Murphy, J., Hallinger, P. and Mesa, R.P. (1985) 'School effectiveness: checking progress and assumptions and developing a role for state and federal government', *Teachers College Record*, **86** (4), 615-41.

Reynolds, D. (1990) 'School effectiveness and school improvement: an updated review of the British literature', Paper presented at the International Conference on the Study of School Effectiveness and the Practice of School Improvement, Boston. (Chapter 1 in this volume)

Seeley, D.S. (1988) 'A new vision for public education', *Youth Policy*, **10** (2), 34-6.

Chapter 10

School Effectiveness and School Improvement in the 1990s

David Reynolds and Anthony Packer

INTRODUCTION

A number of important factors will continue to increase the influence that schools have over the development of young people in the 1990s and beyond. Firstly, the school populations of elementary and, especially, secondary schools are now changing rapidly as children with what we call in Britain 'special educational needs' (children with physical, behavioural or learning problems) are re-integrated into schools with other so-called 'normal' children. This movement is common to all the major industrialized nations of the world (with the exception of some Scandinavian countries who were integrating already) and, whether the integration is total or partial, will put into schools groups of pupils highly sensitive to their school and classroom environment. Assuming that all other factors remain unchanged and particularly that variation between schools continues to exist at least at its present levels, the result of this changing pupil population will be a substantial increase in the influence of the school.

Secondly, and again this is an international phenomenon, the increased policy concern to keep troublesome, delinquent or disturbed children within the normal school setting (rather than utilizing specialist, expensive and clearly highly ineffective special residential homes or units) will put into mainstream schools another group of pupils whom the evidence suggests also to be highly influenced by their schools (Graham, 1988). There is a substantial volume of literature (e.g. Gottfredson, 1987; Reynolds and Sullivan, 1981) which suggests that educational failure and the effects of schools in the generation of this failure may lie behind many of the anti-social demeanours that concerned virtually all industrialized societies in the 1980s. Again, schools' influence on young people will increase because of the greater recruitment of young people highly sensitive to the quality of what they are being offered within their educational settings.

The third process that will increase school influence upon young people is the highly prevalent policy of decentralization of power within the educational system down to the level of the school. There are, of course, substantial variations between countries (and even within North American countries) in the precise nature of the relationships between the increasingly autonomous schools, and the other 'meso' or 'macro' levels of the educational 'state', whether local, provincial or national. In Britain, for example, the major mechanism of quality control will be locally determined market mechanisms of parental choice, whereas in some Australian states the clear intention is to use a range of central state monitoring and inspection arrangements to discover and improve what central data collection shows to be the ineffective schools (see country reports in Reynolds *et al.*, 1989a; Creemers *et al.*, 1989).

Whatever the variation may be across cultures, a common result is likely to be, in the short term at least, a substantial increase in the variation in their quality between schools, since the common factors which all schools had when their school districts or local education authorities were involved with them are being simply removed. In addition to the major influences upon school practice that are to be removed, the huge additional range of powers, roles and responsibilities that will fall upon schools and particularly upon their principals or headteachers, will also increase school variability substantially, because of the ways in which the schools will differ markedly in their ability to cope with rapid externally induced changes, a variability that is likely to be more marked than when the rate of external change was slow. It may be, of course, that mechanisms of local or national quality control will, in the medium to long term, reduce the variability of school quality. In Britain, for example, the clear intention is that schools judged by parents to be ineffective will rapidly lose pupil numbers and will eventually shut, with staff simply losing their jobs (Hargreaves and Reynolds, 1989). In the medium to long term, then, variation between schools in their quality may narrow but in the short term an increase in the effects of schools because of a substantial increase in the variability of schools seems inevitable. It is frankly very worrying that those who are pulsing along in the fervour of the school decentralization movement seem unable to recognize these likely effects.

Superimposed upon these changes which increase - my hypothesis would be *greatly* increase - the effects of schools or school influences, demographic changes mean that governments in major industrialized societies will be faced with cohorts of young people leaving school which are perhaps 20-25 per cent smaller in their overall numbers than five years ago, the result of course of the small secondary school cohorts that have been caused by the dramatic decline in the birth rate in the late 1960s and 1970s. Assuming that the demand for labour in various societies remains roughly the same, no society will be easily able to tolerate in the future the 15-20 per cent of young people who 'drop out', as in the United States, or the 10 per cent of young people who leave school without any formal public examination qualifications at all, as in Britain. Governments, then, are likely to be even more concerned with the quality of educational institutions, with their outcomes and with their schools' effectiveness and possible improvement, a concern that is bound to intensify as the countries of the Far East and the Pacific Basin begin to show economic results from their rapid expansion in the resources available to education over the past five to ten years.

THE SCHOOL EFFECTIVENESS KNOWLEDGE BASE

The need for research and development in the general disciplinary areas of school effectiveness and school improvement is, in my view, likely to be even greater in the 1990s than it has been in the 1980s and 1970s. The increased pressure for educational systems to attain results will be there, but the school systems themselves are likely to have become more heterogeneous in their quality and are likely to be presented increasingly with 'at risk' young people who are likely to have very sensitive reactions to their schools, and over whom they are likely to have a substantial influence. To meet the challenge of this new set of educational circumstances, what needs to be our agenda for the future of research on school effectiveness?

The development of the field over time has been extensively described by myself and others elsewhere (Reynolds *et al.*, 1989a; Creemers *et al.*, 1989; Creemers and Scheerens, 1989), so only a brief outline seems necessary. In both the United States and Britain, studies such as that by Coleman *et al.* (1966), the work of Jencks *et al.* (1971) and the British Plowden Report of the Central Advisory Council for Education (Department of Education and Science, 1967) all concluded that schools bring little independent influence to bear upon the development of their pupils. This period has been gradually followed in both societies by the emergence of a wide range of 'effective schools', 'school effectiveness' or 'school effects' studies that argue for the importance of school influence, beginning in the United States with various case studies and moving on to a wide range of quantitative studies, and in Britain with work by Power *et al.* (1972), Gath *et al.* (1977), myself (Reynolds, 1976; 1982; Reynolds *et al.*, 1987), Rutter *et al.* (1979), Galloway *et al.* (1985) and Gray *et al.* (1986), moving on to the recent studies of Mortimore and his colleagues (1988) in primary schools and Smith and Tomlinson's (1989) work in multi-cultural secondary schools. Work in these two societies has been recently joined by that from the Netherlands, Australia, Canada and by a recent resurgence of studies done in and about Third World societies.

From studies in this wide range of countries, it seems that a number of early simplistic assumptions that were frequently based upon school effectiveness research are now no longer tenable:

- On the size of school effects, it seems that early beliefs that school influence might be as large as family or community influences were misplaced, since a very large number of studies in the past five years show only 8-15 per cent of the variation in pupil outcomes as due to between-school differences (Cuttance, this book, Chapter 4; Bosker and Scheerens, 1989).
- On the causes of school effects, it seems that early beliefs that school influences were distinct from teacher or classroom influences were misplaced, since a large number of studies utilizing multi-level modelling show that the great majority of variation between schools is in fact due to classroom variation and that the unique variance due to the influence of the school, and not the classroom, shrinks to very small levels (Scheerens *et al.*, 1989).
- On the consistency of school effects, it seems that early beliefs that 'effective' or 'ineffective' schools stayed so over quite considerable time periods of five to seven years were invalid, since it now appears that school performance can vary quite rapidly, over two or three years (Nuttall *et al.*, 1989). (The

imminent publication of the academic outcomes of schooling, such as the results of national assessment procedures in Britain, involves utilizing only one year's figures and is clearly a worrying policy if school performance is unstable.)

- On the relative consistency of the performance of schools across a range of outcome measures, it used to be thought that the 'effective school' was so across a range of both academic and social outcomes, yet now we have much evidence that schools need not be effective or ineffective 'across the board'. The Junior School Project of Mortimore *et al.* (1988) showed, for example, a virtually complete independence of schools on different outcome measures, suggesting strongly that academic effectiveness is not necessarily associated with social or 'affective' effectiveness.
- On the question of effectiveness across different groups of pupils, the traditional belief that schools are effective or ineffective for all sub-groups of pupils within them is no longer tenable in view of the evidence that there can be different school effects for children of different ethnic groups, ability ranges and socioeconomic status within the *same* school (Aitken and Longford, 1986; Nuttall *et al.*, 1989).
- On the question of what factors make schools more or less effective, the traditional belief (Edmonds, 1979) that there was a blueprint or 'recipe' independent of school history, context or personnel is no longer tenable, since what is effective may vary in accordance with the context of the social environment of the school's catchment area (Hallinger and Murphy, 1986), with the stage of development of the school itself (Stringfield and Teddlie, 1990) and with the particular outcome measure being considered (Mortimore *et al.*, 1988). Even if the characteristics of effective schools are found to be similar across contexts, the actual *generation* of these characteristics at the level of day-to-day school management may be different, as shown in the American work of Brookover *et al.* (1979) and in a neglected study by Galloway (1983) in New Zealand, where four schools exhibiting low rates of disruptive behaviour exhibited similar 'effective school' characteristics but also contained two autocratic headteachers, one democratic and one of 'mixed style'. The headteachers all generated 'collegiality' among their staff groups and all generated effective school outputs, but they did so in *different* ways appropriate to their own personalities, the dynamics of their local contexts and the stage of development of their school.
- On the last issue of what makes schools effective, it is abundantly clear that there is no cross-cultural agreement on this matter. Assertive instructional leadership from the

> headteacher recurs repeatedly in North American five-, six- or seven-factor theories of school effectiveness and is empirically verified in recent American school effectiveness research (Levine and Lezotte, 1990), but is not an important factor determining school effectiveness in by far the greater part of the Dutch research on effective school practices (Creemers and Scheerens, 1989). Frequent monitoring of pupil performance is a characteristic of some American effective school studies (Levine and Lezotte, 1990), but this is not found in British primary schools, where in the Junior School Project frequent monitoring of school performance was a characteristic of *ineffective* schools (Mortimore *et al.*, 1988).

The resolution of these issues about the size of school effects, their consistency over time, their consistency across outcome measures, their consistency for different types of children within individual schools and the issues concerning the organizational and process factors responsible for school effects clearly necessitates a major research undertaking in the 1990s. Briefly, the research must involve cohort studies, so that the actual increments in children's learning and their progress over time (as well as at a point in time) can be studied. The research needs multiple measures of outside-school or intake factors, probably including pupil ability and a wide range of family and environmental factors, to ensure that the influences of schools are not overestimated because of under-specification of intake factors. Research needs to be multi-level in its research design, so that the variation within schools of different classes, pupil groups, etc. can be handled statistically. School effectiveness studies need to have measures of academic *and* social outcomes, and the measurement of the latter of course involves particular problems if they cannot be simply tapped through use of behavioural measures, since the measurement of pupil attitudes is clearly fraught with difficulty. Research into the factors responsible for school effects needs to continue to consider *which* factors are responsible, particularly since some studies have found it very difficult to explain variation in social outcomes: the study by Rutter *et al.* (1979), for example, could find only seven school process factors associated with possession of a low level of delinquency, by comparison with over twenty associated with possession of a high level of academic attainment. Further issues for the research agenda include the study of *how* school process factors have their effects, *which* process factors are most important in determining outcomes, *which* process factors may lead to the determination of other process factors and the study of the *interaction* between factors, as in the interesting interaction between the classroom level and the school level in ineffective or successful schools (Teddlie *et al.*, 1989).

Vast areas of school life are also under-researched in terms of their possible relationships with school effectiveness, particularly the nature of the effective instructional practices in the effective school, as argued elsewhere in this volume by Creemers, and the curriculum content, organization and knowledge base of effective schools. Crucially, adequate specifications of the levels of resources that are available to schools have in recent years rarely featured as independent school variables, because the widespread criticism of the use of 'quantity of resources' as measures of school quality and school processes that featured in some of the early North American school effectiveness studies (Averch *et al.*, 1971). In the twenty or more years since these studies, inequalities between schools in their levels of resource availability have probably increased dramatically, especially in societies such as the USA where schools are still predominantly locally funded and in societies like Britain where inequalities between geographic and social groups have been maximized deliberately as part of governmental policies. I doubt very much if all school subjects are equally affected by any substantial variations in the availability of school resources, since the teaching of subjects like science is clearly more resource-dependent than that of subjects such as reading or history, but I suspect that were we to use sensitive measures of resources now, and particularly if we were able to measure the relationship between the quantity of resources and educational outcomes at an *individual* pupil level, then resource levels might assume a much larger place in our explanations of school performance.

Our final research needs in school effectiveness are, firstly, for the generation of theories, probably of the middle range variety, which can link together sets of potentially disparate findings in ways that would both structure the field and make it more accessible for practitioners, and secondly for the generation of 'good practice' case studies in which data would be 'sliced' horizontally rather than vertically, thus permitting the proper picture of effective school processes in interaction with each other within one school that is so necessary for any improved practitioner take-up of the insights of our collective school effectiveness work. Further speculations about the future research agenda are available in Reynolds (1985), Reynolds *et al.* (1989a) and Creemers *et al.* (1989).

THE EFFECTIVE SCHOOL IN THE 1990s

I suspect that the 1990s will provide an even more difficult agenda for school effectiveness researchers and practitioners than that caused by attempting to unravel the unresolved problems of the 1980s research base, formidable though that task clearly is. This is because of two further factors.

Firstly, the range of outcomes expected from schools is likely to be significantly enlarged by the addition of various competencies perceived as needed by the world of work (such as ability to access information or social outcomes like ability to work as a part of a team) and by the addition of further competencies required by an increasingly information-orientated society (such as knowing how to learn, knowing how to find out, etc.). Given the nature of these competencies, I suspect that they may not always, or even often, have been produced by the sort of schools that are currently labelled as possessing 'effective' organizational processes. If the future society needs 'active' individuals who have acquired learning-to-learn skills, an ability to work co-operatively and a more active, learner-directed mode of operation, then very new instructional methods will be required, which turn passive learning into active learning, which entail putting more responsibility upon the student and which entail putting the teacher consciously in the role of helping students to learn how to learn. These may be not the sort of skills which would be likely to emanate from the classic models of the effective school, especially in the American formulation, with its ordered climate, assertive headteacher leadership, concentration upon basic skill acquisition, collegial/consensual mentality and concern with conventional academic outcomes. Significantly, where arguments for, and visions of, new kinds of educational processes exist at present, those within these newer traditions see themselves as directly opposed to the sort of educational philosophy and practices that they see reflected within school effectiveness's five- or seven-factor theories (see Cuban, 1988; Holly, 1990).

With the need for new outcomes, then, will come a need to reassess the usefulness of the organizational processes on which we have concentrated our past efforts at describing and analysing, and we will have to move on to attempt the most difficult task of all: that of describing which classroom and school processes may actually be effective in generating the ability to *learn* as well as the ability to think. These are not areas we have concentrated upon in the past.

The second factor making for disciplinary difficulty in the 1990s is that our research agenda will be further complicated by the changed nature of the leadership and management tasks required of teachers and particularly of senior teachers in their schools. These changes are produced by the effects upon management styles of the ways in which schools are increasingly having to compete against each other in forms of educational 'markets', changes that are most marked in Britain with its provisions under the 1988 Education Reform Act but that are also increasingly in evidence elsewhere in the world: as James Coleman said to all countries at the 1990 International Congress for School Effectiveness and School Improvement meeting, if you haven't seen parental choice yet, just wait! The move from having a situation of one 'producer' of education, in the form of a district, state or local education authority, having influences over all schools to a situation of *multiple* producers of the goods of 'education' is ultimately bound to result in increased competition between the producers, all of whom will be chasing the client (the pupil) or, more likely, the client's parents. This competition between producing schools is likely to come immediately, as it has already in Britain, or to follow on in a few years time in other societies, especially if the centralized attempts at quality assurance break down in cultures attempting them.

The result of this process of market competition between schools is to change vastly what is necessary for effective leadership at school level, because it changes the managerial qualities necessary to create an effective school. New managerial skills will be needed:

- a heightened public relations or marketing orientation and an ability to 'sell' the product;
- the capacity to relate to parents;
- the capacity to find sources of support in local communities;
- the capacity to manage rapid change, not to manage a steady state;

- the capacity to motivate staff in times when instrumental rewards like promotion or advancement are rare;
- the capacity to relate to pupils, since the wave of future consumerism will, I suspect, increasingly involve consumer opinion surveys with pupils.

Generally, there will be a decrease in self-initiated tasks and an increase in other directed ones, an increase in role set, greater pressure upon time, the need to monitor school and programme quality and an increased entrepreneurial or brokerage function of matching programmes, personnel and expected markets together. There is even likely to be an increased need for headteachers and senior managers to be financially competent, numerate and perhaps open to the ways in which they can maximize the income from what will be increasingly called their 'plants' (i.e. their schools).

It would be very surprising if the effective headteacher of the 1990s bears more than a very superficial relationship with the effective headteacher as we now describe him or her. The complexity of the situation in which he or she is likely to be, the very real problems of motivation of colleagues, the overload of pressures (and in the case of Britain of policy enactments also) - all these are likely to call for a style of effective headteacher very different to that practised by the thoroughly one-dimensional creatures that stalk through the present-day leadership literature within school effectiveness. It may be, of course, that the effective school as now described and the effective headteacher as now described will remain effective as described in the 1990s, but I doubt that very much indeed. What worked in the 1970s is simply unlikely to travel well to the educational world of the 1990s.

THE NEED FOR PSYCHOLOGY

The difficulty of the task that is facing school effectiveness researchers and practitioners in the 1990s is increased in its magnitude and its effects because of the isolation of the discipline from sources of intellectual renewal in other cognate and related disciplines. School effectiveness research in the United States actually began outside the mainstream educational research community and within the educational system itself it was inspired by the late Ron Edmonds, who of course was a school board superintendent. In Britain, the first four papers published on school effectiveness in the 1960s and 1970s came from a social medicine unit, a child guidance consultant, an epidemiology unit and an institute of psychiatry, not from conventional sources of empirical educational research.

The price that has been paid for this splendid disciplinary isolation is obvious. The reluctance of school effectiveness researchers to undertake research to specify the exact nature of the instructional processes within effective schools is in part explicable by the isolation of the great majority of school effectiveness researchers from the broader traditions of teacher/instructional effectiveness in the United States and elsewhere. Our inability to move beyond the most simple characteristics and typologies of school organizational processes owes much to our isolation from the strong research traditions within educational sociology and the sociology of the school, particularly where the latter has been well researched and documented as in Britain (and to a lesser extent the United States). Our isolation from criminological research cuts us off from the large volume of literature on the role of the school in creating deviant pupils by means of the interactive influence of various within-school factors. One will still learn far more about the reasons for school effects on their pupils from a glance at the compendium of evidence contained in the famous *Task Force Report of the President's Commission on Juvenile Delinquency and Youth Crime* of 1967 than from the accumulated wisdom of school effectiveness studies.

The most important, and damaging, isolation of all for school effectiveness research is from the disciplines of psychology and psychiatry, and particularly from specialities such as abnormal psychology. References to psychological findings and an appreciation of psychological or psychiatric insights are rarely found within the school effectiveness community and, crucially, rarely within the literature on school improvement, with the exception perhaps of Sarason (1971). I suspect this isolation is very damaging, since there are likely to be very complicated interpersonal processes at work in the effective, and particularly in the ineffective, schools that our research tradition has customarily ignored. We have concentrated, to put it simply, upon the first dimension of schooling - the formal, reified, organizational structure - without looking in enough detail at the second - cultural and informal - world of values, attitudes and perceptions, which together with the third dimension - the complicated web of personal relationships within schools - will determine a school's effectiveness or ineffectiveness.

This neglect of school culture and school interpersonal and psychological processes is very costly because I suspect we truly need psychology (or perhaps even psychiatry!) to understand the 'deep structure' of the ineffective school. In our experience, the staff culture in this type of school may exhibit many of the characteristics of the 'inadequate', ineffective or insecure person (see Reynolds, 1987, for further speculations on this theme). These are:

- projections of individual teachers' deficiencies on to the children or the surrounding community and its parents, as excuses for ineffectiveness;
- 'cling-ons' of past practice (we've always done it this way!);
- defences, whereby teachers have built walls to keep out threatening messages from outsiders;
- fear of attempting change because it may fail, associated with a reluctance to risk;
- the fantasy that change is someone else's job;
- the 'safety in numbers' ploy, whereby the staff retreat into a ring-fenced mentality.

The culture, then, will be somewhat weary, fatalistic, used to failure and unused to the risks necessitated by changed organizational practices. It will be the defensive apparatus that is employed by the inefficient and the insecure to protect themselves from any outside influences that may expose them and their inadequacy.

In addition, the third dimension, concerning the interpersonal processes of the staff group, is likely to be psychologically abnormal. The staff are likely to be organized into strongly demarcated sub-groups, with perhaps hostile relations between them. There is unlikely to be any shared value system because the friendship groups act as props to their members' linked professional and personal ideologies.

If this means of characterizing the second and third dimensions of schooling is an appropriate and accurate one, then it must be obvious that the literature on inter-group, psychological, psychiatric and interpersonal processes would considerably aid us in our understanding of effective and ineffective school processes and, most importantly of all, in our understanding of how to improve schools, the issue that we will turn to consider next.

SCHOOL IMPROVEMENT IN THE 1990s

If the 1990s pose real problems for us in terms of the adequacy and validity of our body of knowledge on school effectiveness and its appropriateness at times of rapidly changing educational and societal circumstances, then the same problems are often more apparent in the field of school improvement. The body of knowledge in this area is now extensive and has been excellently described elsewhere by Fullan (1991), so there is no point in reviewing it again. It is clear from this review that intellectually we are beginning to acquire 'good improvement practice' but I suspect from our experiences in Britain that we still have a long way to go, because of the poorly explained and conceptualized psychology of the change process that is in evidence within the improvement literature. It is on this point - the point of how to manage institutional change - that most studies of school improvement are in my view most opaque, most vague and most unhelpful. Indeed, the school improvement knowledge base reminds one of Gertrude Stein's definition of California: 'the trouble is that there's no there, there'.

If one accepts the description of the ineffective school and its organization, its interpersonal processes and its culture offered above, then it is clear that school improvement attempts must take account of the complex web of psychological abnormality and pathology in order to be successful. To assume, as virtually all do, an empirical/rational approach which presumes the rationality and psychological normality of the targeted school is mistaken both tactically and operationally if the school culture, values and interactive processes are essentially non-rational and abnormal. Very little that one reads in the school improvement literature, with the notable exception of the British work by Jones (1988) and the seminal contribution of Elizabeth Richardson's 'Nailsea study' (1973), is of use to us in our task of school improvement, since it does not address the sorts of problems and dilemmas which face those of us who try to bring the knowledge base of school effectiveness to ineffective schools. There may be cultures in which North American school improvement literature may be appropriate and within which it may be effective, but unfortunately in my experience the schools in which we have worked do not fall into this category.

The following example will, I hope, illustrate this point in more depth. More detailed accounts of this attempt to improve a school can be found elsewhere (Reynolds and Murgatroyd, 1985; Reynolds, 1987) and are forthcoming, but, briefly, a team from the University of Wales College of Cardiff was invited by a local school that perceived itself as ineffective and underperforming to join it as 'consultants' to resource the school's improvement efforts. Our consultancy role was to bring to the school the best available knowledge and evidence on school effectiveness, discuss with the school what aspects of the knowledge base were seen as appropriate to its local context and then evaluate the success or failure of the change attempt and feed back the results to the school for further consideration. As we began our work with the teachers in the school, many processes began which the school improvement literature had given us no warning about. These will be taken in turn.

The staff of the school were unused to discussing educational matters, other than at the level of discussion of individual children who might have been 'problems' or who had perhaps distinguished themselves in conventional terms. Introducing educational ideas, the language in which they were couched and their apparently advanced modes of conceptualization into the school caused immense problems, because staff inexperience in handling discussions on complex educational issues resulted in their being unable to separate the personal and the political. They were unable to argue educational 'points of view' without getting personally involved in the process, because of a deficiency of interpersonal and communication skills. Increased interpersonal conflict, a breakdown of some pre-existing relationships and much interpersonal hostility in some cases were the results of our attempt to introduce outside ideas into a school.

We attempted to 'open up' the culture of the school by employing various devices. The 'behind the closed door' mentality, whereby teachers had few contacts at a professional or intellectual level with other teachers, we attempted to end by the introduction of 'pupil pursuit'. This technique involved a member of the teaching staff shadowing an individual pupil through that pupil's entire morning or afternoon of schooling, in order to understand what the school experience and its shortcomings must have looked like for the 'consumer' of education. This tactic generated a rapid further deterioration in interpersonal relations. Many staff realized for the first time the incompetence of their colleagues, having experienced it at first hand rather than merely encountering it through rumour or innuendo.

There were other strategies which we utilized that eventually helped to solidify the staff group and make it re-form around the new body of knowledge that we had interpreted as 'good practice'. We opened up the school's management team through greater democracy, more openness, the keeping of minutes of meetings, etc., thereby encouraging the staff to 'take on' their management and thus solidify in terms of interpersonal relationships as they did it. We introduced some quasi-group work - small group and experiential interventions - to try to repair interpersonal damage. Eventually, although there were numerous individual casualties of the change process (including the headteacher, who retired with an apparent breakdown), the school emerged a stronger and more effective institution and is now more able to handle the complex interpersonal difficulties that school improvement brings.

The world that we encountered at this school was, to return to my theme, far removed from the picture painted of school improvement within educational institutions in the North American school improvement literature. The teachers were unable to engage in rational discourse about the directions in which they should move without a degree of personal growth, both as individuals and in terms of their collective interpersonal processes. The culture of the school, both in the sense of the school's set of taken-for-granted understandings and in the sense of its interpersonal relationships, acted as blocks on change. The knowledge of the rational-empirical paradigm encountered irrationality, emotionality, abnormality and what can only be called personal and group disturbance. Conventional school improvement programmes of the 1980s may 'play in Peoria' but they do not 'play in Wales'.

School improvement in the 1990s must therefore, in my view, move in very different directions to those of the 1980s. It must deal with the culture of schools, as well as with their structure. It must concern itself with the informal world of the school, as well as with the formal world. It must concern itself with the deep structure of values, relationships and interpersonal processes, as well as with the world of behaviour. It must ensure that it takes account of the need to manage the interaction between the body of improvement knowledge and the collective psyche of the school.

Most important of all, the world that schools find themselves in during the 1990s is likely to be, in terms of the direction and orientation of educational change, very different to that which has been deemed appropriate for the utilization of past educational improvement models. Put simply, the 1980s were times when school improvement attempts sought to produce *internally* generated school change. Indeed the whole 'ownership' paradigm was based upon the need for school teaching staffs to own the improvement attempt so that it would be able to pass from the implementation to the institutionalization phases without hindrance. Yet in the 1990s in many countries, like the United Kingdom, it is clear that educational change is now *externally* generated, and the internal organizations of schools are forced to adjust. The introduction in a British context of a 'market choice' system of educational provision, with severe market penalties for those unable to compete effectively, is a major external change to which schools must adjust in institutional terms. The school improvement literature that is on offer is not just deficient because it does not acknowledge the importance of the psychological dimensions of within-school life. It is perhaps highly dated, because it was based on the now inappropriate premise that school improvement attempts are internal, and are not school-based attempts to respond to externally generated change. I would therefore be surprised indeed if the 'good practice' generated by the educational experience of the 1980s were to be an appropriate model for the schools of the 1990s.

I suspect that a productive future for school improvement may lie in its acknowledgement as a discipline that it has been reactive in nature, rebounding from the practice of what it sees as ineffective and inappropriate school improvement strategies but by doing so only rebounding towards equally inappropriate attempts and models. The school improvement strategies of the 1970s were generally based upon acquisition of elite knowledge, were 'top down' and externally generated in orientation, were individually targeted and were predominantly based out of schools (see Reynolds, 1988, for further elaboration on this theme). In opposition to this paradigm came a new emphasis, reflected in the work of Elliott (1981) in Britain for example, upon the importance of relying upon practitioner knowledge, group improvement activity, internally generated 'bottom up' solutions and completely school-based improvement attempts. Yet of course the basic tenets of the new paradigm may be as educationally unreliable as those of the old: reliance upon practitioner knowledge may condemn practitioners to ignorance or even, at best, lead to a futile reinvention of the wheel in each change attempt. Group activity may neglect the crucial factor of individual motivation that lies behind successful improvement: individual greed, occupational ambition and selfishness may be ideologically unsound but still highly effective precursors of school improvement programmes! Likewise, basing school improvement programmes completely within schools may imprison them in an educational jail of poor practice.

School improvement, then, has reactively moved from one paradigm to its opposite, but the future for the discipline, I suspect, lies in its acknowledgement that, as Newman noted, 'The truth does not lie mid way between extremes - it actually lies *in* both of them.' School improvement practitioners should perhaps consider that their knowledge base should not be drawn 'either' from one paradigm 'or' from an oppositional other, but should be drawn from 'both' one paradigm 'and' the other at the same time. To give an example of how this ideological position may be operationalized in practice, we have ourselves been experimenting in Wales with a novel school improvement programme based upon the following principles of a multi-paradigmatic nature:

- the knowledge base was both the effective schools literature and the practitioner-based lore about what made for effective practice;
- the programme relied upon individual teachers' motivation for professional education and upon group activity based in the schools of the participating teachers to ensure permeation within the organizations;
- the programme was located outside the school within the university, although the course was school-focused;
- the programme was 'top-down' in its relationship to school processes (since most participants were senior managers in their schools) but was also 'bottom-up' in that attention was given to group-based techniques at school level to ensure 'ownership';
- the approach was 'empirical-rational' in the sense that the course aimed to generate problem-solving change agents, but also involved giving participants information about group work techniques, the social psychology of organizational life and related psychological and psychiatric insights;

- the orientation was behavioural in the sense of being concerned to change programme participants' behaviour and the behaviour of others within schools, and was at the same time concerned with ensuring attitudinal change in the 'deep structure' of values and relationship in schools.

We believe the results of our programmes to be impressive. Over three-quarters of programme participants changed aspects of their schools' organization, with an average of four major organizational changes per person. Over 85 per cent of these changes had survived in a six-year follow-up study and the schools that had exhibited organizational change had improved in terms of their academic and their social outcomes by comparison with a group of 'control' schools that were not included in the programme (fuller details are available in Reynolds *et al.*, 1989b). Our suggestion is that school improvement should consider suspending its commitment to different paradigms and investigate further the utility of putting together coalitions of what have been all too often seen as mutually exclusive approaches.

CONCLUSIONS

The aim of this chapter has been to present the case that we need a rapid development of school effectiveness and school improvement work in the 1990s. In the case of school effectiveness, the influence of schools is likely to increase, which makes it vital for those with concerns about educational policy that the continuing doubts and uncertainties that exist in the field are more progressively removed. My argument here has been that only a closer allegiance between school effectiveness researchers and the persons and knowledge bases of different disciplines will enable intellectual progress. Psychology, psychiatry and the disciplines concerned with interpersonal relationships were identified as the most important specialities to relate to in future.

In the case of the discipline of school improvement, I have argued that the continued use of the rational-empirical paradigm has neglected the realities of the culture and the interpersonal processes of the ineffective schools, which of course most need improvement and effectiveness knowledge. Such schools have an abnormal staff culture and exhibit a disturbed set of interpersonal relations, and the introduction of improvement programmes and/or effective schools knowledge to them needs to be handled with particular personal sensitivity. School improvement has deep psychological, as well as educational, effects upon schools and it is argued that we need a psycho-therapeutic orientation and psycho-therapeutic mechanisms to deal with this. School improvement programmes and their knowledge base are not, in themselves, sufficient to change schools or their personnel. In addition, the body of knowledge within the 'rational-empirical' paradigm may be well past its shelf life because educational change is now externally, not internally, generated. Multi-paradigmatic programmes are suggested as a possible way forward.

It is clear that the international school effectiveness and improvement movement has major intellectual and organizational tasks ahead, and some of the omens are disturbing. In certain countries school effectiveness has already become associated with a narrow, 'back to basics' orientation to the teaching of basic skills and has therefore become much criticized. There are also unresolved tensions between those who have an 'equity' perspective and who believe that effective schools should help disadvantaged populations particularly, and those who see the drive for effectiveness as something that should extend across all social categories. There are also issues concerned with the definition of effectiveness that wait lurking in the wings to cause dissent and disagreement.

Many of the omens for intellectual progress in the fields of school effectiveness and school improvement are, however, especially encouraging. There are many in educational and social research who still believe that research should not be related to issues of public policy and who view the direct policy orientation and practical concerns of school effectiveness and school improvement as a cause for worry. However, in the early stages of the development of a discipline there is much historical evidence that a problem-orientation or problem-solving approach is most likely to generate intellectual advances, as in the case of physiology, which developed rapidly in the nineteenth century through its close association with the practical needs of clinical medicine. A problem orientation prevents elaborate flights of theoretical and philosophical fancy which often lead into the realms of metaphysics. It does not mean that any of the theoretical problems that will arise from consideration of practical issues should not be investigated. It does mean that theoretical discussion will be erected on the foundation of an empirical, practical knowledge base. If it is true, as I believe, that it is through a proper consideration of practical issues that educational research is most likely to make major theoretical advances in the next few decades, then there is no group of persons who are more practical than those in the fields of school effectiveness and school improvement, and no group of persons who are therefore better qualified to make rapid intellectual progress.

REFERENCES

Aitken, M. and Longford, N. (1986) 'Statistical modelling issues in school effectiveness studies', *Journal of the Royal Statistical Society, Series A*, **149** (1), 1-43.

Averch, H. *et al.* (1971) *How Effective Is Schooling?* Santa Monica, CA: Rand Corporation.

Bosker, R.J. and Scheerens, J. (1989) 'Issues in the interpretation of the results of school effectiveness research', *International Journal of Educational Research*, **13** (7), 741-51.

Brookover, W.B., Beady, C., Flood, P., Schweitzer, J. and Wisenbaker, J. (1979) *School Social Systems and Student Achievement*. New York: Praeger.

Coleman, J.S. *et al.* (1966) *Equality of Educational Opportunity*. Washington, DC: US Government Printing Office.

Creemers, B. and Scheerens, J. (eds) (1989) 'Developments in school effectiveness research', special issue of *International Journal of Educational Research*, **13** (7), 685-825.

Creemers, B., Peters, T. and Reynolds, D. (1989) *School Effectiveness and Improvement: Proceedings of the Second International Congress, Rotterdam, 1989*. Lisse: Swets & Zeitlinger.

Cuban, L. (1988) 'Constancy and change in schools', *Noteworthy*; cited in Holly (1990), *op cit*.

Department of Education and Science (1967) *Children and Their Schools*. London: HMSO. (The Plowden Report)

Edmonds, R.R. (1979) 'Effective schools for the urban poor', *Educational Leadership*, **37** (15-18), 20-4.

Elliott, J. (1981) *School Accountability*. London: Grant McIntyre.

Fullan, M. (1991) *The New Meaning of Educational Change*. London: Cassell.

Galloway, D. (1983) 'Disruptive pupils and effective pastoral care', *School Organisation*, **13**, 245-54.

Galloway, D., Martin, R. and Wilcox, B. (1985) 'Persistent absence from school and exclusion from school: the predictive power of school and community variables', *British Educational Research Journal*, **11**, 51-61.

Gath, D. *et al.* (1977) *Child Guidance and Delinquency in a London Borough*. London: Oxford University Press.

Gottfredson, G. (1987) 'American education: American delinquency', *Today's Delinquent*, **6**, 5-70.

Graham, J. (1988) *Schools, Disruptive Behaviour and Delinquency: A Review of Research*. London: HMSO.

Gray, J., Jesson, D. and Jones, B. (1986) 'The search for a fairer way of comparing schools' examination results', *Research Papers in Education*, **1** (2), 91-122.

Hallinger, P. and Murphy, J. (1986) 'The social context of effective schools', *American Journal of Education*, **94**, 328-55.

Hargreaves, A. and Reynolds, D. (eds) (1989) *Education Policy: Controversies and Critiques*. Lewes: Falmer Press.

Holly, P.J. (1990) 'Catching the wave of the future: moving beyond school effectiveness by redesigning schools', *School Organisation*, **10** (2), 195-212.

Jencks, C. *et al.* (1971) *Inequality*. London: Allen Lane.

Jones, A. (1988) *Leadership for Tomorrow's Schools*. Oxford: Basil Blackwell.

Levine, D.U. and Lezotte, L.W. (1990) *Unusually Effective Schools: A Review and Analysis of Research and Practice*. Madison, WI: National Center for Effective Schools Research and Development.

Mortimore, P., Sammons, P., Ecob, R. and Stoll, L. (1988) *School Matters: The Junior Years*. Wells: Open Books.

Nuttall, D., Goldstein, H., Prosser, R. and Rasbash, J. (1989) 'Differential school effectiveness', *International Journal of Educational Research*, **13** (7), 769-76.

Power, M.J., Benn, R.T. and Morris, J.N. (1972) 'Neighbourhood, school and juveniles before the courts', *British Journal of Criminology*, **12**, 111-32.

Reynolds, D. (1976) 'The delinquent school', in Woods, P. (ed.) *The Process of Schooling*. London: Routledge & Kegan Paul.

Reynolds, D. (1982) 'The search for effective schools', *School Organisation*, **2** (3), 215-37.

Reynolds, D. (ed.) (1985) *Studying School Effectiveness*. Lewes: Falmer Press.

Reynolds, D. (1987) 'The consultant sociologist: a method for linking Sociology of Education and teachers', in Woods, P. and Pollard, A. (eds) *Sociology and Teaching*. London: Croom Helm.

Reynolds, D. (1988) 'British school improvement research: the contribution of qualitative studies', *International Journal of Qualitative Studies in Education*, **1** (2), 143-54.

Reynolds, D. and Murgatroyd, S.J. (1985) 'The creative consultant', *School Organisation*, **4** (3), 321-35.

Reynolds, D. and Sullivan, M. (1981) 'The effects of school: a radical faith re-stated', in Gillham, B. (ed.) *Problem Behaviour in the Secondary School*. London: Croom Helm.

Reynolds, D., Sullivan, M. and Murgatroyd, S.J. (1987) *The Comprehensive Experiment*. Lewes: Falmer Press.

Reynolds, D., Creemers, B.P.M. and Peters, T. (1989a) *School Effectiveness and Improvement: Proceedings of the First International Congress, London, 1988*. Groningen: University of Groningen, RION.

Reynolds, D., Davie, R. and Phillips, D. (1989b) 'The Cardiff programme - an effective school improvement programme based on school effectiveness research', in Creemers, B.P.M. and Scheerens, J. (eds) *Developments in School Effectiveness Research* (Special issue of the *International Journal of Educational Research*, **13** (7)), 800-14.

Richardson, E. (1973) *The Teacher, the School and the Task of Management*. London: Heinemann.

Rutter, M., Maughan, B., Mortimore, P. and Ouston, J. (1979) *Fifteen Thousand Hours: Secondary Schools and Their Effects on Children*. Cambridge, MA: Harvard University Press.

Sarason, S. (1971) *The Culture of the School and the Problem of Change*. Boston: Alleyn & Bacon.

Scheerens, J., Vermeulen, C.J. and Pelgrum, W.J. (1989) 'Generalisability of instructional and school effectiveness indicators across nations', *International Journal of Educational Research*, **13** (7), 789-99.

Smith, D. and Tomlinson, S. (1989) *The School Effect: A Study of Multi-racial Comprehensives*. London: Policy Studies Institute.

Stringfield, S. and Teddlie, C. (1990) 'School improvement efforts: qualitative and quantitative data from four naturally occurring experiments in Phases 3 and 4 of the Louisiana School Effectiveness Study', *School Effectiveness and School Improvement*, **1** (3), 139-61.

Teddlie, C., Kirby, P.C. and Stringfield, S. (1989) 'Effective versus ineffective schools: observable differences in the classroom', *American Journal of Education*, **97** (3), 221-36.

Name Index

Page numbers in roman type indicate a citation within the text; page numbers in *italics* refer to reference lists

Subject Index